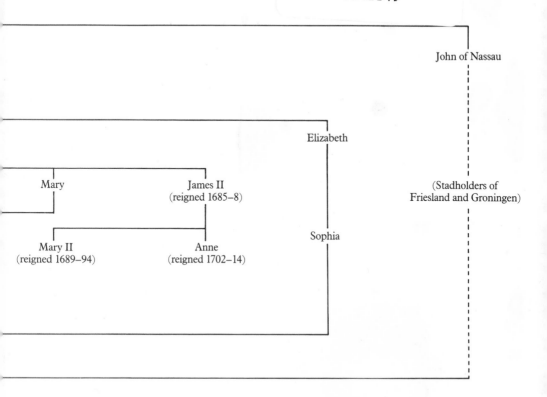

John of Nassau

Elizabeth

Mary   James II
(reigned 1685–8)

(Stadholders of
Friesland and Groningen)

Mary II   Anne
(reigned 1689–94)   (reigned 1702–14)

Sophia

The House of Orange,
Stuart and Hanover

THE BRITISH
AND
THE DUTCH

THE BRITISH
AND
THE DUTCH

*Political and Cultural
Relations through the Ages*

K. H. D. Haley

GEORGE
PHILIP

For Catherine and Rosemary

British Library Cataloguing in Publication Data

Haley, K. H. D. (Kenneth Harold Dobson)
    The British and the Dutch.
    1. Great Britain. Foreign relations with Netherlands,
    1500-1945
    I. Title
    327.410492
ISBN 0-540-01174-6

© K. H. D. Haley 1988
First published by George Philip,
59-60 Grosvenor Street, London W1X 9DA

Printed and bound in Great Britain by
Butler & Tanner Ltd, Frome and London

Contents

ILLUSTRATION ACKNOWLEDGEMENTS

Atlas Van Stolk, Rotterdam pp. 82, 84, 85 (above); Bibliotheek Der Rijksuniversiteit, Leiden pp. 190 (above), 191; British Library p. 192 (below); Het Koninklijk Penningkabinet, Leiden p. 81 (below); A. F. Kersting p. 188 (above and below); The Mauritshuis, The Hague p. 185 (above); The Trustees, The National Maritime Museum pp. 83 (above), 86 (above); National Portrait Gallery p. 190 (below); The National Trust Photographic Library p. 192 (above); Rijksmuseum, Amsterdam pp. 85 (below), 87, 88, 185 (below), 186, 187; Stedelijk Museum de Lakenhal, Leiden p. 81 (above); Vereeniging Nederlandsch Historisch Scheepvaart Museum, Amsterdam p. 83 (below); By courtesy of the Board of Trustees of the Victoria and Albert Museum pp. 86 (below), 189 (above and below).

Introduction

In the history of British relations with other European peoples, the French have inevitably taken the largest place. Most obviously, France faces the English coast across the Channel for hundreds of miles, and at the Straits of Dover is closer than any other neighbour. France is larger and until the nineteenth century was more populous than the British Isles; and Paris (or Versailles) was a rival power centre which could at times contemplate planning an invasion in a way that the native peoples of the Low Countries never could. From the time of the Norman Conquest and the Angévin Empire, to the two Hundred Years Wars of 1340–1453 and 1689–1815, British and French troops fought one another on battlefields ranging from Hastings, Crécy and Agincourt to Blenheim and Waterloo. If the deaths of the fallen really made the field forever England, a large amount of territory would have been accumulated in this way.

Socially and culturally, the attraction of French life and accomplishments has also been powerful. In so far as the British can be persuaded to learn any foreign language, it has usually been French, with the attractions of French literature as a reward. Through France, and by way of Versailles, the British aristocracy proceeded on the Grand Tour in the eighteenth century; and through France and to the French Riviera proceeded those in search of the sun and the Mediterranean in the nineteenth. Paris itself became a magnet to much wider social groups, for its own sake and as the art capital of Europe. France was the destination of most British tourists who visited the Continent, and amongst the delights of French towns, countryside and people, the attractions of French wines played no small part.

Yet it is the argument of this book that even by the side of the French connection the importance of the influence of the Dutch upon British development, especially from the sixteenth to the eighteenth centuries, should not be underestimated. Furthermore, that influence has been exercised in ways which often contrast sharply with the influence of the French, and can frequently be interpreted as suggesting a deeper affinity.

In the first place, in the age of the sailing ship the Dutch were in practice less distant from London and the south-east than were the French. The estuary of the Thames faces those of the Scheldt, the Maas and the Rhine across the North Sea. It is no accident that this developed into one of the great axes of European trade, more important than the trade to the mouth of the Seine or even the earlier trade to the Gironde, until the age of the 'commercial revolution' and the development of transoceanic trading routes. A whole series of east-coast ports, extending as far north as the Firth of Forth, were brought within the orbit of this trade. But naturally it was London, which included one in ten Englishmen in the seventeenth century and through which a far greater proportion of English economic life was conducted, that predominated in it. From Gravesend or by way of Harwich it was possible to get to Antwerp or The Hague more quickly than to Paris until the age of the train ferry and the aeroplane. Until the age of the turnpike, indeed, except in prolonged stormy weather, the Netherlands were less remote from London than the more distant parts of England. Scots could get more easily to Leiden University than to Oxford and Cambridge. Of course Dublin was more removed still from Whitehall and the City.

Relations between the English and the Dutch were not primarily relations of armed struggle. In spite of the myth of the Dutch admiral Tromp sailing the Channel with a broom at his masthead, hostilities were confined to one generation between 1652 and 1674, and another between 1780 and 1813, during the latter part of which it was

The Netherlands in 1550 and 1648.

In 1550 all the provinces, except the Bishopric of Liège, were ruled by Spain. By 1648 the independent
Dutch Republic included the seven northern provinces who sent representatives to the States-
General – Groningen, Friesland, Overijssel, Gelderland, Utrecht, Holland and Zeeland – the sparsely
populated area of Drenthe and the territories known as the Generality taken from Spain in the later
stages of the Revolt. Everything else, except Liège, was Spanish. The areas indicated in the south-
west were conquered by Louis XIV in 1659–78.

Napoleonic domination of Holland rather than the wishes of the Dutch that mattered. Though the naval campaigns in the seventeenth century were particularly hard-fought, with great deeds of daring accomplished by Tromp, De Ruyter, Blake and many lesser sailors, they never entered the national consciousness in the same way as the campaigns against the French. This was partly because, even at the height of the wars, many Englishmen continued to regard the Dutch as potential Protestant allies against Spain or France, rather than long-standing enemies. Thus there was no Lowestoft or Camperdown Square or Blake's column; and there was nothing remotely resembling Waterloo, for land campaigns against the Dutch in Europe were restricted to two expeditions lasting only a few weeks in 1799 and 1809. This was little enough to set against the years in which the two peoples fought together under William III and Marlborough, or the two centuries in which British volunteers served in Dutch pay against the enemies of the Dutch Republic. Nor were the Dutch potential invaders of England (though other forces occupying Dutch territory, whether Spanish, French, or German, certainly were). The only exception to this generalization was the unopposed 1688 landing of William III. A Stuart prince of the blood, as well as a Dutch stadholder, his intervention was requested by some prominent Englishmen and was desired by many more, both Whigs and Tories.

It would be absurd to minimize the three wars of the seventeenth century (though each lasted only two years) to the point of denying that they were the outcome of a much more long-standing commercial and colonial rivalry, and of a deep English envy of Dutch commercial success. Yet in this case of commercial rivalry, as in many others, there were also important connections between the two rivals. The jealousy between them in the Stuart period must be kept in perspective by the knowledge that the United Provinces had long been by far the principal market for English exports and the place where English cloth was finished, and in 1700 almost half the total of English exports still went there. By that date the Dutch Republic no longer supplied as high a proportion of English imports as it had once done, but this was in large measure because it now came second in importance to the plantations with their heavy supplies of colonial produce, tobacco and sugar. Relations between merchants of the two nations engaged in this trade were not always cordial (Englishmen were notoriously xenophobic). However, there could be no denying either its basic importance or the fact that it enabled those Englishmen taking part to divine the causes of the Dutch lead over the rest of Europe in commercial and financial matters. Imitation is said to be the sincerest form of flattery, and it has been well observed that much English economic policy consisted in imitation of Dutch commercial, financial, industrial and agricultural techniques. And in the dissemination of this influence it was important that in each country there should be substantial communities of people who came, not all for purely economic reasons, from the other.

As far back as the reign of Edward III, Flemish immigrants had been encouraged to contribute to the development of an English cloth industry. In the sixteenth century refugees from the tyrannies of Alva came to several provincial centres to foster the so-called 'new draperies'; in the seventeenth century engineers and craftsmen came to drain Axholme and the Fens; in the eighteenth century Dutch businessmen, investors in the National Debt and their agents came to the City of London to pursue their financial and mercantile interests. Round the Anglo-Dutch churchof Austin Friars in London from 1550 onwards, a Dutch community developed which was cohesive but never exclusive. In fact, many of them intermarried with the families of their British business associates and became permanent residents, significant not only for the intrinsic importance of their economic activities but as the conveyors of Dutch ideas and Dutch tastes. The British in Holland were probably more numerous. It has been said, with every appearance of truth, 'that for a variety of reasons, economic, religious, and political, all the people of English extraction scattered over the rest of the continent hardly compared in number with the English permanently resident in the Low Countries'[1], and to these must be added the Scots in Rotterdam and Veere and in the Scots Brigade. The word *resident* needs stressing here – for long periods if not necessarily for life. For a much smaller proportion of British in the Low Countries were gentlemen travellers, or what we should call tourists, than was the case among those who went to France, where indeed there would be much more to see and to occupy them. Most of the British in the United Provinces were there for more practical reasons than just to see the sights. They were Merchant Adventurers, craftsmen of all kinds, soldiers (often founding families and settling there), religious and political fugitives from hostile governments in London (often returning to their native country, when conditions took a turn for the better, with valuable experience of a church not based on tithes and unable to enforce conformity). They were scholars and students, particularly of theology, Roman law and medicine, ministers of religion and freethinkers in a society without censorship. In short, they were people of all kinds and from every social class. Through them, a traffic flowed along the route between the facing estuaries, not only in goods but also in ideas and tastes (literal as well as metaphorical, for they included gin). From the United Provinces came paintings and painters, books and newspapers and maps, tiles and delftware, turnips, cabbages and tulips, Dutch ribbon looms, the example of brick buildings, and models for Dutch gables, barns and furniture.

The largest gap was in a knowledge of Dutch vernacular literature, unless indeed Vondel's *Lucifer* had an influence on Milton; for in contrast to French, the Dutch language remained 'double Dutch', even to most Englishmen in the Netherlands, unless they learned it in the course of a commercial apprenticeship, and the literary did not need it, for most books published were in Latin or French. On the other hand, a knowledge of English literature flowed in the reverse direction. It was through the Netherlands that Shakespeare and Milton became known on the Continent, as well as Lockian philosophy and Newtonian science, just as Englishmen became familiar with the practice of religious toleration and with a more liberal intellectual atmosphere than was usual in their own country.

Such topics as these will therefore receive some attention in the following pages, along with the course of Anglo-Dutch political relations (including the involvement of each country in the internal politics of the other) and the development of economic co-operation and rivalry.

I have therefore provided not a lengthy formal bibliography but footnote references which indicate not only the sources of quotations, but the main works in which further information can be found on

general topics mentioned in the index. Where no place of publication
is given it is in the United Kingdom. If I have tried to avoid the
natural temptation to multiply references to those great scholars who
have previously worked on the Anglo-Dutch connection, such as Sir
George Clark, Professor Geyl, and Professor Charles Wilson, I hope
this will not obscure the extent of my debt to them, and particularly
to the last mentioned, the doyen of Dutch studies in this country at
this time. The spelling and punctuation of quotations have been
modernized. I hope the whole will be at least some small repayment
for the pleasures I have received in discovering Dutch cities, the
Dutch countryside, and the Dutch people.

K. H. D. Haley
Sheffield, 1988

CHAPTER ONE

From Boniface to Erasmus

U ntil at least the middle of the sixteenth century, Englishmen applied the name 'Dutch' indiscriminately to all those people living on the north-western coasts of Europe, from at least the Weser to Dunkirk, who spoke a Teutonic language. In the modern Dutch tongue the kindred word *duits*, like the German *deutsch*, does not refer to the inhabitants of the Netherlands, but to those of Germany. For the Tudor Englishman there was a similar lack of precision in contemporary usage of the word 'German' to that of the word 'Dutch'. In 1550 the charter of the Anglo-Dutch church of Austin Friars, which was to be for many years the centre of the Anglo-Dutch community, granted the building for the use *Germanorum aliorumque peregrinorum* (of Germans and other foreigners). The young Edward VI in his journal simply allocated it to 'the Germans', irrespective of the fact that the majority of the congregation certainly came from the Netherlands part of the dominions of the Hapsburg emperor, Charles V. On the other hand, in 1567, when the same ruler no longer ruled over both Germany and the Netherlands, official returns of the number of foreigners in London still referred to 'Dutch' without a special category for the Germans and Flemings. It was essentially the success of the rebels against Spain in the seven provinces of the northern Netherlands, which made it necessary to find a separate word to describe them. A certain amount could be done with the aid of provincial terms like

'Hollanders' and 'Zeelanders', but ultimately a word was needed to cover all the inhabitants of the new Republic who spoke its main language. That word was 'Dutch'; beyond the eastern frontier were the 'Germans'; while across the southern frontier, in Flanders and that part of Brabant which remained under Spanish rule, as well as Artois and the Cambrésis which were later to be annexed by Louis XIV, the words 'Fleming' and 'Flemish' were used. But the differentiation was only very gradual. It was, for instance, unclear in the plays of Jacobean dramatists, and even Clarendon, writing after the Restoration about the havoc wrought by the English privateers in the second Anglo-Dutch war, referred to the practical difficulty of distinguishing between Dutch and German prizes. 'The Hanse Towns of Hamburg, Lübeck, Bremen, and the rest ... had the worst luck; for none of them could ever be distinguished from the Dutch. Their ships were so like, and their language so near, that not one of their vessels were (*sic*) met with, ... but they were brought in.'[1] He could have added that the difficulty was compounded by the fact that 'Dutch' crews included many North German sailors.

Though it would be foolish to draw too hard and fast a line between Dutch, German and Flemish in early modern times, this book will be mainly concerned with the first of these categories in the two hundred years after the outbreak of the Revolt against Spain. But clearly there were relations between the Netherlands and the English (and Scots) before the Revolt and an introductory word is necessary about them.

Contacts between the peoples on the opposing shores of the North Sea date back at least to the time of the barbarian invasions of the fifth century. At this time, the Saxon tribes who had moved west of the River Weser into 'Frisia' were impelled to migrate further by over-population and by a rising high-water level which made the artificial dwelling-mounds or *terpen* no longer adequate. They then took some Frisians with them in their attacks upon the eastern shores of England. It has often been said that the Frisian language, which differs from Dutch and is still spoken in areas of the modern province of Friesland, but was once spoken over a much wider area, is the language most closely related to English. A long tradition to this effect, far from being a theory of modern philologists, may be represented by the work of the poet Starter. An Englishman by birth, who lived in Leeuwarden, he wrote Frisian poetry in the early seventeenth century, and went so far as to claim that men 'of the noble Frisian race conquered all England with their lord Engisto'.[2] Apart from linguistic evidence, archaeology has shown close affinities between the culture of the Frisian *terpen* and that of the early Germanic invaders of England. It has also been suggested that comparisons can be made between the social systems of East Anglia in particular and of 'Frisia' (by which is meant here the coastal strip from the Scheldt to the Weser).[3]

If 'Saxon and Norman and Dane are we', it may well be then that there is at least a dash of Frisian as well. But between the fifth and ninth centuries Frisian influence was not limited to participation in conquest and settlement. As early as this there were already close trading contacts. The Frisians came to play an important part in the economy of north-western Europe as middlemen between the Rhineland, England and Scandinavia. They sailed much further afield than East Anglia or London. Notably they sailed to the Humber; archaeological discoveries at York suggest what has been called a *vicus Frisonum*, a distinct area in which the Frisian traders lived. Similar discoveries at Hamwih (early Southampton) also suggest a strong Frisian connection. In the late seventh century there emerged a kind of Anglo-Frisian coinage, the sceattas, which were struck on both sides of the North Sea and were so similar in weight and type that it is often difficult to distinguish between those from English and those from Frisian mints. Most have come to light in Walcheren.[4]

This Frisian trade reached its height between about 750 and 850. The English contribution, however, was not only in providing slaves, furs, and other commodities. Within half a century of the conversion of Northumbria to Christianity, missionaries were crossing to preach to the Frisian heathen. A visit by Wilfrid, Bishop of York, in 678–9, was followed by a much longer mission by another Yorkshireman, Willibrord (trained in Ireland), who was sent to preach the gospel to the Frisians in 690 and made it his life's work. A tradition was preserved that the success of the Anglo-Saxon missionaries was no doubt due to the similarity of language; 'so their St Willibrord preached in these lands in the same tongue as he preached in England, which without doubt was at that time the natural language of both these countries'. However this may be, Willibrord, in the course of a long life, became an archbishop and made his base at Utrecht, close to the Frisian border on the River Ijssel. He had numbers of English helpers, of whom the most famous was St Boniface. Most of the latter's work was done further east in central Germany, but his missionary career began in Frisia (716) and ended there many years later when he was martyred at Dokkum, in the modern province of Friesland, in 754. Nor was this traffic across the North Sea, mostly of Northumbrians, only one way, for young Frisians like Liudgar were sent by their abbot at Utrecht (a pupil of Boniface) to study at York. Alcuin, who crossed from York to the great river port of Dorestad on the Rhine in 780, asked his former pupils from York to send hymns and to fill 'the boats of the Frisians' with them.[5]

The commercial activities of the Frisians, as the carriers of the northern seas, and the missionary activities of the English were both cut down by the incursions of the Vikings in the ninth century. Dorestad, hitherto the most important commercial centre of north-western Europe, was raided four times and was finally captured in 863, so that its name survives only in a famous later painting of the mill at Wijk-bij-Duurstede. Frisia reverted from being a trading centre to being a base for Viking raids, many of which (like the earlier invasions of the Saxons) must have been mounted from the estuaries of the Scheldt and the Rhine. According to the Lindisfarne Annals, there were Frisians in the invading Viking fleet in 854–5. But it is equally true that when King Alfred wanted to create an 'English' navy, he turned for assistance to the obvious source, and Frisian mercenaries, some of them even mentioned by name among the casualties, were on Alfred's ships in 896.

Though the seafaring qualities of the inhabitants of the Netherlands were thus known early to the English, they tended to fade from prominence in the centuries that followed. It was hundreds of years before the Dutch could be said to have recovered a major part of the carrying trade of Europe, and even then it could not be said that it was the inhabitants of Friesland and Groningen who did so. The result of the Battle of Hastings, the relationship between England, the Angevin Empire and France, and the wine trade from Bordeaux once again made the Channel more important than the North Sea. No powerful ruler, threatening or inviting attack, dominated the Netherlands, which after the splitting-up of Charlemagne's empire tended in practice to dissolve into counties until in the fifteenth century many of them became part of the Duchy of Burgundy. It was only in the sixteenth century that Charles V combined all the famous 17 provinces under his rule.

It was the growing symbiosis between English wool and the Flemish cloth industry which eventually led to a new relationship between the peoples of England and the Netherlands (and principally the provinces of Flanders and Brabant). But in the intervening period, in spite of the paucity of records, there are enough glimpses also of trade between ports in the northern Netherlands and east-coast ports of England to confirm the obvious probability that commerce continued without much publicity. Though merchants from the Dutch member-cities in the Hanseatic League of German trading cities cannot have been so prominent as those of Hamburg, Bremen and Lübeck, they must have been present among the residents of the League's London base in the Steelyard by the end of the Middle Ages.

From at least the thirteenth century the fishermen of the Zeeland islands and the villages near the mouth of the River Maas began to fish near Great Yarmouth, with the aid of privileges given by Edward I. It was another century before improved methods of curing herring were discovered. In the meantime it was to the advantage of all parties to land catches at Yarmouth, the beginning of a long association. But the ships of Zeeland and Holland were also in demand by Englishmen to transport their expeditions. In 1326 Queen Isabella, mother of the prince who was to become Edward III, used a fleet of herring busses, said to number 140, to convey her troops from Dordrecht to England. Henry V hired ships in Holland and Zeeland for the Agincourt campaign and later expeditions. In 1471 Edward IV landed at Ravenspur near the mouth of the Humber, having sailed from Flushing in ships of Holland and Zeeland (said with some exaggeration to number 500), provided by his brother-in-law,

Charles the Bold, Duke of Burgundy. Other naval contacts between the English and Dutch were less official and less well-recorded. But smuggling always has to be in some sense a co-operative enterprise, by subjects if not governments, and the crews of pirate ships are rarely restricted to one nationality. That Englishmen knew of the provinces of Zeeland and Holland as sources of ships and sailors is certain; and it is highly probable that the process had begun by which Dutch seafaring terms entered the English language, from *ahoy* to *yacht* and including *skipper* and *smuggler* and many others.

In the fourteenth and fifteenth centuries, however, the export of English wool to the booming towns of Flanders was far more important, followed by the development of a native cloth industry, with the aid of immigrant Flemish workers, for export to the Low Countries. By the beginning of the reign of Edward III the supply of English raw wool to Bruges and Ypres, Ghent and Antwerp was so essential that Edward was able to use the threat of an embargo to try to pressurize the Count of Flanders into joining an anti-French coalition. When this failed, he used the same threat to turn the cloth towns against the Count, in full alliance with himself. It was at Ghent that Edward assumed the arms and title of King of France in 1340, and in the Scheldt off Sluis that he won the first naval battle of the Hundred Years War.[6] But the wool trade was not only with Flanders. When in 1337 Edward granted a monopoly of the export of wool to a syndicate of wool merchants, it was to Dordrecht that the wool was to be shipped. Later, when the merchant Company of the Staple was given the monopoly of the export of wool through Calais, the growing cloth industry of Leiden depended upon it, and in the last half of the fifteenth century the men of Leiden were buying up at Calais almost half the total number of woolfells exported from England.[7]

It was Edward III who encouraged Flemish weavers and also some Zeelanders to come to England to stimulate the cloth industry with their knowledge of craft processes. The inducement was, according to tradition, that 'they should feed on fat beef and mutton, till nothing but their fullness should stint their stomachs ... their beds should be good, and their bedfellows better, seeing the richest yeomen ... would not disdain to marry their daughters unto them, and such

English beauties, that the most envious foreigners could not but commend them'. In practice the Flemings were not always as popular as they had been led to expect, and those who 'could not say Bread and Cheese but Brot and Cause' suffered in the Peasants' Revolt of 1381, as they also did in the London riots against foreigners on 'Evil May Day', 1517. English immigrants in the Netherlands never had to face anything comparable.[8] But, though recent authorities no longer assign to them quite the same importance as older ones, there can be no doubt that they passed on their skilled techniques, for instance in Norfolk and Coventry.

The cloth exports which resulted found their way to the Low Countries through the Fellowship of Merchant Adventurers, primarily a chartered body of London merchants. However, there was a time when York and Newcastle Merchant Adventurers had an independent existence, and 'interlopers' who ignored the official monopoly became increasingly common. In the reign of Edward IV the Merchant Adventurers eventually established themselves at Antwerp, whence they traded with Holland, Zeeland, Brabant and Flanders. At the height of their prosperity in the first half of the sixteenth century, following Henry VII's new charter of 1501, they sent four fleets a year to the Scheldt, with a quota of exports for members which was intended to set up a kind of cartel. The Fellowship had a governor with 24 elected assistants, and civil and criminal jurisdiction over its members in foreign fields. In theory all who paid the fees could enjoy the privileges of the Fellowship, but gradually Londoners came to dominate merchants from the outports. London's position facing the Low Countries was one reason why commercial life was concentrated there.

It might be thought that the obvious advantages to both parties of this central trade, first in wool, and then by 1500 to a much larger extent in cloth, unfinished or part-finished, would lead to political harmony. But if the needs of trade fostered the connection, it was also true that the needs of politics made an interruption of trade a useful tactic – and one which encouraged retaliation. Grants of privileges and the imposition of embargoes alternated, at least from the time of Edward I. The most important factors in this were the attitudes of the rulers of the Netherlands to the Hundred Years War with France and the dynastic ties of the English kings; often these were interlinked. A daughter of Edward I had married a count of Holland, but a more important marriage was that between Edward III and Philippa, daughter of the Count of Holland and Hainault (by that time under the same ruler), which was part of the arrangement with Queen Isabella in 1326. As previously mentioned, this encouraged Edward in his attempts to bring about an anti-French coalition at the beginning of the Hundred Years War, but equally he did not hesitate to use an embargo when it would suit his policy. In 1383 the counties of Flanders and Artois fell to Philip, Duke of Burgundy, through his marriage to the heiress. This marriage was designed to bring Flanders back under French influence, but, in fact, it had the opposite effect, provoking the start of the well-known feuds between the Armagnac and Burgundian branches of the Valois royal family of France. As a result, political and economic interests combined to lead successive dukes of Burgundy to cast their influence, and Flemish resources, on the side of England when the Hundred Years War was resumed by Henry V.

In 1433 Holland and Zeeland followed Brabant and Limburg into the territories of the Duke of Burgundy, two years before he withdrew from the English alliance at the Congress of Arras. From then on a far greater part of the Netherlands (though still only two of the seven provinces which later achieved their independence in the Dutch Republic) was under the Burgundians than under any ruler since the break-up of Charlemagne's empire. In the Wars of the Roses their influence was cast on the side of the Yorkists, until the Magnus Intercursus of 1496 with Henry VII provided for political peace and economic friendship. It did not end all disputes, but it inaugurated a more settled period and indeed the Intercursus was appealed to as a basic document for over 150 years.[9]

In the meantime merchants from Scotland, on the whole less harassed by political complications, had also developed a profitable trade with the prosperous towns of the Low Countries. The exchange of luxury goods from Flanders for Scottish hides, coarse cloth, salt and eventually coal was sufficiently important to attract privileges for those merchants involved in it. Until the fourteenth century it was principally carried on at Bruges, and later at Middelburg.

The ledger of Andrew Haliburton shows that he was living in the Netherlands and conducting business at Middelburg and Bruges between 1492 and 1503, and he was then addressed as Conservator of Scottish privileges in the Low Countries. Between 1506 and 1541 the Scottish Staple, supposedly regulating all exports to the Low Countries, alternated between Middelburg and Veere, a smaller port on the island of Walcheren. Though naturally the trade was never as important as that of the Merchant Adventurers, it is significant not only that it warranted careful regulation by James V of Scotland, but that Middelburg and Veere (and on occasion Antwerp) made rival bids to attract the Staple to their ports. Veere bid highest, and from 1541 was the sole Staple port, though what goods were covered by the Staple was never precisely defined. In the seventeenth century it was disputed whether the profitable commodity of coal, which went then to the much more convenient port of Rotterdam, was included. There was an interruption in the years 1573–8, when trade up the Scheldt was cut off by the rebel Sea Beggars. But in 1578 the prospect of north and south Netherlands combining seemed so good that, in their eagerness to attract the Scots once again, the magistrates of Veere made a new agreement. Their concessions were a nice mixture of commercial, practical and spiritual inducements: quantities of beer and wine free of excise for the Scots factors, powers for the Conservator to judge all quarrels between Scots, and the use of the choir of the great church, with more excise-free beer and wine for the ministers. After the recapture of Antwerp by the Duke of Parma for Philip of Spain, however, Veere was permanently cut off from that city and the southern Netherlands, while it was not centrally placed for trade with Holland and the northern areas which gained their independence. We shall return later to the subject of Scots trade with the Dutch after the Revolt. For the present it is relevant to note that in places like Culross on the northern shores of the Firth of Forth the crow-stepped gables and pantiled roofs of some houses still show signs of the old traffic with the Low Countries. They form a counterpart to the gabled fronts of houses still preserved on the picturesque quayside at Veere, which the Scots factors made their headquarters until the eighteenth century.[10]

If the Netherlands took two-thirds of English cloth exports and were the main outlet for Scots trade, the influence of Burgundian culture was wide ranging upon all those in many walks of life who were in contact with it. It is too large a subject (and not merely a Dutch one) to be covered adequately in the course of a few introductory pages of a book focusing on Anglo-Dutch relations after the Revolt.[11] Suffice it to say that Englishmen had already, by the beginning of the sixteenth century, formed the habit of looking to the Netherlands for new crafts, new fashions and new skills. In the use of bricks and gables, pilasters and glass, overmantels and furniture, tapestry and linen-fold panelling, choir-stalls and bells, lace and jewellery, Flemish influence abounds. It is to be found alike in the history of art and architecture and in the history of printing. Caxton, who was Governor of the Merchant Adventurers in Bruges from 1462 and led a temporary exodus to Utrecht from 1464–7, printed in most cases on paper made in the Low Countries, and in the early sixteenth century many printers working in England were Flemish. According to a well-known rhyme, hops were said to have come into the country from Flanders in the year of the Reformation; and another tradition has it that when Catherine of Aragon wanted a good salad she sent to Holland for it.

In religion there were no dramatic developments, but in 1349 there were already signs of the religious unorthodoxy for which the Netherlands were later known to Englishmen. In that year 'more than 120 persons of Zeeland and Holland, coming through Flanders unto London, sometime in the Church of St Paul, sometime in other places of the City, twice in the day, in the sight of all the people, from the loins unto the heels covered in linen cloth, all the rest of their bodies being bare, having on their heads hats with red crosses before and behind, everyone in their right hands a whip with three cords, each cord having a knot in the middest, beat themselves on their bare bloody bodies going in procession, four of them singing in their own language, all the others answering them.'[12] But more important than the unorthodoxy of the Flagellants was the more mild, rational, tolerant and scriptural unorthodoxy of Erasmus of Rotterdam (c. 1466–1536). The great Dutch scholar made a short stay at St Mary's College, Oxford, in 1499 (in the course of which he became acquainted with the humanist scholars Colet, Grocyn,

Linacre and More) and another stay at Cambridge in 1505–6. He made a third and longer visit after the accession of Henry VIII when there was talk of his becoming Lady Margaret Reader in Divinity there. His views of the country and the university tended to vary with the prospects of preferment, but he paid compliments to English scholars and recalled Cambridge evenings 'spent in perfectly delightful talk' (in Latin). His work on the Greek text of the New Testament was stimulated by Colet, and it is tempting to connect this with the emergence, within a decade of Erasmus's departure in 1514, of a group of Reformers at Cambridge. But the evidence suggests that he had few pupils there. His personal contacts with English scholars were not with later Reformers, but with people like More (in whose house he wrote the *Encomium Moriae* when confined by an attack of lumbago), who remained loyal to the Catholic Church. Insofar as there is truth in the claim that 'the English reformation began at Cambridge, and the Cambridge movement began with Erasmus'[13] this was not the result of known personal contacts but of his books and particularly his work on the New Testament. In the world of scholarship the Erasmian influence upon a whole generation was profound, and it is noteworthy that in 1547, and again in the reign of Elizabeth, copies of Erasmus's *Paraphrases* were ordered to be placed in every parish church.

In the prosperous, industrialized, densely populated, urbanized and culturally advanced area of the Netherlands, the Dukes of Burgundy had replaced a collection of scattered counties by a state. This state was far from being centralized, but it promised to become more so and held the equivalent of almost half the population of England. It is impossible to say whether a new independent state could have established itself alongside the others in the whole of the Netherlands, for the area was absorbed into the dominions of the Hapsburg family. The provinces of the Netherlands descended to the Emperor Charles V (born at Ghent in 1500) and thence in 1555 to his son Philip II of Spain, along with the Spanish empire in the New World, Milan, Naples and the dominance over Italy; a younger branch ruled at Vienna. The addition of the Dutch province of Friesland in 1515 was followed by that of Utrecht and Overijssel in 1515, Groningen in 1536, and Gelderland in 1543. The 17 provinces of the area now comprised the whole of modern Holland, Belgium (apart from the bishopric of Liége which enjoyed a special status) and areas which now form part of northern France. They were rich, populous and cultured, and there was nothing to foreshadow the later split between north and south, which was a consequence, not a cause, of the Revolt later in the century. But the link with Spain, the largest of European powers, inevitably meant that they were dragged into conflict with Spain's great opponent, France. At the same time, this subordination of the Netherlands to the political interests of Spain, coupled with Spanish persecution of Protestant heresy at the time of the contemporary English Reformation, transformed the relationship between the English and the Dutch.

CHAPTER TWO

Allies against Spain

It has been well observed that 'the Duke of Alva's arrival in Brussels in August 1567 was one of the turning points of western European history'. The army that he brought with him to support Philip II's authority was not only a menace to the local provincial and municipal liberties of the Netherlanders, but a strategic threat to Elizabeth, her councillors and the majority of her people. Within five years, during which Mary Queen of Scots fled across the English border and became the focus for the Revolt of the Northern Earls, Alva's tyrannical rule 'made Spain rather than France appear to most Englishmen as the prime national enemy'. His troops, soon reinforced to 25,000 and eventually to 50,000 men, were lodged, according to Cecil, 'in the very counterscarp of England'.[1] Protestant heretics in the Netherlands were by no means the only ones to dread the activities of Alva and his Council of Blood, but they had specially urgent reasons for doing so. In England zealous Protestants were particularly concerned with the possibility that Catholic conspirators supporting Mary would look to the army of the head of the Counter Reformation. It was natural that Protestants in both countries should seek to make common cause, with the support of many secular-minded people who feared subjection to Spain.

Philip II's decision to appoint Alva which led to these consequences was not at all inevitable, but in the previous thirty years there had been signs of a cooling of relations between England and Spain. The English Reformation and Henry VIII's divorce had meant that he had to be wary of Charles V's possible intervention in support of his aunt Catherine of Aragon and her daughter Mary. Nothing came of that, but there were early links between English Protestantism and that in the Netherlands, where Antwerp was not only a great financial and commercial centre but a centre for the new heretical ideas. There the first Protestant heretic was martyred in 1523; there the Merchant Adventurers became acquainted with Protestant literature; there were the printing facilities which Tyndale used for many reprints of his New Testament of 1526 (based on Erasmus's edition of the Greek text). In his later years Tyndale resided in the English house of the Merchant Adventurers at Antwerp, and they presumably subsidized his work and facilitated the smuggling of his Testament into England. Following the Henrician Reformation, the process began by which those out of favour with the ecclesiastical authorities in one country sought refuge in the other across the North Sea, and Netherlanders came to escape from Charles V's Placards against heresy. Not all of these were welcome. A proclamation against Anabaptist 'strangers' in 1535, the year when Anabaptist excesses at Munster (just across the Netherlands border) extended not only to adult baptism and to a new and sectarian conception of the Church but to polygamy, social revolution and a reign of terror, probably referred to Dutchmen. Three were burnt at Smithfield in 1538 to demonstrate Henry VIII's orthodoxy. Even in the less intolerant reign of Edward VI, the boy-king made an entry in his journal to the effect that 'a certain Arian of the Strangers [Church], a Dutchman, being excommunicated by the congregation of his countrymen, was after long disputation condemned to the fire'.[2] But less heterodox fugitives from the Netherlands were better received, and of the many ecclesiastical buildings vacated at the Dissolution of the Monasteries, the church of the Austin Friars was allocated to them by letters patent in 1550. The historian of the church estimates their numbers at six to eight hundred, presumably adults, and assumes that the majority were south Netherlanders, as the congregation's early ministers certainly were.[3]

At first sight the reign of Mary Tudor stopped these trends, for the Queen's marriage to Philip II seemed to involve England more deeply than ever in a Spanish alliance, and the members of the Dutch Reformed Church took to flight once more. But the long-term result of the presence of a Spanish king and Spanish aristocrats in London was a considerable increase in their unpopularity, and at the accession of Elizabeth, England reverted to Protestantism. The Dutch Protestants returned in 1559–60, and were granted their petition that 'the poor religious refugees might not be molested'; this time they were put under the supervision of the Bishop of London, Grindal, who had reluctantly to deal with a case in which the Dutch martyrologist, Haemstede, fell out with his church.[4] The political need to guard against France by preserving tolerable, if cool, Anglo-Spanish relations did not prevent the Governess of the Netherlands, Margaret of Parma, and her minister Cardinal Granvelle from reacting against the activities of English privateers by banning the import of English cloth. Nor did it prevent Elizabeth from retaliating by forbidding all imports from the Netherlands. During the period of the embargoes the Merchant Adventurers explored the possibility of transferring their Staple to Emden and Hamburg, and some of the local pamphlets against Granvelle may have been unofficially printed in England. Though trade between England and the Netherlands was resumed at the end of 1564 the links were no longer so cordial as they had once been.

By the year of Alva's arrival the Bishop of London's certificate of aliens recorded the presence in the City of 2993 'Dutch' (over the age of 14) out of 3760 foreigners there.[5] Though Germans as well as Flemings must have been included in this category, it is likely that around 2000 were members of the Austin Friars congregation. Some Englishmen had reservations about them. Thus the chronicler Stow recorded that they came 'with their wives, children and whole families, and that in such abundance, that, whereas before their coming large houses in London were plenteous, and very easy to be had at low and small rents, and by reason of the late dissolution of the religious houses many houses in London stood vacant, and not any man desirous to take them at any rate, were all very suddenly inhabited, and stored with inmates, to the great admiration of the

English nation, and advantages of landlords and leasemongers'.[6] Another return of 1568 gave the houses 'pestered with the greatest numbers of them'. The sect called the Family of Love, associated with the German Hendrik Niclaes but in England primarily the work of Christopher Vittels, a joiner from Delft who translated Niclaes's writings, evoked attacks by a pamphleteer who claimed he had been told that there were about a thousand members in England, and reviled 'the drowsy dreams of a doting Dutchman'. A royal proclamation of 1580 ordered that their books be burnt and the sectaries imprisoned, and bills for the suppression of the sect were discussed. The fact that two Dutch Anabaptists were burnt in great agony in 1575 was a further indication that English sympathies with religious unorthodoxy were not unlimited. Yet the fugitives from Alva clearly excited sympathy in the years after 1567, not only in London, but in a number of provincial centres. In the second largest city, Norwich, a church was opened in Blackfriars in 1569; in Yarmouth in 1570 the Queen licensed 'divers strangers of Holland, Zealand and other parts of the Low Countries ... being of late years upon lamentable occasion come into this our realm' to carry on their trade of fishing; in Sandwich there were said to be four to five hundred; and there were communities at Maidstone (1567), Colchester, Canterbury, Stamford (1572), Rye, Dover and elsewhere. In East Anglia they were responsible for the introduction of the manufacture of new cloths, the so-called 'new draperies' of lighter and often cheaper fabrics. Their success received encouragement in some official quarters, for instance at Colchester (where the congregation numbered several hundred), and inspired jealousy in others, but in the time of Alva sympathy naturally predominated. At Norwich, where there were said to be 4679 aliens (Walloons or French-speaking natives of the southern Netherlands, as well as Dutch) by 1582, one immigrant reported: 'You would never believe how friendly the people are together, and the English are the same and quite loving to our nation.' The historian Van Meteren, another immigrant, gives a picture of the English which may be contrasted with English pictures of the Dutch in later pages. Like those it says a good deal by implication about the writer's own nation.

'The English are a clever, handsome, and well-made people, but, like all islanders, of a weak and tender nature.... The people are bold, courageous, ardent, and cruel in war, fiery in attack, and having little fear of death; they are not vindictive, but very inconstant, rash, vainglorious, light and deceiving, and very suspicious, especially of foreigners, whom they despise. They are full of courtly and affected manners and words, which they take for gentility, civility, and wisdom. They are eloquent and very hospitable; they feed well and delicately and eat a great deal of meat; and as the Germans press the bounds of sobriety in drinking, these do the same in eating, for which the fertility of the country affords them sufficient means....

The people are not as laborious and industrious as the Netherlanders or French, as they lead for the most part an indolent life like the Spaniards; the most toilsome, difficult, and skilful works are chiefly performed by foreigners, as among the idle Spaniards.... They keep many lazy servants, and also many wild animals for their pleasure, rather than trouble themselves to cultivate the land....

The English dress in elegant, light, and costly garments, but they are very inconstant and desirous of novelties, changing their fashions every year, both men and women. When they go abroad riding or travelling, they don their best clothes, contrary to the practice of other nations....

Wives in England are entirely in the power of their husbands, their lives only excepted ... yet they are not kept as strictly as they are in Spain or elsewhere. Nor are they shut up, but they have the free management of the house or housekeeping, after the fashion of those of the Netherlands and others their neighbours. They go to market to buy what they like best to eat. They are well-dressed, fond of taking it easy, and commonly leave the care of household matters and drudgery to their servants. They sit before their doors, decked out in fine clothes, in order to see and be seen by the passers-by. In all banquets and feasts they are shown the greatest honour; they are placed at the upper end of the table, where they are the first served; at the lower end they help the men. All the rest of their time they employ in walking and riding, in playing at cards or otherwise, in visiting their friends and keeping company, conversing with their equals (whom they call *gossips*) and their neighbours and making merry with them at childbirths, christenings, and funerals; and all this with the permission and knowledge of their husbands, as such is their custom. Although the husbands often recommend to them the pains, industry, and care of the German or Dutch women, who do what the men ought to do both in the house and in the shops, for which services in England men are employed, nevertheless the women usually persist in retaining their customs. This is why England is called the paradise of married women. The girls who are not yet married are kept much more rigorously and strictly than in the Low Countries.'[7]

In 1572 the Spanish ambassador guessed that there were 20,000 of his master's subjects who had found shelter in England and who looked for Alva's overthrow by the Prince of Orange, William the Silent. The latter not unnaturally looked to Elizabeth for assistance and in 1568 Cecil did allow the Dutch churches to collect money for him. In 1571 William's brother, Louis of Nassau, even proposed an alliance of France, England, and the German Protestants to expel the Spaniards from the Netherlands. As their reward England would gain Holland and Zeeland, France would get Flanders and Artois, and the rest would go to William. The two most zealous Protestants on Elizabeth's council, Walsingham and the Queen's favourite, Robert Dudley, Earl of Leicester, both supported the project 'in respect of the spiritual fruit that may thereby ensue.'[8] But, precisely because France would thereby move into Flanders, Lord Burghley (as Cecil had now become) did not. At the same time, Elizabeth was wary of driving Philip II into war when her own position was threatened by the arrival of Mary, the Rebellion of the Northern Earls, the Ridolfi plot and the papal bull of excommunication and deposition. No direct answer was made to this first proposal for the incorporation of Holland and Zeeland into her dominions. She was prepared to make a nuisance of herself to Alva; she had seized for herself the treasure ships bringing a much-needed Genoese loan to pay his troops in Plymouth harbour at the end of 1568, thereby provoking Alva's embargo on trade with England and seizure of English goods and ships. She retaliated with a counter embargo of her own. Her proclamation forbidding the Dutch refugees to send help to William in 1568 was only a gesture. In the following years the Spanish ambassador in London, De Spes, complained bitterly of help given by the inhabitants and governors of English ports to pirates, English and Dutch, who preyed on Spanish shipping. Prizes were brought in openly to Dover, which De Spes described as the biggest robbers' den in Europe, and the booty seized by the Sea Beggars was sold in English ports. Though the Privy Council took action on paper and, for instance, banned English sailors from serving on the privateers, De Spes complained that the practice was winked at, and even that Spanish prisoners were kept in Dover town jail until ransomed. Attempts to make a distinction between peaceful, pious refugees from the Netherlands and those who 'under colour of religion and piety lately entered at sundry ports and creeks into the realm' were hardly likely to satisfy him, but in December 1571 he was expelled from the country. In September 1571 the Sea Beggars' leader, Count de la Marck, himself visited London.[9]

The extent of the English government's deliberate connivance in the activities of the Sea Beggars in the years 1568–71 is difficult to gauge. In this context, it was natural for Spaniards at the time, and some historians in later ages, to suspect that Elizabeth's famous order to the Sea Beggars, on 1 March 1572, that they should leave her ports, which was followed by their seizure of a new base at the Brill (near the modern Hook of Holland), was concerted with de la Marck. However, these suspicions probably had no basis in fact: the privateers, who were indiscriminate in their seizures of shipping, were a nuisance to English and Hamburg merchants, while Elizabeth was making overtures for a renewal of trade with the Netherlands and could not have wanted to co-operate with the Sea Beggars in the diplomatic situation which existed. In any case the far-reaching consequences of the seizure of the Brill, beginning the Dutch Revolt against Spain, could not have been foreseen.[10]

At all events, de la Marck immediately appealed to Elizabeth for arms and munitions. Within three weeks of the seizure of the Brill volunteers were being raised in support of the Sea Beggars. Burghley noted: 'Here is all covert means used to let them of the Low Countries pass home to the help of the liberty of the country,' and hoped that the Dutch would succeed by their own exertions and without having to call in the French. The volunteers were, it is true, financed by the Dutch community at Austin Friars, but the first contingent, some 300 strong and led by Thomas Morgan, mustered before the Queen at Greenwich. 'All this is done so publicly that one is bound to believe that the Queen and council willingly shut their eyes to it,' reported the disgusted Spanish ambassador. Morgan's men reached Flushing on 7 June, and were followed a month later by Sir Humphrey Gilbert with a thousand more. When Gilbert was shut out of Flushing by the governor, the townsmen demanded that 'their ancient friends and neighbours' be allowed back, with 'such a general affection ... as both tears were shed and their own beds presented to the Englishmen though they should lie on the ground themselves'. What the people of Flushing did not know was that Morgan and Gilbert were in correspondence with Burghley, and that Gilbert's instructions were concerned with guarding against the occupation of Flushing by the French, which might be permanent, rather than with giving strong backing to the revolt, whose outcome seemed very doubtful.[11]

These English troops – and Welsh, for the recurrence of the names Morgan, Williams and Price reminds us how many of the countrymen of Shakespeare's Fluellen were among them – were followed by Scots, who were given leave by their Privy Council on 21 June 1572 to pass to the wars in Flanders. In the following year one John Adamson was given permission to set out for the Low Countries with 130 soldiers 'for serving in the defence of Goddis trew religion agains the persequutoris theirof'. The historian of the Scots Brigade[12] comments on the tendency of historians to describe the English as 'volunteers' and the Scots as 'mercenaries'. The motives of both must have been mixed. Some no doubt fought for the cause of liberty, political and religious, and genuinely sympathized with the rebels; but many must have fought, in the words of one of them, 'for knowledge sake, fame and entertainment'. It would be difficult to know how much 'entertainment' they received in the modern sense of the word, but in its sixteenth-century sense of 'maintenance' they received little in the early years, when the supply of pay, food and equipment was exceedingly erratic. By October 1572 difficulties over pay from the Dutch assembly of the States-General were such that English volunteers were considering offering their services to the Spanish commanders. Eventually one of them, Sir Roger Williams, did accept an invitation to serve with the Spaniards for a short time 'having spent all my crowns, and being loth to return into England without seeing something'.[13] Gilbert and many of his men returned to England, and later a point was reached at which 'many bands of 150 were not able to muster sixty, and those in such poverty and misery as was lamentable to behold'.

Elizabeth and Burghley were so doubtful of the rebels' chances and so reluctant to commit English resources that at one point in the summer of 1573 one of Burghley's agents was sent to suggest that the unequal struggle would be better brought to an end. In the crisis year of 1574, in which the Dutch fought off the enemy at the siege of Leiden, the English were so far from rendering assistance (apart from a handful of volunteers) that the Privy Council had ordered the seizure of all ships from Flushing in retaliation for their 'insolencies'. What this meant was that the Sea Beggars cut off the resumed English trade up the Scheldt to Antwerp. Seizures of English ships by privateers claiming the authority of William, Prince of Orange, caused much ill-feeling in the following years. In Holland and Zeeland it was reported that Englishmen were criticized as 'those that do put on religion, piety and justice for a cloak, to serve humours withal and please the time, while policy only is made both justice, religion and God'.[14] Early in 1576 Elizabeth did agree to receive Marnix de St Aldegonde, who brought a request from the Prince of Orange that she should take Holland and Zeeland into her protection, and lend them money in return for the cession of Flushing, the Brill and other towns as security for repayment. But she declined this first offer of 'cautionary towns'. There was more support for the rebels elsewhere, and it is significant that in the House of Commons a Privy Councillor had to divert a proposal by several members that she should accept the Dutch offers.[15]

In 1576 the situation was transformed by the 'Spanish Fury', the mutiny of the unpaid Spanish troops at Antwerp. It now seemed that it might be possible to combine all 17 provinces of the Netherlands and not merely the two, Holland and Zeeland, which had hitherto been in revolt. In July 1577 the Spanish ambassador in London found the whole Privy Council in favour of going to their assistance against the new Governor, Don John (who privately had dreams of using the Netherlands as a springboard to send aid to Mary Queen of Scots, an aim which would have accorded with Elizabeth's fears). And Elizabeth herself seemed convinced. She told her envoy, Davison, to assure the States-General that if Don John refused to send the Spanish troops away she would support them against him. She also told Davison to let the Prince of Orange know how willing she was to befriend his cause, and to tell him that she had five or six hundred troops about London which she would send at once if he wanted them. But the States-General now hung back. 'When Elizabeth offered to lend money, it was unwise to give her time for second thoughts,' and she changed her mind and offered mediation.[16]

It has been suggested[17] that at this point Elizabeth missed a great opportunity to encourage the emergence of the whole of the Netherlands as a unified independent state. The polarization into north and south, Protestant and Catholic, was only just beginning, and the 17 provinces together could have secured their freedom from Spain. Consequently, they could have formed a barrier to Louis XIV and Napoleon: 'Not only Marlborough's wars but Wellington's too were a consequence of the late sixteenth-century division of the Netherlands.' But it is impossible to be confident of such a historical 'might have been'. No doubt these years represented the best chance of preserving the unity of the Netherlands. However, it is surely probable that the social, religious, personal and political tensions which led within two years to the separate Unions of Utrecht (the seven northern provinces which came to form the Dutch Republic) and Arras (the ten southern provinces which remained Spanish and Catholic) would still have had a disruptive effect. And without excusing Elizabeth's hesitations and changes of mind, which drove her own councillors to distraction, or trying to see in them a greater consistency and far-sightedness than could realistically be expected in constantly changing circumstances, we may conclude that Elizabeth might well have been wary of the risks involved in a confrontation with the greatest power in Europe until she had no practical alternative. She had burnt her fingers badly in the first French religious war; within the last decade she had had reason to appreciate the danger to the internal security of her kingdom, and Mary Queen of Scots was still a prisoner in Sheffield Castle. She was always conscious of the meagreness of her resources, and knew that in addition to her own expenses she would be called upon for loans which might or might not be repaid. Furthermore, there could be no certainty of military success against the far greater military experience of the Spanish tercios. When war did in fact come in 1585 the military position had deteriorated, but this could not have been certainly known in 1577. Rather than gamble on a hazardous co-operation with an uncertain States-General, it seemed better to avoid clear-cut decisions, and to hope that the aim of getting the Spanish troops out of the Netherlands while retaining Philip II's nominal suzerainty could be achieved by the rebels' own exertions. To this end she would offer her mediation, but would send men and money only if the rebel forces were on the point of collapse.

The result was that by 1584 the situation had become much blacker in Holland and Zeeland, which were again the nucleus of the Revolt. A new Governor of diplomatic as well as military ability, the Duke of Parma, had recovered most of the south for Spain; the man who had done most to co-ordinate the Dutch effort, William the Silent, was assassinated and his son was a Spanish prisoner; and Parma laid siege to the great prize of Antwerp, which would cap all his previous conquests. Even now Burghley drew up arguments against intervention. The Dutch were an ungrateful people, much given to mutinies and corruption, divided against themselves even to 'the very bowels' of their towns, and the leaders of the forces sent to their aid were likely soon to be at loggerheads with the leaders of the Dutch. Yet by now Philip II, should his hands ever become free, was more likely than ever before to take action against the heretic Queen, and the risks of intervention had to be run. In August 1584 Elizabeth declined what was effectively an offer of sovereignty, but permitted the levy of 1500 troops with the aid of contributions from the Dutch churches in England. It was not until June of the following year that a deputation arrived to renew the offer, in return for men to relieve Antwerp, which by then was in dire straits. In the Treaty of Nonsuch (10 August 1585) she took the plunge. She still refused to take on the responsibilities of sovereignty, but she undertook to send an Englishman of rank who, with two colleagues, would sit in the Dutch executive Council of State. She would send and pay for 6000 troops as long as the war lasted, and as security for the repayment of her expenses she would garrison Flushing and the Brill, at the mouths of the great waterways, at her own cost. The cost of 6000 men was reckoned at £126,000; actual payments over the two years 1585–7 were estimated by the Privy Council at £313,000, but may have been more.

At first sight these numbers might seem too pitifully small to make much difference. Yet 6000 men, together with the volunteers already present, constituted a substantial portion of the total Dutch forces of 30,000 (apart from the civic militias) – at least on paper, for there were both 'dead pays' (casualties kept on the muster rolls so that officers could draw their pay) and deserters. Nor was £126,000 a negligible sum, in that it amounted to about half the Queen's ordinary revenue in peacetime. The figures were appreciable; but the drawbacks were in the quality of the troops and their leadership, and in the deficiencies in their pay and upkeep.

The 2000 pressed men who were sent to help in the relief of Antwerp arrived too late to be of any use. The question was what could be done to restore the situation in the following year, and the Queen's answer was to send the Earl of Leicester. This choice of the Earl of Leicester has been much criticized because his mission was such a disastrous failure. It is easy to dismiss him as her 'favourite', and to assume that she chose her 'Sweet Robin' because of their sentimental relationship, though precisely for that reason she was reluctant to let him go when the time came. The fact is that to English and Dutch alike, no one could have seemed a more suitable choice. For many years he had been regarded as the leader of those in the Privy Council who advocated a 'Protestant' foreign policy, and for this reason the Queen's envoy in Brussels had written to him in 1577: 'I find the Prince [of Orange] the most desirous in the world of your lordship's coming over, and it is the string he daily harps on.' Others might have been abler, but none could have better indicated the Queen's commitment to the Dutch cause, and there would have been great disappointment if he had not come. It is also true that, as we shall see, co-operating with the local Dutch authorities would have been a difficult task for anyone. It had frustrated the French Duke of Anjou when he had been protector of the rebel provinces in 1582–3, and it had taxed all the charm and the powers of conciliation of William the Silent. In their offer of sovereignty to the Queen, the States-General had been concerned with obtaining full commitment to their cause, rather than with putting themselves under English authority. When that offer had been declined Leicester had been given a seat on the executive

Council of State, but even this was of little use to someone who did not speak Dutch. Nevertheless, despite this, the inadequacy of his support from home, and his not unnatural ignorance of the complexities of the internal Dutch situation, the fact remains that his stay in the Netherlands was a failure.

The author (probably Walsingham) of *A Declaration of the Causes moving the Queen of England to give aid to the Defence of the People afflicted and oppressed in the Low Countries*[18] declared that 'in respect that they were otherwise more straitly knit in ancient friendship to this realm than to any other country, we are sure that they could be pitied of none for this long time with more cause and grief generally than of our subjects of this our realm of England, being their most ancient allies and familiar neighbours, and that in such manner, as this our realm of England and those countries have been by common language resembled and termed as man and wife'. This cordial statement of the relationship, with its curious reference to a 'common language', raised the question why, in that case, the Queen had not gone to the rescue earlier. But the *Declaration* claimed that many friendly messages had been sent warning Philip to restrain the tyranny of his governors, while the Dutch had been restrained from yielding their subjection to any other prince. Seeing that all this had been in vain, 'and joining thereunto our own danger at hand by the overthrow and destruction of our neighbours, and access and planting of the great forces of the Spaniards so near to our countries, with precedent arguments of many troublesome attempts against our realm', it had been decided to send troops 'to defend the people and their towns from sacking and desolation'. The garrisoning of Flushing and the Brill was said to be only temporary, and 'for sure access and recess of our people and soldiers in safety, and for furniture of them with victuals and other things requisite and necessary' till those countries recovered their ancient liberties.

The months after Leicester's arrival in support of these high-sounding sentiments 'happened to be the first meeting of really large numbers of Englishmen and Dutchmen from every social layer'.[19] He was received with prodigious pageantry on the theme of *Quos Deus conjunxit homo non separet*. At Delft the banquets alone cost £1104, including £742 for wine, and at Amsterdam there were even aquatic monsters in the pageantry – 'whales and others of great hugeness', who seized his ship and towed it to land. There was a propagandist and a political purpose in all the display. It was intended both to demonstrate the addition of England's resources to the populace and to obtain further English commitment by inducing Leicester to accept the title of Governor-General, something which, much to the Queen's anger, he was not reluctant to do.

The disillusionment was correspondingly great, on both sides. In the first place, he was in no position to work the military miracles which were expected of him. The State Papers Foreign show that for some years there had been frequent reports of the bad condition of the English volunteers whom he found there. Poorly paid by the States-General who were their masters, they either deserted or solved their problems by seizing what they needed from the local population they were supposed to be defending. Our men at Ath, wrote one officer, have not a piece of bread to put in their mouths, and 'stand in terms' to treat with the enemy, yet the States are readier to pay other garrisons that are in no necessity 'than to send us victuals to live withal.... If there be no present order for us, our men will all go serve the Spaniard.' Ill-trained, ill-fed, ill-clothed, and mutinous, their actual numbers were much less than their strength on paper. Though Leicester made his own financial problems worse by diverting to these volunteers some of the money intended to pay the troops he brought with him, the 'old ragged rogues' inevitably contaminated the newcomers. 'It is no marvel our men run fast away. I am ashamed to write it, there was 500 ran away in two days, and a great many to the enemy.... There is of our runagates 200 brought again from the coastside. Divers I hanged before the rest, and I assure you they could have been content all to have been hanged rather than tarry.'[20] In these circumstances it is not surprising that he gained only minor successes, and that these were offset by some notable instances of English, or Irish, treachery. The town of Zutphen, which is associated in England with the famous words of the mortally wounded Sir Philip Sidney to his water-bearer that another's need was greater than his own, was also the same place where Rowland York betrayed the fortifications to the enemy. Sir William Stanley and his predominantly Irish troops handed over

Deventer to the enemy, and unpaid mutineers, largely German but under English command, handed over Geertruidenberg in 1589.

In war there are always problems when foreign troops are stationed in the land of an ally and these are always more noticeable when the war is not going well. There were mutual recriminations, the worse because there was some justification on both sides. Sidney's company on garrison duty at Flushing was described as 'the worst accommodated of all our soldiers, amongst a people of a froward and perverse disposition'; frequent clashes between townsmen and soldiers were reported until Sidney suggested the creation of barracks. One colonel thought 'these nations ... need a good schoolmaster, with the thunderbolt of Jupiter in his hand, to make them know themselves and their superiors', while another correspondent said that 'we begin to grow as hateful to the people as the Spaniard himself'. In 1587 the Queen's envoy, Buckhurst, after asking leave to return on the ground that he did not know the language and had to work through interpreters, wrote to Walsingham: 'As we have been never free from the daily and continual complaints of the States, in that her Majesty's bands are so weak, and so far from the number contracted both of horse and foot; so have we on the other side made the like daily against them, for that the English in their pay are so miserably used for want of pay, so that daily they cry out, and are ready to perish for want.'[21]

Such exasperations would have been more easily soothed had there been a greater semblance of co-operation between the Queen's representatives and the Dutch authorities. Leicester was quite unused to any system but that of a monarchical court and Privy Council, and finding that his authority was far less in practice than he had been led to expect by his initial welcome, rapidly grew to dislike the 'monstruous [sic] government' of the Republic. He not only had to deal with the assembly of the States-General, containing delegations from each of the seven provinces which had constantly to refer back to their principals for instructions. He also had to deal with separate States or assemblies in each province. In particular the States of the province of Holland (by far the most important province, containing most of the large towns) were difficult to manage. They in turn combined delegations from 18 towns, from Amsterdam downwards, and one delegation representing the nobility of the province. The 'regents' or ruling oligarchies of the towns (perpetuating themselves in the main by co-optation) by no means confined themselves to local municipal affairs, but had views on all matters of policy. Though often irritatingly parochial in their attitudes, these 'regents', most of them merchants, were also often more enlightened than Leicester would give them credit for, and he should not have written them off as his social inferiors, supposedly ill-informed about matters of state.

Privately he called them churls, tinkers, bakers and brewers and hired advocates. Unwisely he established himself at Utrecht, which was nearer to the military front but some distance from the towns whose regents he should have cultivated. There he fell into the hands of a group of zealously Calvinistic exiles from the south with whom, as the patron of Puritans, he had natural affinities. But he was removed from the Holland oligarchs. He could not understand why the Dutch persisted in trading with the enemy; he dismissed the argument that this was necessary to build up their financial strength to sustain the war effort as mere justification of private profit. By June 1586 he was already writing to the Queen of his desire 'to get into my hands three or four principal places in north Holland', so that she should 'both rule these men and make war or peace as you like'.[22] There was in fact a futile attempt to gain control of Leiden, and not long afterwards he left the country. The total lack of an official farewell was a marked contrast to the effusive welcome, and Leicester's own medal bore the words: *Non gregem sed ingratos invitus desero.* (I am not deserting my flock, but reluctantly leaving ungrateful people.) His successor, Willoughby, though a better soldier, was no more popular.

Yet in spite of these strains, the alliance survived. The English auxiliaries had their drawbacks, but they were sufficiently useful to make the States-General unwilling to lose them. The death of Sir Philip Sidney, Leicester's nephew, was regretted by a wider circle than the Leiden humanists who wrote Latin elegies. When Elizabeth, in pursuance of her usual policy of keeping as many irons in the fire as possible, sent commissioners to open peace negotiations with Parma at Ostend, they were fearful that they would be abandoned to Spain. (It was in fact scarcely a fortnight before the Armada sailed up the Channel.) Yet the negotiations never made much progress. In the last resort Dutch and English needed each other. For the Dutch the English alliance, if nothing else, produced another enemy for Spain and diverted Spanish resources from the steady reconquests which Parma had been carrying out in the Netherlands in preparation for the Armada. For the English, the Revolt kept Parma's formidable army occupied, and they knew that, if the Dutch went under, their own turn would come next.

These mutual benefits were exactly illustrated in the defeat of the Armada. It was 'equipped with wood, pitch and rope almost entirely conveyed on Netherlands ships from the Baltic'[23] and there was no co-ordinated plan by English and Dutch fleets to resist it. Yet the ships of Justin of Nassau performed a useful function by blockading Parma's ports and preventing his soldiers from emerging; the Armada's destruction meant not only salvation for England but a great gain for the Dutch cause. It is not without significance that Elizabeth did not recall her troops from the Low Countries to meet the danger until 26 July 1588, and then withdrew only a thousand from her contingent. In both countries 26 October was a day of thanksgiving.

Success against the Armada did not immediately make relations much more harmonious. The States denounced the betrayal of Geertruidenberg, which was handed over to the Spanish in 1589; and Walsingham himself, a natural sympathizer with the cause of Protestant rebels, wrote that he wished that 'our future and theirs were not so straitly tied as it is, so as we cannot well untie without great hazard'.[24] There were loud English complaints of the States' 'manifest ingratitude' and 'feebleness of help' in joint expeditions, and the ambassador complained of 'the rude and intractable nature' of the leading Dutch politician, Oldenbarnevelt. For some time the English desired the establishment of a really effective executive under a prince, like William the Silent's son Maurice of Nassau, with whom they could deal as with any other royal head. They wanted to see the replacement of a system in which so many people had to be consulted. At the very least, they wanted the authority of the Council of State, on which Queen Elizabeth had her two representatives, to be restored.[25] From about 1590 relations steadily took a turn for the better. Bodley, the English ambassador, still complained that 'he never perceived hearty good will in any one of this people toward Her Majesty or any of our nation, ... but in a cause of any moment you shall see them so falter in the duties of affection as a man would hardly credit ... But what will you have? It is not possible to draw wine out of vessels full of vinegar.'[26] Nevertheless, the English gained more confidence in Oldenbarnevelt's administration and the Dutch gained more confidence in the English soldiery. One factor in this was that Willoughby's successor, Sir Francis Vere, was not governor-general but sergeant-major-general and had only military duties. He was an able soldier, and he struck up a good comradeship in arms with Maurice of Nassau, distinguishing himself particularly in the battle of Nieuport and in the defence of Ostend. Outside military matters his interests were limited and uncontroversial. Five Veres were killed and two wounded in the Dutch cause. In many ways his civilian counterpart was George Gilpin, who was first interpreter to Sir Thomas Bodley and then in 1593 his successor as member of the Council of State and ambassador, in fact though not in name. He had lived in the Low Countries since his student days, spoke fluent Dutch and had indeed become quite Dutch in his ways, sending his sons to the new university at Franeker. Like Vere, he was also a sympathizer with the rebel cause and had no sophisticated political ambitions.[27]

As the 1590s proceeded, the troops under Vere's command became more professional, better paid and equipped, and better trained in the new scientific methods of Maurice of Nassau, to whose army Protestant would-be soldiers came from all over Europe as to a modern school of warfare. Gilpin wrote that the States regarded them as their greatest strength in the field. Sometimes, like English soldiers in Wellington's armies, they seemed, on first enlistment, decidedly unpromising material. In 1602 the Privy Council drew up orders 'for the apprehending and sending to the port at Yarmouth all rogues, vagabonds, idle, dissolute and masterless persons, which cannot make a good account of their living, being of strong and able body, to be sent over for Her Majesty's service in the Low Countries'. More men were pressed 'whose absence would be a benefit to their native countries'.[28] It is not surprising that there were still frequent desertions at Ostend. Nevertheless, it is clear that by 1600 the English troops, as well as the Scots who even earlier had been described to Parma as giving more trouble than any other foreign troops in the Dutch service, were both a substantial (perhaps one-third) and a valuable part of Maurice of Nassau's army. At the battle of Nieuport, 800 of the 1600 casualties were English. The garrisons of 850 men at Flushing and 650 men at the Brill were also much more disciplined forces.[29]

At sea the Dutch also made a contribution to allied expeditions, and after the joint attack on Cadiz in 1596, the Dutch admiral Duivenwoorde was amongst those knighted aboard ship. But there were also causes of friction. There was continuing English resentment against the persistent Dutch trade with the enemy, and at the same time there was Dutch resentment against indiscriminate seizures of ships trading with Spain, which inevitably included Dutch ones.

With the familiarity produced by time, even the Queen softened in her attitude, and condescendingly told the Dutch ambassador Caron that 'your state is not a monarchy and we must take everything together and weigh its faults against its many perfections'. On a later occasion, with all the diplomatic flattery of which she was capable, she even went so far as to say that 'we kings ... require, all of us, to go to school to the States-General'.[30] The decision of her successor, James I, to make a separate peace with Spain, contrary to England's treaty obligations, was not too much of a blow to the Dutch. Though the Anglo-Spanish treaty of London in 1604 left them to fight on alone, Oldenbarnevelt was not too bitterly aggrieved provided that he was allowed to keep the English and Scots troops in Dutch pay, reinforced by disbanded soldiers from Vere's army. By 1604 the Dutch were in no great danger of losing their hard-won independence. Though the treaty signed by the Dutch and Spaniards in 1609 was formally only a truce, for all practical purposes the seven northern provinces were now a separate Republic, leaving the ten southern provinces under Spanish control.

There remained the problem of the repayment of the English expenses under the terms of the Treaty of Nonsuch, and of the 'cautionary towns' of Flushing and the Brill which English forces had been allowed to garrison as security. Years of warfare had meant that the debt had grown to an amount which the Dutch could not repay in total. On the other hand, James had an urgent need for cash to help solve his financial problems and the maintenance of the garrisons was costly. Accordingly an agreement was reached in 1616 by which James, having claimed £600,000, accepted £100,000 plus three further half-yearly instalments, bringing the total up to £215,000, decidedly less than the money owing. The garrisons were allowed to join the English and Scots regiments already in Dutch pay. As a last vestige of the Nonsuch arrangement it was agreed that the English ambassador, Sir Dudley Carleton, should continue to sit on the Council of State on a purely personal basis until the end of his tour of office. Since the Dutch over the years had steadily entrusted more effective power to the States-General, largely evading the Council of State on which England was represented and making its duties mainly administrative, this arrangement was only a formality. It came to an end in 1627. Until that time it was one factor which led James, who had no great liking for rebels against a legitimate sovereign, to adopt a patronizing attitude to the Dutch; he was the leading Protestant prince whom they ought to follow. Pamphleteers also supported jealousy of Dutch commercial success by alleging 'ingratitude' and exaggerating the contribution of English services to the cause of Dutch freedom. The futilities of English policy in the middle years of Elizabeth's reign were forgotten in the successes of the later years.

It is not easy to evaluate the extent of the English contribution to the Dutch cause. Often the amount of direct help was less important than the diversion of Spanish resources from the struggle to subdue the Revolt of the Netherlands. Without this the Dutch position would have been exceedingly precarious in the years after the fall of Antwerp. Though Henry IV of France also joined the number of Philip II's enemies from 1589–98, by that time Spain's best opportunity had been missed. The failure of the Armada was not final, but it at least gave the Dutch a breathing space. Had it succeeded, it is not easy to see how the Dutch could have escaped falling back under Spanish influence. The Dutch, however, could also claim (though curiously it seems they hardly ever did) that they performed a comparable service to England by drawing off the force of Spanish efforts in northern Europe for nearly twenty years before Elizabeth had, at last, in her own interests, to intervene against the head of the Counter Reformation. The gratitude should have been mutual.

From the war came memories, lasting at least half a century, of a struggle against a common enemy, and there remained a constant reminder of it in the English and Scots troops which continued to form a substantial part of the Dutch army, in peace and war. The numbers varied, but from 1628 there would usually be three regiments in the Scots Brigade and three English regiments with ten companies in each, and originally there were supposed to be 150 men per company. English and Scots together might have formed a quarter of all the infantry. Their competence in support of Maurice's solid and scientific tactics was acknowledged. *The Exercise of Arms* (1607) has been described as 'the English version of the training-manual of Prince Maurice's troops'.[31] As time went on, they inter-married with the local population, as Sir Thomas Morgan did in 1589. As so many loose women were following Scots soldiers to the Netherlands, the Conservator at Veere was told in 1581 to see that no shipmasters 'ressave or transport any women in their shippis or veschellis towardis the pairtes foirsaidis in tyme cuming, bot as salbe notourlie knawin to be menis wyffis, women of gude reputatioun in lyff, and having necessar and knawin affaires their'.[32] Whether because of this official ban, or more probably for more natural reasons, the number of Dutch names in the baptismal and marriage registers of the Scots Brigade's chaplains increased as time went on (particularly after 1700) and this was not entirely owing to the Dutchmen who found their way into these regiments. As for the English troops, when in 1592 some companies were ordered to form an expeditionary force to Brittany, 'there were so many men married in the country, belonging to Sir John Pooley's company, that the order for their removal was cancelled'.[33] Yet if this intermingling between British and Dutch and the foundation of families in Holland was important, so too was the number who returned to England (there were comparatively few who returned to Scotland). The Civil War is often thought of as being fought largely by amateurs like Cromwell, but officers with Low Countries experience were at a premium.

For the King they included Sir Jacob Astley, Sir Thomas Glemham, Lord Goring and Sir Richard Grenville; while the Parliamentarians (rather more numerous) included Essex, Sir Thomas Fairfax (and others of his family), Skippon and Monck, who had, he said, been bred in 'a Commonwealth where soldiers obeyed commands, but gave none'. But there must have been many lesser gentlemen who paid briefer visits to the front, and who had been 'a soldier swallowlike, for a summer or only a siege'. On the whole, those who had seen service in the Netherlands wanted England to take part on the Dutch side when, after the outbreak of the Thirty Years War, the Dutch struggle with Spain was resumed in 1621. Some ex-officers were said to 'live in garrison in the good town of London and hold their council of war in a tavern. These are those which are the cause of laziness and ignorance of our youth; for they will teach them to roar and vapour....'[34] Other Englishmen, however, had more responsible reasons for believing that their country ought to be on the Protestant and Dutch side once again, and for doubting the policy of the Stuarts and the idea of a Spanish marriage for the Prince of Wales. For such people the first single-sheet English corantos, giving news translated from Dutch corantos, were printed in Amsterdam for sale in England in 1620–1. Thereafter, even when printed in London, they drew heavily upon material often directly translated from the Dutch newspapers. In the words of the title of a Ben Jonson play, Amsterdam was *The Staple of News* for the English public, and it has been calculated that in the decade 1622–32 between sixty and seventy per cent of the news material in the English periodical press originated from the Netherlands, particularly from Amsterdam. This situation only came to an end when, at the height of the Thirty Years War, a ban was imposed by Star Chamber decree, perhaps after Spanish complaints.[35] Englishmen who were interested in the European conflict had another reason for looking to the Netherlands, this time to The Hague and later to Rhenen, near Arnhem. The 'Queen of Hearts', Elizabeth, daughter of James I, and her husband Frederick found shelter in the Dutch Republic when they were evicted from the Kingdom of Bohemia and their hereditary dominions in the Palatinate. There, preferring (so it was said) her dogs and monkeys to her numerous children, she continued to receive her faithful English visitors even after her husband's death, an exiled Protestant victim claiming the support of her brother Charles I and his Protestant people.

Yet the attitudes of other Englishmen to their neighbours across the North Sea were ambivalent, and it is to the jealousies and rivalries, which grew alongside a tradition of hostility to Spain, that we must now turn.

CHAPTER THREE

Mammon and God

In February 1587, a fortnight after the execution of Mary Queen of Scots, Job Throckmorton in the House of Commons urged the acceptance of the Dutch offer of the sovereignty of the Netherlands, which he described as 'an evident sign that the Lord hath yet once more vowed himself to be England'. 'The very finger of God directs us to the Low Countries, as though to say: "There only is the means of your safety, there only is the passage laid open unto you, there only, and nowhere else is the vent of your commodities".' Money talks, and a committee drafted a petition to the Queen offering a large benevolence, even a voluntary yearly contribution, should the Queen accept sovereignty. Elizabeth saw that the matter proceeded no further, but it is noteworthy that there is no sign of opposition to these sentiments in the Commons.[1]

Only six years later the House held a long debate on the report stage of a bill directed against the retail sale by aliens of foreign wares brought into England. At the bar, counsel for the city of London set out the case against alien (Dutch) retailers, on the ground that 'strangers' wares are better than ours, which causeth that our retailers have no sale of their wares. They sell cheaper, though their wares be as good as ours. And by this reason they have factors beyond the seas that are their friends and kinsfolk, and so they save that charge.... Their retailing, beggaring our retailers, makes a diminution of the Queen's subjects. Their riches and multitude makes our estate poorer and weaker.' He answered the argument that it would be uncharitable to take action against refugees for the sake of religion by saying, in effect, that charity begins at home. There followed a sharp debate on these lines in which one member maintained that 'the riches and renown of the city cometh by entertaining of strangers and giving liberty to them'. Another argued on the other hand that 'the exclamations of the city are exceeding pitiful and great against these strangers; nay had not these latter quiet times in their own countries and our troubles made many of them retire home, the citizens would have been in uproar against them.' The committee failed to agree, and there was another debate, in which it was stated that there were twenty retailers in London with a turnover of £10 to £20,000 a year, and this money was sent out of the country. Then Raleigh, who, being no friend of Spain, might have been expected to favour the refugees, spoke against the argument of charity. 'Religion is no pretext for them, for we have no Dutchmen here but such as come from those provinces where the gospel is preached, and here they are disliking our Church. . . . The nature of the Dutchman is to fly to no man but for his profit. . . . The Dutchman by his policy hath gotten trading with all the world into his hands, yea he is now entering into the trade of Scarborough fishing, and the fishing of the Newfoundlands, which is the stay of the west country. They are the people that maintain the King of Spain in his greatness [by their "trade with the enemy", presumably]. . . .' An amended bill eventually passed the Commons but was rejected in the Lords.[2]

To these two quotations may be added a third, from someone not unsympathetic to the Dutch, the letter-writer John Chamberlain. He wrote in 1598: 'One of the chiefest reasons I can hear for it [peace] is a kind of disdain and envy at our neighbours' well-doing, in that we, for their sake and defence entering into the war and being barred from all commerce and merchandise, they in the mean time thrust us out of all traffic to our utter undoing (if in time it be not looked into) and their own advancement.'[3] The antiquary Camden complained that the Dutch 'by war grow rich whereas all other nations are impoverished'. The 1590s were in fact the period of the Dutch 'economic miracle', when Englishmen began to feel the weight of their competition and to struggle against it.

The problem of jealousy of the Dutch immigrants, which was exemplified in the Commons' debate of 1593, diminished with the passage of time, the birth of children in England, and their assimilation into the community. Presumably some commercial co-operation also helped. There were disturbances in the year 1593, when 'malicious libels' were set up on the wall of the Dutch churchyard in London, and again in 1595. In the former year a return compiled by order of the Lord Mayor reported a total of 4570 strangers (men, women and children) born abroad and 2534 born in England. Out of 3429 adults, 1376 were members of the Dutch Church (as against 1910 in 1568) and about as many were French speaking, including Walloons. By 1635, however, the Dutch Church put its membership at only 840. Under the early Stuarts there were complaints about Dutch (or Flemish) engines for tape, lace and ribbons, by which one man could do the work of seven Englishmen. There were also renewed complaints of Dutch merchants sending large sums of money abroad which may have been connected with the foundation of the Bank of Amsterdam; in 1617 they were called upon, as a community, to advance large sums of money to finance James I's trip to Scotland. The Dutch lived in neighbouring areas: Ben Jonson talks of going:

To Shoreditch, Whitechapel and so to St Katherine's [near the Tower]
To drink with the Dutch there and take forth their patterns

though this reference to the breweries may be another instance of the confusion between Dutch and Germans, which still persisted in Jacobean dramatists. Nevertheless, the Dutch community shrank as the population of London increased, and the process of assimilation went forward. The rivalries between English and Dutch merchants, fishermen and sailors on opposing sides of the North Sea were more deep-seated.[4]

Apart from the Dutch 'trade with the enemy', which ceased to be a problem when James made peace with Spain in 1604, the most obvious rivalry was concerned with fishing. Fishing for herring was not only extremely profitable, but it was carried on systematically within sight of the British coasts (Raleigh's fears that a bitter rivalry would extend to the Newfoundland Banks did not materialize). Many hundreds of herring busses began work off the Shetlands every year on St John's Day (24 June) and worked their way southwards along the east coast of Scotland and England, following the shoals of herring until they reached the mouth of the Thames early in December. The fish were caught and cured by a process invented by the Zeelander Beukelsz in ships designed for the purpose, and the catch reached a value roughly comparable to the total export value of the English cloth industry. Inevitably there were incidents when Dutch fishermen landed on British coasts. There were the usual disputes over nets set out to dry, though there was a long tradition of co-operation in the Yarmouth area which was carried on when Dutch refugees from Alva settled there. But the real grievance of Scots and English was that 'their' fish were being caught in 'their' waters and were being used as the foundation of Dutch prosperity. For apart from the intrinsic value of the catch, exports of salted herring to the Baltic and Mediterranean made it easier to bring back valuable return cargos from those areas. Furthermore, in addition to finding employment for the fishermen, the industry sustained a whole series of ancillary tradespeople, such as shipbuilders, rope-makers, sailmakers, and coopers. Statesmen such as Burghley saw the fisheries as a source of seamen and a national asset for that reason alone; and English pamphleteers saw them as the basis for the whole of the economic success which they envied.

At first many of these pamphleteers did not preach hostility. Instead, they wrote in terms of the need to emulate the hard work and success of an ally, and argued that the Queen's subjects could be encouraged to do so. In 1601, John Keymor, giving exaggerated figures which were often repeated by later writers, guessed that of 20,000 Dutch ships, giving employment to 400,000 men, 4100 were fishing vessels and of these 2000 were herring busses. The perception was of an expanding industry and prosperity for all. 'And not a beggar there, every one getting his own living, is admirable to behold; that the poor man, though he be blind, and have but one hand, will get his own living by turning the wheel for making cables and cordage, and another that has not one leg, will get his own living sitting on a seat with knitting, and making of nets and hooks; every boy and wench, from 10 and 12 years and upwards, will get his own living by winding hemp, spinning yarn, making twine and thread for nets. So idleness, beggary and penury will be driven out of this land. . . .'[5] But neither the hope of riches nor the prospect of finding a solution to the problem of poverty, which was pressing in 1601, attracted investors, perhaps because those Londoners with capital were remote from the fishing centres, or because direct competition with the Dutch was an unattractive proposition. As a result, admiration turned to resentment and a demand that the Dutch should pay for a licence to fish.

Among those who thought in this way was James I, ever on the look-out for means of increasing his income. At the end of the thirteenth century Edward I had encouraged men from Holland, Zeeland and Friesland to fish in the waters off Yarmouth, and since then several treaties, including the Magnus Intercursus of 1496, had referred to similar privileges. These were not officially called into question in England until the reign of James I, though in 1577 John Dee, the well-known mathematician and astrologer, wrote a pamphlet in which he called for foreigners to be made to pay one tenth, or £100,000 per annum, for the right to fish.[6] In Scotland, however, attempts had been made to take restrictive measures and to enforce them, and it was to this tradition that James I belonged. In May 1609 he issued a proclamation calling upon foreigners to pay for a licence.[7]

It was not enforced, largely because James I needed Dutch support in a diplomatic crisis over the succession to the German principalities of Cleves and Jülich, but the demand had been made. As in Dee's pamphlet, it was more and more linked with a demand that the royal sovereignty over British waters be acknowledged. There was some difficulty over what exactly constituted British waters, but essentially the claim was that foreign vessels meeting British warships should acknowledge sovereignty by striking the flag, lowering the topsail, and, if armed, saluting with a cannon shot. This has often been regarded as a matter of mere protocol, and certainly patriotic feelings entered into it. It has been questioned whether the salute was 'a theme fitter for scholars to fret their wits upon than for Christians to fight and spill blood about' or 'a glory fitter for women and children to wonder at than for statesmen to contend about'. Yet there were very practical issues underlying it. The Dutch might have been not unwilling to give way, purely as a matter of civility; but the concession of the sovereignty over the seas would be a basis for a claim for payment for the right to fish in British waters. Accordingly, the arguments of the great Dutch 'father of international law', Grotius, in *Mare Liberum* (1608), were called upon. They had originally been devised to counter Portuguese and Spanish claims to exclude the Dutch from the East and West Indies. Now they were applied to deny Britain's claim to sovereignty over the seas round the British Isles and to assert Dutch freedom of navigation and fishery there.

A third source of competition which became urgent from the 1590s, and to which the British could find no immediate answer, was merchant shipping. The Dutch devised the famous fluyt or flute ship, which was cheaper to construct and more economical to run than the merchantmen of any other nation, especially where bulk cargos were concerned. Unarmed, simply rigged, and fitted with more labour-saving winches and tackle, it needed a smaller crew (perhaps even ten to the English thirty) who, according to the English, contented themselves with hard fare whereas the English wanted their meat and beer. The Dutch version was that English mariners had more stomach for the mess deck than for hard work. It was commonly estimated that Dutch freight rates were a third to a half lower for the same voyage. All that could be done to remedy the situation was to issue a royal proclamation in 1615 enjoining the King's subjects to freight English ships in preference to foreign bottoms. But the English merchants persisted in using Dutch ships, seeing no point in handicapping themselves by paying higher freight charges and therefore having to set higher prices for their goods. Dutch ships had long outnumbered English vessels entering the Baltic (in 1562 by 1192 to 51); even much of the English trade to France came to be conducted in Dutch ships. Dozens of Dutch ships also loaded tobacco cargos from Virginia and Maryland for Europe as that trade developed.[8]

Not only lower freight charges but also greater financial and commercial expertise favoured the Dutch. Before the Revolt, shipping had long been largely in the hands of Hollanders and Zeelanders rather than the Antwerpers themselves. Amsterdam, for instance, had conducted its 'mother trade' in Baltic corn which was basic to prosperity while Antwerp was the commercial and financial capital. After the recapture of Antwerp by Spain in 1585 many Antwerpers preferred to emigrate to the freer atmosphere of the north, which now offered greater commercial opportunities. They took with them their trading experience, connections all over Europe, and knowledge of exchange and insurance techniques to add to those which the citizens of Amsterdam already possessed. Printed bills of exchange and marine insurance forms were in use in the 1590s, and in 1609 the Bank of Amsterdam was founded, solidly based on the municipality and not on private credit. This made the deposit and transfer of money much simpler. Credit became easier and rates of interest lower. The Bank was a great source of envy to English merchants for nearly a century, and they clamoured for one until the Bank of England was founded in the reign of William III. Dutch trade was further assisted by the existence of communities of Dutchmen who settled not only in London but also in the areas with which they traded: Gothenburg in Sweden was essentially Dutch in origin, and until French policy turned against them in the reign of Louis XIV, the Dutch were numerous in Normandy and western France. The English could at first do little to counter these advantages. A striking illustration of this is to be found in the trade to Muscovy, which had been opened up following Willoughby and Chancellor's expedition in the reign of Queen Mary, and the grant of privileges to the Muscovy Company by Ivan the Terrible. By the middle of the seventeenth century there were only two English ships in Archangel where there had once been 17, and there were thirty Dutch ships. The superior competitive powers of the Dutch had triumphed over the lead gained by the earlier English arrival.[9]

There were other disadvantages which the English brought upon themselves by mistaken policy. The Merchant Adventurers, unable to return to Antwerp, moved to Middelburg in 1582 and set up a Court there in 1598. In 1591 Amsterdam tried to attract them by offering the Begijnhof, where the English church shortly came into existence, as the site for their Court, and the Merchant Adventurers briefly considered a move to Amsterdam on two later occasions. In Middelburg they asked for good healthy air, better attention to improving the state of the streets, and permission to import English beer to treat their clients! But their trading monopoly was now under attack by their own countrymen. 'Interlopers' who paid no fee to join the fellowship traded to Flushing in spite of the English garrison there. More serious were their activities in Amsterdam, where the municipality did little to discourage them. Worse still was the hostility of rival merchants in London. For a long time the trade of the Merchant Adventurers had been in unfinished cloth, which was dyed and dressed in the cities of Holland, leaders in Europe in these as in other industrial techniques. Merchants who wanted to break into the trade pointed out that the value of the cloth was greatly enhanced by such finishing processes, especially the dyeing; if they could be carried out in England the increased profits would fall to Englishmen instead of Dutchmen. Alderman Cokayne and a syndicate pressed this attractive argument upon James I. The King's hope of deriving increased revenue from the cloth trade, together perhaps with 'sweeteners' to suitable men at Court, brought about the granting of a patent to Cokayne for his 'project' and the cancellation of the monopoly possessed by the Adventurers in 1614. The intention was to prohibit the export of undyed and undressed cloth altogether (as foreshadowed in some Tudor statutes) but the result was as the Adventurers had foreseen: Englishmen could not produce dyed and dressed cloth in sufficient quantity and quality. The States-General retaliated by banning its import into the United Provinces for the sake of their own competing industries. Cokayne himself may have been partly influenced by the desire to take over the Adventurers' monopoly of the exportation of unfinished cloth for his own company. Although an essential part of his scheme had been to ban the export of unfinished cloth in the interest of stimulating that of the finished product, he soon declared that the English industry could not yet produce enough dyed and dressed cloth, and asked for permission in the meantime to export unfinished cloth himself. The result was a disastrous drop of about a third in cloth exports between 1614 and 1617, compelling James to abandon the scheme. With the aid of Dutch money the Merchant Adventurers bought their charter back from him. After the early depression years of the Thirty Years War they recovered some of their former prosperity, settling first at Delft in the Prinsenhof, where William the Silent had been murdered, then at Rotterdam; but they had to contend with more competition from interlopers, at which local authorities connived. It was only in the course of the century that Englishmen were able to exploit their possession of unlimited raw wool, whose export they banned, to rival the Leiden industry and reduce the Dutch technical lead in finishing and dyeing.[10]

Finally, there was rivalry over the trade to the Indian Ocean and further East, where valuable spices were the original lure. Here the Dutch had a substantial lead. In the 1590s, the decade of the 'economic miracle', they had made several expeditions. Jacob van Neck had returned from one of these in 1599 with so much pepper, cloves, nutmeg and mace that backers received an interim profit of a hundred per cent. Oldenbarnevelt persuaded those interested of the political, financial and commercial advantages of combining in one company, and the Dutch East Indies Company received its charter from the States-General in 1602. James Lancaster had returned from his pioneering voyage round the Cape in 1594. This, and an English translation of Jan van Linschoten's Dutch account of his experiences in the Indian Ocean which appeared in 1598, had stimulated the founding of the English East India Company three years earlier in 1599. But whereas 6,500,000 florins of capital, the equivalent of more than the English national revenue in a year, were rapidly subscribed to the Dutch Company, the English had an initial capital of only £30,000, later augmented to £72,000 and including £4000 from an Amsterdammer. Furthermore, whereas the Dutch Company sent 55 great ships in its first seven years, the English sent 12 ships in nine years. It was the Dutch who broke into the dominance of the Portuguese in the Spice Islands, justifying their freedom of trade by Grotius's arguments. But thereafter they sought to obtain a monopoly of trade and to keep the English out, arguing that they, rather than the English, had borne the cost of opening up the trade routes and establishing forts. There were the inevitable disputes over seizures of ships and conflicting relations with native potentates. The island of Pularun, occupied by the English and seized by the Dutch in 1617, re-echoes through the diplomatic records for the next fifty years. The name Amboina resounded even longer. In 1623 some English merchants were tortured and put to death for an alleged conspiracy against the Dutch governor of the island, and the story of this atrocity was constantly repeated in anti-Dutch pamphlets and in Dryden's play *The Massacre of Amboina* (1673). Two hundred years after the 'massacre' had taken place, Sir Walter Scott was complacently ignoring any British atrocities, and pontificating that 'it has always been remarked that the Dutchman, in his eastern settlements, loses the mercantile probity of his European character while he retains its cold-blooded phlegm and avaricious selfishness'. Even Scott described the play as 'the worst production Dryden ever wrote', and the critic Saintsbury endorsed this verdict on 'the one production of Dryden which is utterly worthless except as a curiosity'. Yet when Dryden or any other writer had to whip up hostility against the Dutch, memories of Amboina were always revived.[11]

Most of the main points made by anti-Dutch pamphleteers in the three Dutch wars can be found foreshadowed in writings of the first quarter of the century. It is not without significance that Thomas Mun's famous pamphlet, *England's Treasure by Foreign Trade*, begun in 1622 and in manuscript by the 1630s, could be printed by his son, with absolute relevance, in 1664.[12] In the reign of James I these rivalries created tensions with the view, inherited from the previous reign, of the Dutch as natural allies. James did not share that tradition, and had little inclination to approve of a people who had rebelled against their lawful sovereign. On the other hand he was prone to patronize people who could be regarded as 'junior Protestants' and would follow his advice on matters of foreign policy and religion. He considered himself entitled to intervene in the election to a chair at Leiden University of the theologian Vorstius, whose name had once been linked with his own and whose allegedly Socinian (Unitarian) heresies he was therefore anxious to repudiate. James wanted his books to be burnt in the United Provinces as they had been in London, Oxford and Cambridge. Oldenbarnevelt could see no justification for James's obstruction of the appointment, though reluctantly he consented. From this episode James derived a suspicion of Oldenbarnevelt which eventually led him to use his influence against the Dutch statesman and, as we shall see, to send representatives to the Synod of Dort.[13] The greatest restraints upon James were his lack of sufficient resources to do more than bluster, and his need to maintain good relations with his protégé to serve as a counterpoise to Spain. With delaying tactics he could be diverted, as he had been from his proclamation on fishing in 1609. This dispute, never formally settled, was made worse when James granted a monopoly of whaling rights in Arctic waters to the Muscovy Company because of Willoughby's discovery of Spitsbergen in 1553. Dutch boats, attacked as interlopers, claimed that van Heemskerk had discovered it first in 1596, and in 1614 a Greenland Company was set up. The whalers clashed over the right to boil blubber on the island of Spitsbergen.

The result was a series of clashes, disputes and conferences (always held in London) which decided nothing about fisheries, sovereignty or the East Indies. On one occasion a Scots official, trying to collect payment for the right to fish off the coast of Scotland, was carried off to Holland, and in return two Dutch captains in the Thames were seized as hostages. The Dutch were apologetic but maintained their rights. At the conferences, Grotius was among the Dutch representatives, and, as one voluble talker to another, the great scholar found little favour with James I. There was even a scheme for a working union of the two East India Companies, but even if this had found favour with the merchants in Europe, it was never likely to materialize in distant seas when voyages took many months. After another long, expensive and entirely fruitless embassy in 1621, James gave the Dutch ambassadors 'a short and good answer', which was in fact neither short nor good. 'Surely you are like leeches, bloodsuckers of my realm, you draw the blood from my subjects and seek to ruin me.... I would not endure it [the whaling dispute] either from France or Spain, do you think I either can or will bear it from you?' In the previous year he and his favourite the Duke of Buckingham discussed with the Spanish ambassador, Gondomar, the idea of a partition of the Dutch Republic, in which Britain would receive Holland and Zeeland. However, it is impossible to tell how seriously this was intended and how far it was just a device for spinning out time. The idea of a partition was revived during the

Madrid negotiations of 1623 for the marriage of Prince Charles to a Spanish infanta. 'Their best friends who for the common considerations of religion and neighbourhood always wished them well, cry out upon them for the continual injuries and insolences we receive from them,' wrote John Chamberlain. When the news of Amboina was received, the government was so apprehensive of rioting that they ordered 800 men to stand watch on Shrove Tuesday, 1625. Chamberlain, normally well enough disposed to the Dutch, wanted England to take vengeance by seizing Dutch ships and 'hanging up upon Dover cliffs as many as we should find faulty or actors in this business'. 'The King', he wrote, 'takes it so to heart that he speaks somewhat exuberantly, and I wish he would say less so he would do more'.[14]

Yet these jealousies of the Dutch, on the part of both King and people, which under other circumstances might have led to war, gave way once more to the need which King and people had of the Dutch. The breakdown of the marriage negotiations at Madrid led Charles and Buckingham to go on to the policy for which many had clamoured – the policy of war with Spain and intervention in the Thirty Years War for the recovery of the Palatinate for the 'Queen of Hearts' (Elizabeth, daughter of James I). To this end an alliance with the States-General was obviously indispensable. The pamphleteer Thomas Scott called up the ghost of Queen Elizabeth to tell her people how grieved she was to see the Dutch without England's assistance in the fight against Spain; he believed the Dutch to 'come of the same race originally that we do, as our speech witnesseth'.[15] Puritans who believed the fortunes of Protestantism on the Continent to be at stake had an obvious incentive to think in this way. James remained reluctant, but was overborne by his son and his favourite. After Charles's accession the last restraints were removed, and the Treaty of Southampton was followed by another example of Buckingham's 'summit diplomacy' in a personal visit to the Hague and another treaty there. This time there was no mention of English subsidies to the Dutch; on the contrary, Buckingham planned to pawn some of the crown jewels, but they were refused by the Amsterdam market.

The old Anglo-Dutch alliance was thus revived, but with far less success. The Dutch contributed twenty ships to the Cadiz expedition, which in contrast to the Elizabethan attack was an ignominious failure. An expedition under the *condottiere* Mansfeld, intended to help recover the Palatinate, landed once more at Flushing but was also far from reviving the Elizabethan glories. 'Such a rabble of raw and poor rascals have not lightly been, and go so unwillingly that they must rather be driven than led.' Their sufferings, partly the result of maladministration as bad as anything in the early years of the Elizabethan war, were not compensated for by any striking success. Of 12,000 conscripts, it was reported that only 600 were left, and they were surviving by eating horses and cats. The eighteenth-century practice was foreshadowed, however, when the subsidies to Denmark (also an English ally) were remitted by bills of exchange, mostly drawn on Amsterdam: Philip Burlamachi, financial agent to the English crown, had a convenient brother-in-law, Philip Calandrini, through whom he maintained business links with that city.[16] Yet this period, supposedly of co-operation, also saw the revival of an old source of irritation, the Dutch trade with the enemy (although the Treaty of Southampton had forbidden it), and the growth of a new one. When England, as the result of a remarkably mismanaged foreign policy, found herself at war with France as well as Spain, Dutch neutral ships trading with France were seized as prizes by English privateers. From protests against this sprang the Dutch claim of 'free ships, free goods' which was to recur over the next hundred and fifty years in English wars in which the Dutch were neutrals.

This was not the only way in which seamen of the two countries were at odds, for in the Dutch blockade of the port of Dunkirk (still in the Spanish Netherlands at this time) it was claimed that Dutch ships were allowed to enter the port while English ones were seized. Sir William Monson, an inveterate naval enemy of the Dutch, drafted 'a project how to war upon Holland, if hostility ever happen betwixt us' and went on to 'a project how to compass the possession of the Island of Wakerland [Walcheren] if the King of England will compound with the King of Spain for that island'. He advocated propaganda to detach the Zeelanders from Holland.[17]

Charles I signed the Treaty of Madrid with Spain in 1630, and in the next decade, to the intense dismay of Puritans, England remained neutral and benevolent to Spain while the United Provinces sustained the Protestant cause against the Hapsburgs. Privately, Charles reverted in 1630–1 and 1634–5 to negotiations with Spain for a partition of the United Provinces and English naval assistance against them.[18] Publicly he once more took up the issues of the fisheries and sovereignty of the seas, and tried to forbid his subjects to serve on Dutch men-of-war and merchant vessels. In none of these areas was he very successful. There was renewed admiration and jealousy of the Dutch fisheries, which even supplied London with lobsters from the north of England, 'which is never practised by the English'. They also transported great quantities of oysters into Holland, 'which causeth the decrease and dearness of oysters among us', and used lampreys from the Thames for bait in northern seas, 'and this is the cause of the scarcity and dearness of this fish in London'.[19] The Earl of Seaforth successfully settled Dutchmen in distant Stornoway on the island of Lewis. But the Fishery Society in London, which it was intended to encourage, turned out to be one of those good ideas that everyone approves but no one backs very vigorously in the face of an established competitor. Nor did the King achieve very much in his attempts to make the Dutch at least pay for the right to carry on their fisheries, by virtue of his claim to sovereignty over the seas.

It has been said that Charles was responsible for 'the most extreme claims to dominion on the neighbouring seas that had ever been put forward by an English king'. From 1631, there was an increase in demands on foreign ships to lower their flags and topsails and it has been suggested that in 1635 the fleet courted an incident with the Dutch over the salute. In the same year Selden's *Mare Clausum*, written by order of James I in 1618 but hitherto unpublished, was recast and brought out to counter the arguments of Grotius's *Mare Liberum*. The Dutch envoy was referred to it in 1636 when he was told that Charles was sending out the fleet financed by his ship-money tax to enforce his right to call upon foreign fishermen to pay for a licence. Some herring busses did pay, but the Dutch admiral Van Dorp was ordered to protect the fishermen against injury, and the unexpectedly small yield of £504 scarcely suggested that the cost of the expedition was worthwhile. Whether for that reason, or because of the outbreak of the Bishops' Wars, or because once again the problem of the Palatinate meant that some Dutch diplomatic support might be needed, Charles did not repeat the experiment. He waived his right, so he said, as a favour only.[20]

In the minds of many Englishmen, jealousy of Dutch economic success warred with the feeling that the Dutch were 'on the right side' against Spain and with a dislike of the policy of benevolent neutrality towards Spain. To Puritans especially, the deficiencies of Charles's foreign policy were all of a piece with the enforcement of an Arminian conformity within the Church of England by the King and William Laud, who became Archbishop of Canterbury in 1633. The irony is that the Dutch name 'Arminian' was applied to this religious policy by its critics, and that in fact the influence of James I had been heavily used against Arminianism in Holland. Now 'Arminianism' in England led many of its opponents to seek refuge in Holland. These complexities can best be understood by first contrasting the religious systems of the two peoples.

Both states were officially Protestant, and yet their Protestantism was of a different kind. In England the Elizabethan church settlement had provided for a church which was largely traditional in its organization (except that it no longer had the Pope at its head). It was governed by bishops appointed by the monarch. Its clergy were appointed by them, by the crown or by lay patrons, and they were paid, directly or indirectly, largely from tithes, which all lay people were liable theoretically to pay. Unless the clergy could evade it, they wore the surplice and other traditional garments, and used the Book of Common Prayer. Everyone had a legal obligation to attend the parish church every Sunday. No other faith was officially tolerated, and there was censorship of all printed books. There were some, to whom the name of Puritan was increasingly applied, who criticized this church as being insufficiently reformed in its vestments and its Prayer Book. From the middle of Elizabeth's reign there were some who wanted to replace the episcopal organization by a church of a more presbyterian kind, with consistories (church councils of clergy and elders), classes (representatives of local churches meeting together) and synods. There were very few who wanted a system of voluntary congregations, self-supported and without any connection with the state. Such critics came to look more and more to the freer situation in the Dutch Republic.

There, following the Revolt, the seven United Provinces had swept away all bishops and ecclesiastical hierarchies and the Reformed Church had its consistories, classes and provincial (though not, as a rule, national) synods. The ministers were appointed by the classes, though the approval of the burgomasters of the towns was required. On the other hand, they were paid a salary by the municipal authorities from the proceeds of the church property which had been taken over, instead of being dependent upon tithes. Though all office holders were supposed to be members of the Reformed Church (a provision often evaded), there was no compulsion upon anyone to attend public worship. There were far more Catholics than in England, whose numbers were increased after further conquests from the southern Netherlands in the 1620s and 1630s, and whose services were connived at. There were Jews and there were many other types of Protestant, in particular, Mennonite Baptists (named after their leader Menno Simons). In a state where people of many faiths congregated, for reasons of commerce, there was no censorship.

At the end of the sixteenth century, the Church of England and the Dutch Reformed Church, different as they might be in other respects, shared a doctrine dominated by Calvinism. The theology of 'double predestination', according to which the elect were fore-ordained by God to eternal bliss and the remainder of mankind to eternal punishment, had been developed to a greater degree than that laid down by Calvin himself. The ideas of the Leiden professor of theology, Arminius (1560–1609), gave more scope to human free will, and led to much dispute in the Republic between his followers, the Remonstrants, and the orthodox Counter Remonstrants. They also excited attention in Cambridge before the end of Elizabeth's reign. Richard, or 'Dutch' Thomson, fellow of Clare College, 'a debosh'd drunken English Dutchman' according to Prynne, had met Arminius in Holland, and his own book, *De Amissione et Intercisione Gratiae et Justificationis*, was printed posthumously in 1616 not in England but in Leiden. Arminius himself criticized William Perkins, the favourite theologian of the English Calvinists, in an *Examen* of the latter's book *De Praedestinationis Modo et Ordine*. At first James I's views on the controversy were hesitant. Amongst his friends was Lancelot Andrewes whose private views on free will did not coincide with the full Calvinist doctrine, and in 1610 he told delegates from the States: 'I have come to the conclusion that nothing certain can be laid down in regard to it. I have myself not always been of one mind about it, but I will bet that my opinion is the best of any, although I would not hang my salvation upon it. My Lords the States would do well to order their doctors and teachers to be silent on this topic.' His experience of the Kirk in Scotland led him to sympathize with the efforts of civil authority to damp down the vehemence of the Calvinist Counter Remonstrants. But he resented the use which Oldenbarnevelt made of a letter to this effect in 1613, and the most distinguished of the Arminian Remonstrants, Grotius, did not help matters when he talked to the King: 'By reason of his good Latin tongue, he was so tedious and full of tittle-tattle that the king's judgment of him was that he was some pedant full of words and of no great judgment.' This was pot and kettle with a vengeance.

James tended to see Socinian (Unitarian) ideas in those of Arminius and his Remonstrant disciples. When William the Silent's younger son Maurice of Nassau supported the cause of orthodoxy and national unity against Oldenbarnevelt's support for more liberal views in religion and the political rights of the province of Holland, James's influence was cast more and more on Maurice's side. He had disliked Oldenbarnevelt since the time of the Vorstius affair, whereas he made Maurice a Knight of the Garter. He also tended to think that only a prince could be depended on to save the United Provinces from anarchy. The Counter Remonstrants were allowed to use the English Church in The Hague when other churches were closed to them, and 'no single individual did more to urge the Calvinists forward' than the English ambassador, Carleton. His plea to the States-General for a national synod to settle the matter was printed in Dutch, and the Arminian reply, *De Wegschaal,* only excited Carleton's and James's indignation. After Oldenbarnevelt's overthrow and arrest (and James did nothing to urge that the old and distinguished statesman should not undergo his death sentence) James sent English representatives and one Scot to the Synod of Dort. This reaffirmed Calvinist orthodoxy in the Dutch Reformed Church. Since the proceedings were in Latin, foreign representatives could easily follow them and, though they did not play an especially prominent part, they were given a place of honour. They also lent their name to the decisions which were taken and to the expulsion of the Arminians. Foreign delegates were each paid ten guilders a day by the Dutch and sent home with a gold medal and 200 guilders each.[21]

All these events attracted considerable attention in London where a play, probably by Fletcher and Massinger, *Sir Johan van Olden-barnevelt*, presented the statesman as the author of a conspiracy against Prince Maurice under the cloak of a religious movement. When the accession of Charles I in 1625 was followed by the spread of doctrines of free will, and when the advocates of these secured marked royal favour to the dismay of those who believed that pre-destination was the central doctrine of their Calvinist faith, it was natural for the label 'Arminian' to be pinned upon the innovators. The well-known Resolutions of the House of Commons in 1629 declared that anyone seeking to introduce 'Popery or Arminianism or other opinion disagreeing from the true and orthodox Church' should be reputed a capital enemy to the kingdom and common-wealth. Yet this English Arminianism extended into areas beyond the theology of Arminius. Its ritualism and sacerdotalism, its stress on the sacraments, its view of the authority of Church and King and Archbishop Laud's attempts, by censorship and other means, to impose conformity upon others would have been repudiated by Dutch Arminians like Episcopius. His motto of *in necessariis unitas, in non necessariis libertas, in utrique caritas* ('in essentials unity, in doubtful matters liberty, in all things charity') was quite foreign to Laud's intolerance. Englishmen who did not find Laud's régime congenial, or were in disfavour with the ecclesiastical authorities, sought refuge across the North Sea in the land of toleration. Here, after about 1630, Calvinism was predominant but Arminians (along with other unofficial groups) were an indulged minority.

The flight of English dissidents to the Netherlands was by no means a new phenomenon in the 1630s. Indeed, within twenty years of the flight of Dutch and Flemish refugees from Alva to England, English Puritans, who regarded the Church of England as insufficiently reformed in its Prayer Book and discipline, had begun to flee in the opposite direction. Of course not all the Englishmen in the Dutch territories were Puritans. There was always the official element, such as the ambassador at The Hague and his household, and some army captains, who might have chaplains fully acceptable to the Queen and her Archbishop Whitgift, and employing the Book of Common Prayer. But there was inevitably a tendency for those who did not find preferment in the Church of England easy to obtain or congenial, to seek opportunities in the Netherlands where they could either minister to English merchants and garrisons, or to congregations whom they took with them from England. There were Presbyterians and Independents (Congregationalists) who, if they could not get a chaplaincy to the Merchant Adventurers or to an army garrison, might be prepared to accept a salary (often of £100 per year) from the city burgomasters and even affiliation to a classis (or assembly of local churches) of the Dutch Reformed Church. There were Separatists (repudiating all connection with the civil authority) and sectaries of various kinds whose congregations were self supporting. For all, and for Puritans who remained in England, there were printers who were prepared to publish their books, which could not have appeared in their native country. Notable among them in Elizabethan times was Richard Schilders of Middelburg, who after being himself a refugee in England, where he was admitted to the Stationers Company, returned to his homeland around 1580 and became printer to the States of Zeeland. He printed books for both Presbyterians (including a 'Middelburg Prayer Book') and Separatists over a long period: 44 survive in the British Library.[22]

Amongst the early Presbyterians there were some famous names in the history of the denomination. Thomas Cartwright, after escaping arrest in England in 1573, preached to the Merchant Adventurers at Antwerp and later at Middelburg before returning to enjoy the patronage of the Earl of Leicester. He declined the offer of a chair at the University of Leiden in 1580. Until the capture of Antwerp by the Spaniards, the English congregation there 'seems to have powerfully influenced the domestic Puritan movement in a Presbyterian direction'. Henry Jacob, on the other hand, returned to found what has been described as the first Congregational church in England. As for the Separatists, Richard Browne, after whom the

Brownist sect was named, was in Middelburg with a small congregation from Norwich in 1581–3; and other congregations were much more long lasting. Some congregations naturally fell under the influence of the Dutch Mennonite Baptists. Later in the seventeenth century Richard Blunt of the English Particular Baptists went to Rijnsburg, submitted to total immersion and seems to have introduced the practice to England.[23]

By 1610 Amsterdam had at least five English congregations, four of them Separatist. The most famous group of Separatists who availed themselves of the indulgence they found in the Netherlands was the Nottinghamshire group from which the Pilgrim Fathers sprang. Under the leadership of John Robinson they moved from Amsterdam to Leiden, either because of dissensions within the Amsterdam Separatists or because they sought employment in the Leiden cloth industry for the clothworkers among them. A minority of the community of perhaps 300 decided to emigrate across the Atlantic under William Brewster, not because of intolerance from the magistrates but because they feared that a longer stay in Leiden would lead to assimilation into Dutch society, which they were reluctant to contemplate. The voyage of the Pilgrim Fathers accordingly started not from Plymouth, as is often popularly thought, but from the small Dutch port of Delftshaven. The Separatists' famous pastor, John Robinson, who was 'versed in the Dutch language', stayed behind with the majority. The emigrants' fears of assimilation were borne out to the extent that when he died Dutch professors and preachers attended his funeral, and his widow, children and some friends joined the Dutch Reformed Church.

It is ironical that tourists often associate the English church in the Begijnhof at Amsterdam with Robinson, by virtue of the monuments to him and to the early Separatists which it has since acquired. The church, which still exists, may claim to be a memorial to the Dutch toleration from which the Pilgrim Fathers benefited, but it was in fact strongly anti Separatist. The church was essentially Presbyterian after the building had been made available to a congregation under John Paget, previously chaplain to the military commanders Sir Horace Vere and Sir John Ogle. The congregation included the major English merchants in Amsterdam and numbered between 400 and 500 members in the first half of the seventeenth century when membership was at its height. It was part of the Amsterdam classis of the Dutch Reformed Church, and the burgomasters, who paid the minister's salary as they paid that of Dutch ministers, expected to influence the choice of minister in return. On the whole, co-operation with the Dutch authorities, municipal and ecclesiastical, was reasonably good. Problems could arise between English and Dutch, for instance over the profanation of the Sabbath, on which the English took a much severer line. When the Dutch wife of an English member sold fruit from her shop on Sundays this raised disciplinary issues. It should be said that this stricter English sab-batarianism was not confined to Presbyterians. One of the reasons given for the emigration of the Pilgrim Fathers was 'the little good we did, or were like to do to the Dutch in reforming the Sabbath'. Dutch consistories (church councils) might promote Sunday observ-ance, but magistrates did not enforce it. Englishmen commented that Sunday was used 'for the holding of dance schools, beer and brandy-wine parties, lotteries, sales, juggling, fairs, auctions, hiring servants, baking and brewing, digging ditches, or for lying in the churchyard during the sermon. On Sundays the aldermen met, contracts for repair of dykes and canals were put out, the militia marched through the city with music and banners flying. Stores were open for business and taverns too,' and ships were unloaded. The English delegation at the Synod of Dort complained, and for the English congregations in the United Provinces society was tolerant, but it was also secular.[24]

By the time of Archbishop Laud there were altogether some thirty English Reformed churches in the different towns of the Republic.[25] The number of Separatist, Baptist and sectarian congregations is much more difficult to compute, for their history is not continuous and their records are much scantier. The Reformed churches were often affiliated to the Dutch church and accommodated by the Dutch authorities in the disused church and monastic buildings. Until the 1630s their members (unlike the Separatist congregations) might consist principally of those with business in the Netherlands, rather than refugees, but their pastors would almost all have been unac-ceptable at home. The Queen of Bohemia had her own chaplain and a religious establishment closer to the Church of England, which held separate services in the English church at The Hague. The ambassadors attended the English Reformed Church services, but even these, and the services for the English regiments, tended to be Puritan in style until the time of the Laudian attempt to enforce uniformity. The chaplains of Sir Horace Vere, governor at the Brill and commander of the English forces, included people like Paget and John Burgess, who had been deprived of his benefice in 1604. At The Hague, he 'with the consent of his people, ordered things in that congregation as to receive the communion sitting at the table, to leave out the cross in baptism, and surplice in all divine service'. Burgess's son-in-law and successor from 1611–19, William Ames, who had left his fellowship at Cambridge after being suspended from the exercise of his ecclesiastical functions by the vice chancellor, acquired a much greater fame. Though the English ambassador sat in his congregation, he was eventually dismissed for allegedly taking part in Brewster's Pilgrim Press at Leiden which published books obnoxious to the English government, and Sir Dudley Carleton obstructed his appointment to a chair at Leiden University. After serving as a paid theological adviser (on the orthodox Calvinist side) at the Synod of Dort, he was Professor of Theology at Franeker from 1622–32. He wrote the treatise *De Conscientia*, which Tawney described as 'the most influential work on social ethics written in the first half of the seventeenth century from the Puritan standpoint': between 1630 and 1670 it had ten Latin, four Dutch and two English editions. He wrote prefaces for, and oversaw the printing of, manuscripts sent by friends in England; and three sons of the Puritan Lord Saye and Sele were amongst the students at Franeker.[26]

For the last few months of his life Ames was assistant at Rotterdam to the Independent (Congregationalist) Hugh Peters, or Peter, who was to achieve greater notoriety for his sermons at the time of Charles I's trial in 1649, and as Cromwell's chaplain. Rotterdam came to have the largest English and Scots community of all. English merchants were so numerous that the place was described as 'Little London', while the north-western sector of the town was the quarter of the Scots, who were more numerous than in the official Staple at Veere, and included many in the expanding coal trade. There were also 'skippers' underlings and tappers of beer and [English] makers of tobacco pipes'. Peters enlisted Dutch financial support (he and Ames receiving salaries from the city authorities) and reorganized the church on a stricter Congregational model, with a new covenant for which women as well as men voted. He opposed the use of the Book of Common Prayer and used none of the Church of England rites. His church reached a membership of a thousand or more before dissensions led him to depart for New England in 1635 and eventually to greater notoriety as Cromwell's chaplain. We shall return to his admiration for Dutch models in his *Good Work for a Good Magistrate* (1651).[27]

Between 1621 and 1635 some of the English and Scots churches were even organized into a classis. In the 1630s, however, Laud's attempt to enforce conformity to his Arminian policies in England extended to an interest in the English churches in the Netherlands, at the same time as a wave of refugees from his policies increased the numbers of their congregations.

English governments had never been indifferent to these congregations of dissidents who established themselves across the North Sea. In Elizabethan times they had been mostly concerned with Separatists and sectaries of all kinds. An example of this was when Burghley added to the draft instructions to a new governor at Flushing an order to co-operate with the magistrates in seeking to rid the town of sectaries such as Anabaptists and Libertines, lest Her Majesty's subjects in the garrison be infected.[28] In the next reign there was a rather unsystematic concern with the printing of obnoxious literature by the Pilgrim Press and others, and occasional interference with the appointment of individuals like Ames. But Laud's interference was typically more energetic, under the stimulus of people like Edward Missenden, deputy of the Merchant Adventurers at Delft, who in 1632 submitted a statement of the Abuses of the English Churches in the Low Countries. In this he attacked them as 'seminaries of disorderly persons. And albeit that some men may think that the land's well quit of them, for that they are beyond the seas, yet there they do more harm than they could do here, in or by corrupting our nation; writing scandalous books; holding continual correspondence with the refractories of England.' He added that 'the

Merchant Adventurers' preachers in the Low Countries are the chief of those refractories there.... They will observe no forms of prayer nor admit any liturgy....'[29] Laud tried to enforce Anglican conformity upon all those he could reach, using as his agents the new ambassador, and informants who used the Book of Common Prayer and reported others who did not. Under pressure, the Dutch authorities withdrew legal support from the English classis, which collapsed in 1635. He tried to insist that all British ministers with the English or Scots regiments or the Merchant Adventurers (who could not risk losing their charter) should be approved by the King and conform either to the Prayer Book or to the official Dutch Reformed Church. Over other town churches he had less influence, except when there was a vacant pastorate which had to be filled with the approval of the authorities. He had some success. But English clergy who were for a time in the Netherlands included men like Philip Nye and Thomas Goodwin. They were later to become leading Independent members of the Westminster Assembly of Divines, which was set up by Parliament during the Civil War to reform the liturgy and government of the Church of England.

Wren, the Bishop of Norwich, was accused of driving out fifty godly ministers and causing '3000 of the King's subjects (many of whom using trades employed 100 poor people each) to go into Holland and other places beyond sea'. In the long run these lay reinforcements may have been as important as some of the ministerial 'stars'. Many returned to Yarmouth when the rule of Charles I and Laud broke down in 1640–1, so that the Rotterdam church has been described as 'the mother church of Congregational Dissent in Norfolk'. There were emigrants from Yorkshire and Cheshire as well as East Anglia. These refugees were responsible for a flow back to England of books and pamphlets which Laud was quite unable to suppress. One of his correspondents complained bitterly that 'the Brownist libellers, and other such malicious spirits, resemble a smitten hydra, which having its head chopped off, springs forth with several more heads'. In response to ambassadorial pressure on the States-General, the authorities of one town might reluctantly take some lenient action against a printer, Dutch or English, but this could easily be evaded by a timely flight to another town. The town councils could scarcely be expected to object to some products of the presses, however inconvenient they might be to the English government. Of the countless Bibles, many were not the Authorised Version but the Geneva edition, 'the worst, and many of the notes were partial, untrue, seditious, and savouring too much of dangerous and traitorous conceits'. 'For the books which came thence, were better print, better bound, better paper, and for all the charge of bringing, sold better cheap. And would any man buy a worse Bible dearer, that might have a better more cheap?' In 1687 one printer proudly boasted that he had printed 'more than ten times a hundred thousand Bibles', and though this is an obvious exaggeration, other printers certainly printed them in thousands.

Other Puritan literature was more virulent, and in some cases it derived from authors in England and not from exiles. William Prynne's works were printed both in English and Dutch. His *News from Ipswich* had a Dutch equivalent, *Wat nieuws uyt Ipswich in Enghelandt*, and there was even an abridged edition of his blockbuster *Histrio-mastix*, by a printer with an English wife. John Lilburne actually began as an apprentice in Holland, where he had books printed at Delft and was later to be accused of shipping to England 10,000 to 12,000 copies of the *Litany* of another Puritan martyr, John Bastwick. Prynne's printer was fined 300 guilders, the maximum penalty under a placard of 1621 against scandalous books (paltry in comparison with the profits to be made), but neither he nor Lilburne's printer was silenced. Laud's correspondents were helpless to deal with pamphlets in which 'bishops are dragged forth as thieves and murderers, vermin, great foxes, spiritual wolves, prelatical dogs, crocodiles, asses, dunghill worms, locusts, venomous snakes and Amalekites to be put to the sword'.[30]

Much of this radical Protestantism was identified with the young. In the country to which they or their parents had fled, they came into contact with an official Calvinist Church which was not based upon tithes, which had no bishops, which enforced no recusancy fines and which had in practice to tolerate a considerable diversity of opinion (even Arminian, after about 1630). In the Republic there was no preliminary censorship of the large numbers of printers, and the only penalties upon works which had appeared, however scandalous, were light and easily evaded. It has been suggested that Presbyterian practice was better known through Holland than (before 1638) through Scotland or France. Apart from New England, Independent practice was scarcely known outside the English churches of the Netherlands before 1640. As for the sectaries of all kinds, Englishmen who visited the Netherlands were in a position to see that, contrary to a commonplace of political theory, the toleration of several faiths within one state did not create chaos and confusion. The consequences for England between 1640 and 1660 are obvious. The new ideas of the Puritan Revolution were not worked out in a total void; often there was an element of imitation, though this did not extend to the practical toleration of Catholic worship which existed in the Dutch Republic.

Many of these ideas were conveyed by books or by returning exiles in 1641, and also by merchants who crossed the North Sea or maintained close business connections. Apart from the obvious Londoners, commotions in Yarmouth were blamed on 'continual intercourse with those of Amsterdam'. In York the most obstinate Puritans were merchants with extensive foreign connections in the Netherlands, and the same was true in Newcastle, where several traded with Amsterdam. There were also the Dutch congregations in London and other provincial centres which marred the conformity of the Church of England. Laud argued, with every appearance of accuracy, that by his time many of their members were not refugees at all, but had been born in England, and that they were reduced in number. From this he drew the conclusion that they could easily attend their parish churches instead. Ultimately this was enjoined only upon those born in England, and some preferred to go to the Netherlands.

For these reasons many Englishmen, in spite of all the commercial jealousies listed in the first half of this chapter, felt an affinity with the Dutch at a time when their struggle with the old enemy, Spain, still continued. Such men viewed with dismay the benevolent neutrality which Charles I extended to Spain, even allowing the transport of Spanish troops and money through English ports. Against this background, in 1639 a Spanish fleet under Oquendo found itself penned against the English coast near Beachy Head by the Dutch admiral Tromp. Before the Battle of the Downs, Charles I temporized between the parties, asking the Spanish governor at Brussels for £150,000 protection money and supplying Spain with gunpowder. But characteristically he was left behind by events. His ship money fleet had to look on while Tromp destroyed all but seven of Oquendo's 77 ships in English waters. This might be an affront to English claims to sovereignty in the Britannic seas; but the victory was very welcome to those who saw it as a triumph for the Protestant cause in the Thirty Years War. Dissatisfaction with Stuart foreign policy was one cause of the discontent which found expression in the 1640s. It was not assuaged by the marriage of Charles's nine-year-old daughter Mary to the 14-year-old William, son of the Prince of Orange, whom Tromp brought across the sea in 1641. Parliament's Nineteen Propositions of 1642 contained a demand 'that your Majesty will be pleased to enter into a more strict alliance with the States of the United Provinces, and other neighbouring princes and states of the Protestant religion'. Four years later the Parliament which had made this demand had won the Civil War, and after six years the independence of the Dutch was at last recognized by Spain. No one could have foreseen that within ten years the British and Dutch would be, not allies, but at war with one another.

CHAPTER FOUR

The Dutch (or English) Wars

By 1651 there was a Protestant Republic in both countries, and many Englishmen naïvely supposed that a natural basis existed for co-operation, in which (of course) the Dutch would accept English leadership. The English monarchy had been abolished early in 1649 after the execution of Charles I. There had been a Dutch Republic since the abjuration of Philip II's authority in 1581. Moreover the House of Orange, which (though holding no hereditary offices) had exercised great influence by virtue of William the Silent's services to the cause of independence, had lost its ascendancy. Under William's sons Maurice of Nassau (died 1625) and Frederick Henry (1625–47) and grandson William II (1647–50), the House seemed to be on the way to dynastic rule, but William II died prematurely from smallpox in November 1650 and was succeeded by a posthumous baby, William III. In the two northern provinces of Friesland and Groningen, a cadet branch of the family occupied the position of stadholder (literally lieutenant), who since the time of Spanish rule had had responsibilities connected with law and order. But in the rest, including the dominant province of Holland, the stadholderate, together with the Captain-Generalship of the armed forces of the Republic, was left unfilled. The field was open to the oligarchic regents in the States-General and the States of Holland, and the latter's adviser, known in Oldenbarnevelt's day as the Advocate but now as the Grand Pensionary. To this office

John de Witt succeeded in 1653. The House of Orange was left leaderless, crippled by conflicts between the baby's mother and grandmother, and it was in the interests of the regents to see that it was never in a position to repeat the coup which William II had attempted against Amsterdam in 1650. But at the same time it was in the interests of the English Republicans to see that the House of Orange was not in a position to aid its Stuart relatives by marriage. Equally, episcopacy had just been swept away in the churches of England, Scotland and Ireland, just as it had been in the Dutch Republic since the Revolt, and there might seem to be a basis for a régime which was Calvinist, yet tolerant (except of popery) in them all. And there was, in foreign policy, the tradition of common hostility to Spain.

Yet this community of interest proved more apparent than real. Although many Dutch Calvinists had hoped for a Puritan victory through Parliament in the Civil War, they no more approved of the public execution of a lawful monarch on the scaffold than did English and Scots Presbyterians. They could justify their own abjuration of Philip II's authority, but a public execution was horrifying. Clarendon, who was at The Hague at the time, later recalled that 'there was a woman at The Hague, of the middling rank, who, being with child, with the horror of the mention of it fell into travail and in it died'.[1] The States-General and the States of Holland limited their horror to condolences to the Prince of Wales, whom they addressed simply as King Charles II of Scotland, where he had been officially proclaimed; and they assembled in a body to bid Charles farewell on his departure for Scotland. They had no reason to take more positive action. At the same time, they now had no urgent reason to consider England as a potential ally against Spain, which had brought its long war with the Dutch to an end by recognizing the independence of the United Provinces in the Treaty of Münster in 1648. Furthermore, tension between Dutch and English sailors and merchants had greatly increased in the past decade. The existence of the two parties in the Civil War, Royalist and Parliamentarian, had meant that each considered itself entitled to seize the cargoes of neutral Dutch ships trading with the other; and both parties traded to the ports of Flanders. Damage to the States' merchants ran into several hundred thousand guilders at the hands of English privateers. Both Royalist and Parliamentarian privateers encroached upon Dutch waters, and the possibilities for disputes were endless.[2] Nor did they come to an end with Charles I's surrender, for Royalist privateers continued to operate from Irish ports until 1650, and sometimes tried to sell captured English prizes in Dutch ports. Thereafter there was an undeclared naval war between England and France in the course of which English privateers, armed with official letters of reprisal, stopped Dutch ships carrying French cargo and seized it as prize goods. Matters developed to such a pitch that the Court of Admiralty threatened English sailors with punishment if they persisted in ill-using Dutch sailors to compel them to acknowledge goods as French when in reality they were nothing of the sort.[3] All this revived, in a much more acute form, the tensions of 1627, the English claiming the right of search while the Dutch maintained the old maxim of 'free ship, free goods'. Naturally great irritation was caused among the Dutch who suffered. But in spite of the ill-feeling which resulted, the Dutch had no interest in pursuing a policy of aggression in European waters, for it would do more harm than good to Dutch trade.

On the English side too, victory over Charles I gave people leisure to reflect on all the old jealousies of the Dutch.[4] The whaling dispute had faded out, but all the other disputes persisted and were indeed exacerbated by the consciousness that Dutch trade had profited from the English preoccupation with the Civil War. At the same time, the ending of the war of independence with Spain in 1648 made possible a surge in Dutch trade to the Mediterranean with which Englishmen could not easily compete. The Rump of the Long Parliament took over the Stuart demands for money in return for a licence to fish for herring and for the salute in acknowledgment of sovereignty over the seas. It is significant that Sir John Borough's *The Sovereignty of the British Seas*, which had been written for Charles I in 1633, was published in 1651. In the same year appeared Benjamin Worsley's *The Advocate, or a narrative of the state and condition of things between the English and Dutch nations in relation to trade ... as it was presented in August 1651*. He argued that just as Spain had aimed at 'the universal monarchy of Christendom', so the Dutch had 'aimed to lay a foundation to themselves for ingrossing the universal trade, not only of Christendom, but indeed of the greater part of the known world'. He rehearsed the old arguments of the beginning of the century: the wide-ranging trade of the Dutch, the 2000 herring ships, the virtual spice monopoly, the advantage of cheap freight rates so that 'they can undersell us even in our countries', low interest rates, the bank of Amsterdam, and so on. Yet when all this had been said, what he advocated was not war but an improved trading policy to enable Englishmen to compete. Again, the appointment of a Council of Trade on which prominent merchants sat did not mean that the Rump Parliament and its Council of State immediately went over to a warlike policy. More research needs to be done into the conflicting mercantile interests at this time. It is fairly clear that East India interests wanted to break into the Dutch position in the East Indies. The statement has been repeated equally positively that the undoubted enthusiasm of the Fifth Monarchists and other radical sectaries for the war was attributable to the fact that they included many clothworkers who saw English and Dutch cloth exports as being in competition. The difficulty about this theory is that the United Provinces were still England's best customer for her cloth exports, and it is not easy to see precisely how the cloth industry would have benefited on balance from war and the dislocation it would cause.

At all events, the Commonwealth's ambassadors, Strickland and St John, were sent to The Hague in April 1651 not to deliver an ultimatum but to ask 'that the two commonwealths may be confidential friends, joined and allied together for the defence and preservation of the liberty and freedoms of the people of each against all whomsoever that shall attempt the disturbance of either state by sea or land, or be declared enemies to the freedom and liberty of the people living under either of the said governments'.[5] Behind this lay an implicit request both for the expulsion of the English Royalists whose turn it now was to take advantage of the freedom of refugees in the United Provinces, and for a still closer form of union. The Dutch evaded both, having no wish to expel refugees or to enter into any commitment which might subordinate them to English policy. They offered colonial and commercial co-operation in return for

(*Above*) *Women spinning*, by I. Swanenburg. One of four paintings depicting processes in the cloth industry which was so important to both the English and the Dutch.

(*Below*) Medal struck for the Earl of Leicester on the occasion of his departure from the Netherlands in 1587. He claims to be leaving, not a faithful flock, but ungrateful people.

Zutphen and its surroundings. The scene of the military operations in which Sir Philip Sidney was mortally wounded.

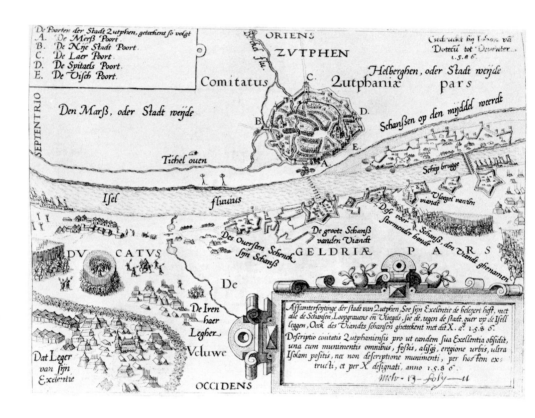

(Above right) The Dutch fishing fleet which aroused so much jealousy on the part of the English in the early seventeenth century. Painting by A. van Salm.

(Below right) Skirmish between Dutch and English ships in the 1st Anglo-Dutch war. Painting by Vroom.

—82—

The Synod of Dort, 1618, which proclaimed Calvinist orthodoxy. Engraving by Visscher, showing the synod in session with the representatives of James I in the places of honour near the president's chair.

A Dutch satirical print referring to the 2nd Anglo-Dutch war. In such prints the lion is always Dutch, and the dog English. Here the lion is shown defending his stockade, with heavenly aid, against the dog's attempts to break in.

Satirical print of Charles II. When turned upside down he is shown as a hyena, again referring to the Dutch view that they were on the defensive against the English.

(*Above*) Painting of the *Royal Charles* brought into Dutch waters after her capture in 1667, by L. Bakhuizen.

(*Left*) Medal of the Peace of Breda, 1667, by Christoph Adolfz.

The Linen Cupboard, by P. de Hooch. English travellers marvelled at the house-proud domesticity of the Dutch wife, as shown in this depiction of middle-class life in the seventeenth century.

The Portuguese Synagogue, Amsterdam, was much visited by Englishmen at a time when there was nothing like it in England. Painting by E. de Witte (1617–92).

freedom of fishing, navigation and commerce. The Englishmen's entry into The Hague had been accompanied, not by an enthusiastic welcome from fellow Protestants and Republicans, but by the insults and abuse of the exiled Royalists and their Orangist friends. Chafing at this reception and at the subsequent failure to achieve the closer union for which he had been sent, St John returned to England, to be in all probability the main instigator of the famous Navigation Act. This tried to satisfy English shipping and commercial interests by stipulating that all imports must be in English-owned ships or those of the country of origin.

In the long run this measure, extended by further acts in 1660 and 1663, clearly damaged the Dutch carrying trade. Its immediate effect must not be exaggerated. The Dutch were adept at finding loopholes in it and there was ample opportunity for quibbles over the ownership of vessels. Moreover, English merchants themselves sought exemptions for the importation of timber from the Baltic, having too few ships which were suitable for carrying it themselves. The prohibition on the importation of fish caught by those who were not British subjects was ineffective, and bills to repeal it were introduced in 1656, 1657, and 1658. Dutch ambassadors tried to get the act repealed, but it is a myth that it was the direct cause of the war which began in the following year, for the Dutch would not have rated it so essential as to justify hostilities. What the act undoubtedly did was to add to the sense of rivalry between the two countries, and to strengthen the ill-will which had begun to submerge the attitude that they were natural allies in international affairs. One incident would be enough to inflame this situation to the point of war.

This incident came in May 1652, when the English claim to the right of search of Dutch merchant ships and the Dutch determination to resist it at last led to an armed conflict off Dover. The conflict was more the outcome of misunderstanding than of deliberate intention. Tromp had received instructions to protect the merchantmen from search, and when his fleet encountered that of the English admiral, Blake, there was confusion over whether he had paid the full salute which Blake expected. Even after a fight lasting two hours in which Tromp lost two of his ships, the States-General instructed Tromp to strike the flag when necessary and sent an embassy to London; but the rising tide of popular opinion on both sides made this appeasement fruitless. On 6 July the States-General ordered Tromp to miss no opportunity to attack the English fleet and 'to do all imaginable damage to it', and Blake had already sailed to attack the herring fleet.

The three Dutch wars, or *engelse oorlogen* (English wars) to the Dutch, which followed had certain features in common. In skill and bravery the two fleets were well matched (though the English had an advantage in the weight of guns) and neither could achieve a really decisive victory. Under seventeenth-century conditions naval battles were usually indecisive. Wind, smoke from the gunpowder used and difficulties of communication made it hard for admirals to co-ordinate tactics. Battles were often followed by recriminations between colleagues, who complained that others had shirked the struggle, whether from cowardice or from factious or treasonable motives. Often both sides claimed victory. Even successful battles could not be followed up by an effective pursuit. In victorious fleets the rigging had often been crippled and the Dutch in particular could escape into shoals near their coasts where the English could not easily follow. In 1666 and 1667 the English raided the Vlie and the Dutch raided the Medway, but it was never possible to follow up a victory by invasion. Even close blockade of either the Dutch harbours or the mouth of the Thames was difficult to keep up for any length of time: the sick and wounded had to be landed. For the English the need to refit after the Dutch concentration of fire into their rigging, and the need to reprovision, taxed all the resources of their dockyards. While this was being done, opportunities were being missed, and as naval operations were confined to fair weather, usually between May and September, it was difficult to do all that was necessary. Time was short and so were stores, particularly as so little was known about methods of preserving food and drink. Complaints about the victualling of the fleets were chronic. To quote one English report from July 1653, 'Of several ships the men have come to me ... and showed me their beer, bread and butter, against which there is such a cry (and very justly), for it's such that in the dearest time that ever I knew I neither saw so bad laid in by state nor mart. Here is witness the men do drink water rather than beer, and the butter is most unfit for men of all the rest. And they must take pork now in harbour which was salted before December last ... or none ... Divers of the men fall sick, who impute it to this stock of victuals.'[6] Conditions in the war of 1665–7 were worse, and the English suffered more than the Dutch, in provisions as in delayed pay, because they had much inferior supplies of money and credit. They needed a press gang, whereas the Dutch did not.

For the English it was therefore a question how long they could afford to sustain a war; for the Dutch the problem was how long they could sustain the dislocation of trade which ensued. They laboured under the disadvantage of depending much more than the English upon the worldwide trade which was interrupted. To make matters worse, their ships from the East Indies, the Atlantic, the Mediterranean and western France had to run the gauntlet in sailing up the Channel. Indeed, winds, tides and currents led them to sail near to the English rather than the French coast, so that they were prey to English privateers. They might attempt the alternative of the long journey round the north of Scotland, but they might still be intercepted in the North Sea before reaching the safety of home ports. Moreover, the herring fishery, since it operated so close to the British shores, was particularly vulnerable and its interruption hurt not only fishermen but also the many who depended indirectly upon the industry. It is true that the English suffered from the risk to colliers bringing coal from Newcastle – war always meant a steep rise in the price of coal in London. 'They are above £6 the chaldron, and scarce to be had for money. A merry fellow last week went through the City crying coals at 3d the bushel, and as the people gathered about him to know where, he told them at Rotterdam stairs....'[7] English supplies of the all-important timber and naval stores from the Baltic were also likely to be interrupted by Dutch attacks, or the stopping of traffic through the Sound by their Danish allies.

Nevertheless, the Dutch suffered far more. In the war of 1652–4 the English seized at least as many ships as there were already in the whole of their merchant navy. These ships not only greatly reinforced the English fleet in terms of numbers, but also gave it the technically advanced 'flutes' or the purpose-built herring busses which were so much better than the English equivalent. The result was a boost for the English shipping industry greater than the initial gains from the early years of the operation of the Navigation Act.[8] In the second and third wars the Dutch had a more efficiently organized convoy system, but there were inevitably delays and, for instance, there was always great rejoicing when the rich East Indiamen reached port safely through the North Sea.

The Dutch, therefore, missed no opportunity for entering into peace negotiations. This did not mean, however, that De Witt, who was Grand Pensionary and had most influence over Dutch policy between 1653 and 1672, was prepared to make the kind of concessions which might lead to greater English demands later. At the same time, there were Englishmen who regarded the Dutch as potential allies against either the Hapsburgs in the 1650s or Louis XIV in the 1660s and 1670s, and so fought them stubbornly but with reluctance. For this reason, as well as the cost, the wars were shorter than the land wars against Louis. In 1653, for instance, after victory off the Texel, a sea-captain wrote: 'I pray God make this mercy a further blessing unto us in the preserving a good peace betwixt us both, who have been so long formerly and so useful one to the other.'[9] But the most important person who thought like this in the first war was Oliver Cromwell himself. Only one of a Council of State of 42 when the war began, he seems to have been swept along by the general trend to war after the incident off Dover, and pressed on with the need to fight it once it had begun. However, he became increasingly anxious to reach a settlement, particularly after he became Lord Protector in 1653.

In 1652 the five admiralties, based at Amsterdam, Rotterdam, Middelburg, Hoorn and in Friesland which composed the rather disjointed Dutch naval administration, and their commanders Tromp, Witte de With, and De Ruyter, were already finding it difficult to meet their commitments to protect the trade arriving from all quarters. The battle of the Kentish Knock (in Dutch, Theemsmond – most of these battles have two names) was reckoned by the English to be a victory, but if so it was scarcely an emphatic one. That winter, the first of these wars, the fleets sought to continue operations, and on 30 November/10 December (according to the calendar used) Tromp won a much clearer victory from Blake off Dungeness ('de Singels'). Presumably, the myth of Tromp sailing the Channel with a broom at his mast-head related to the period after this. At the end of February, however, Blake inflicted severe losses upon him off Portland. On 11 June he had the better of another battle off the Gabbard, a shoal east of Harwich (Nieuwpoort), and when Tromp put out again, he was defeated and killed off Texel (Ter Heide). Monck, who won that battle, was unable to stay on the coast, having to return home for repairs and further provisions, but it was at this time that the Dutch suffered most damage to their trade and fishing. Their ships had either to run a very real risk of seizure or to remain within port. The fishing fleet dared not venture out, so that 'we are fair to eat old pickled herring instead of new, for which the English are cursed by the commons with bell, book, and candle...'.[10] Yet though brought to this not very terrible privation, and to far greater losses, so that Orangist sentiments against the régime were heard, they were not brought to their knees. In the following winter the English were quite unable to press home their advantage. Moreover, the Dutch negotiators who were sent to London found that, though the radical sectaries in the Barebones Parliament and elsewhere still zealously favoured war, Cromwell, whose political authority was growing, was more and more reluctant.

His priorities in international affairs were quite different. When in 1652 Hugh Peters instigated a petition from the Dutch congregation at Austin Friars for a resumption of negotiations, he offered to support it. He harked back to the old Elizabethan days when England and the States-General fought Spain together. In his childhood an Englishman had sat on the Dutch Council of State, and in June 1653, in conversation with the ambassador Nieuport, he even suggested that two or three Dutchmen should sit in the English Council of State, and that Englishmen should sit in the Dutch Council of State (which he must have assumed to be of comparable authority). He favoured the closest possible union short of amalgamation, for both commercial and religious reasons. In the heat of the battles the Council of State went further, demanding complete amalgamation – *una gens, una respublica* – with equal privileges in trade, though with laws continuing to be separate. Two months later the Dutch engineer Vermuyden drew up a paper providing for an offensive and defensive alliance and assigning the trade with Asia and Brazil to the Dutch, while England took the trade to the rest of North and South America.[11] Such proposals must rank among the oddest ever made to an enemy in wartime. But nothing came of these plans for union, any more than the States-General's offer of sovereignty to Elizabeth. Cromwell rapidly came to the conclusion that such ideas were unrealistic, and after the dissolution of the Barebones Parliament and his elevation to the Protectorship, he and his new Council of State contented themselves with far less.

The terms were in fact much more moderate than might have been expected in the previous summer. The Treaty of Westminster (1654) enforced no payment for the right to fish, and the provisions for the right of the salute were sufficiently vague for them to be anything but a final solution to the problem. England's only gains were the promise of the island of Pularun in the East Indies, which was so far distant that the Dutch East India Company could not be obliged to hand it over; and the Act of Seclusion. By this act the province of Holland bound itself not to accept the Prince of Orange as stadholder, nor to consent to the States-General accepting him as Captain-General. It was thought that this would prevent the Stuarts' relatives from coming to power in the United Provinces. This was little enough for two years of hard fighting. Englishmen, particularly Royalist courtiers after 1660, retained memories of a war in which there were supposedly easy pickings to be made from the seizure of Dutch prizes, and East India interests resented the failure of the Dutch to give up Pularun. De Witt, on the other hand, drew the moral that he must build up the strength and organization of the Dutch fleet, so that his merchants and fishermen should not again be exposed to such losses. He was so successful that, whereas on the whole the English fleet was better organized in 1652-4, the reverse was true when the next war came along.

Until the fall of the Commonwealth in 1660 relations were not exactly cordial and the mercantile community in London was little better disposed than before. But the government had more important priorities, such as its war with Spain. At the Restoration it is noteworthy that Cromwell's former secretary of state, Thurloe, briefed

Charles II's Chancellor, Clarendon, with a memorandum on Anglo-Dutch relations which went back ten years over the pre-war negotiations, so that there was no likelihood that the issues would be forgotten.[12] Charles II embarked for his return voyage to England by way of Holland, but neither his memories of The Hague in the grim years of 1648 to 1650 nor the festivities which were put on for his benefit in 1660 were calculated to make him feel much affinity for the States. On the contrary, he felt no liking for De Witt and the other regents who obstructed the claims of his sister, Princess Mary, and his nephew, Prince William, to the traditional offices of the Orange family. The gifts, including a *fijnschilderij* ('fine painting') by Dou, did not make up for the failure to conclude a large loan. When he departed from Scheveningen he took with him an already well-developed interest in naval matters. Yet though he was no lover of the Dutch Republic he was restrained from war for four years, and entered it unwillingly even then, as did Clarendon and Lord Treasurer Southampton. He knew how insecure, inadequately financed and under-equipped his new government was to fight a war, and he was particularly disturbed when De Witt was successful in making a treaty with Louis XIV in 1662 which included an agreement that each country should defend the other's freedom to fish.

What eventually swept him into war was essentially an unusual conjunction between the City of London and influential courtiers. From James, Duke of York downwards they invested in a corporation of the Royal Fishery, but this company, even when led by James as governor and 32 assistants, was, in Pepys's words, 'so ill-fitted for so serious a work' that it was never likely to be more successful than its predecessor under Charles I. More serious was the Royal Africa company, which included James and many of the same people; indeed it met weekly under James's chairmanship in his quarters at Whitehall. As refounded in 1663 with a new charter, it included not only James, Prince Rupert, the Queen and Queen Mother, the second Duke of Buckingham and Sir Henry Bennet (Secretary of State), but people with more practical experience from the City. Its aim was not only to engage in the usual trade to the Gold Coast, and to obtain the gold at the head-waters of the Gambia of which

Rupert had heard on his expedition to Africa in the early 1650s, but to take part in the slave trade. Since about 1640 there had been a great boom in sugar production in the West Indies, and this meant an increased demand for slaves for the sugar plantations of all nations. It seemed to be a profitable speculation for the merchants, but since the Dutch West India company was already established in forts on the Gold Coast, competition and clashes were likely. Through James and the courtiers of the Africa Company, the use of ships from the Royal Navy could be obtained for their expeditions. Between 1661 and 1664 there followed incident after incident as the English tried to break into the virtual monopoly which the Dutch enjoyed in the supply of slaves.

It was probably this combination of interests which was decisive in overcoming the reluctance of the King and his senior ministers – not that they were fundamentally better disposed to the Dutch, but they knew how unprepared for war the country was. But other long-standing colonial problems existed. The East India Company, still trying to break into the Dutch trade with the Spice Islands, cherished its Amboina legend and its grievances over the failure of the Dutch East India Company to hand over Pularun. A great deal of diplomatic energy was devoted to attempts to seek satisfaction over seizures of ships in the Indian Ocean – far more than they were worth. In fact, one can detect the beginnings of the process by which the Dutch company concentrated on the Archipelago, from its headquarters at Batavia on the island of Java, while the English concentrated on forts in India itself, at Bombay, Madras, and eventually in Bengal, importing Indian textiles as well as pepper from Malabar.[13] But though there were ample profits to be made by both companies, it took time before separate spheres of influence were distinguished either by the men on the spot or by those in Europe. At the same time there was conflict in the area at the mouth of the North American river discovered by Henry Hudson, an English explorer sailing in the Dutch service. The resulting Dutch colony of New Amsterdam was a particular nuisance to the English in view of the act of 1663 laying down that all goods from the American colonies should be exported either to England or to other plantations. The Dutch could make use of this loophole to continue their trade with

Maryland and Virginia. In support of their navigation policy the Council for Foreign Plantations trumped up a claim to the Dutch colony, which was duly seized in the spring of 1664, almost a year before there was an official war between the two countries, and rechristened New York after its new owner, the Duke of York. At the time it seemed much the least important of the colonial areas of conflict.

Diplomatic 'brinkmanship' on both sides contributed to the outbreak of war. Sir George Downing, the tough, cantankerous and unco-operative ambassador in The Hague, was a survivor of the Commonwealth period who was frustrated by the repeated delays caused by the Dutch constitution. Matters seemed to be referred endlessly to and fro for decision, from commissioners to States-General, and from States-General to their principals in the provincial States. Remembering the last war, he thought that a policy of bluster would overcome these evasions and lead the Dutch to back down on the outstanding issues. De Witt, on the other hand, thought that in the last resort the insecurity of the Restoration government and its financial weakness would lead it to temporize, and was determined not to encourage further demands by making concessions. He was right in that a petition from the House of Commons, presented by Sir Thomas Clifford and offering money in support of warlike action to settle grievances, was not followed by immediate action. But the tide of opinion at court and in London was running steadily towards war, and this was only confirmed when Sir Robert Holmes's expedition to attack forts on the Gold Coast was followed by the recapture of all but one by De Ruyter. De Witt had to use a trick to get De Ruyter's instructions for this 'beating to dirt at Guinea' of his English rivals passed by the States-General, a fact which suggests that he could not have been confident of unanimous support.

The hopes of English courtiers for naval commissions, and glory and profit from captured prizes, now pushed Charles over the brink. According to Clarendon, there were even some who talked of 'making all ships which passed by or through the narrow seas to pay an imposition to the king, as all do to the King of Denmark who pass by the Sound.'[14] Such sentiments were greatly encouraged when the House of Commons passed a vote for two and a half million pounds, a vote so enormous that Clarendon had to explain to his readers what the word 'million' meant. 'This brave vote gave the king the first liking of the war';[15] but unfortunately it was not as large as it first sounded. It was to be collected over three years, not one; and the first year's instalment, spent before it had been collected, was largely devoted to repairing the ships and replenishing the stores which had been left in a poor state at the Restoration. Charles II later told the French ambassador that all the rope came from Amsterdam.[16] Further aids were voted in October 1665 and January 1667, but the result of the war was as much dependent upon credit as upon blows, and in this the Dutch were vastly superior. Though Downing, using his Dutch experience, tried to encourage investors and contractors to lend to the exchequer as to a sort of 'bank', the financial situation grew worse and worse. Contractors and dockyard workers could extract payment by embezzlement, but seamen had to accept payment by 'tickets', which they resold to moneylenders at a discount.

The second Anglo-Dutch war was therefore one of the few wars in British history which began with a victory and ended with a disaster. The Dutch strategy was, as so often, to seek out the English fleet, but they were badly defeated by the Duke of York and the Earl of Sandwich off Lowestoft, and the commander 'foggy Opdam' was killed. Once again there was no effective pursuit of the fleeing enemy. The eventual scapegoat was the courtier Henry Brouncker, James's gentleman of the bedchamber, 'a person throughout his whole life never notorious for any thing but the highest degree of impudence, and stooping to the most infamous offices, and playing very well at chess'.[17] He was alleged to have ordered the master's ship to slacken sail overnight in order that the heir to the throne (and himself) should not awake in the middle of the enemy fleet next morning. It is more probable that those in command were well aware of the danger of being amongst the enemy, on a lee shore amid shoals.

Still, the poets celebrated the victory, from the well-known *Annus Mirabilis* of Dryden and the *Instructions to a Painter* of Waller to the effusions of the anonymous poetasters:

Poor silly Holland, how canst thou withstand
Great Britain's King? He'll shake thee from his hand,
As Paul the viper did into the flame,
He'll cause thee tremble at his dreadful name ...

Another poem begins with one of the most remarkable pieces of apostrophization in English bad verse:

Gout! I conjure thee by the powerful names
Of Charles and James, and their victorious frames,
On this great day set all thy prisoners free
(Triumphs command a gaol delivery).
Set them all free, leave not a limping toe
From my Lord Chancellor to mine below.
Unless thou giv'st us leave this day to dance
Thou'rt not th'old Loyal Gout, but com'st from France.[18]

From the time of the fleet's withdrawal to refit, things began to go wrong. Shortage of money made difficulties for the refit. Seizures of prizes were disappointing, and the attempt to catch the returning Dutch fleet from the East Indies failed at Bergen. The three richest captures, all East Indiamen, led to a scandal and the removal of Sandwich, when the officers plundered some of the cargo below decks; and the only ally to be found was the Bishop of Münster, while the French eventually kept their treaty obligations to the Dutch and joined in the war. Though they did very little, their very presence raised strategic problems. Soon Charles came to want a way out of the war; but he could not afford to make a peace less honourable than Cromwell's, and De Witt was so far from making concessions that he would agree to nothing more than a peace in which each side retained its conquests.

De Witt had coped with a wave of defeatism in the Republic after Lowestoft and had worked to reorganize and re-energize the fleet. His reward was a considerable victory by De Ruyter in the Four Days Battle of 1666, at the beginning of which Prince Rupert was diverted by false intelligence that the French fleet was sailing up the Channel. The English soon retaliated in the Two Days Battle (St James's Fight) and Holmes's Bonfire of shipping in the roadstead of

–99–

the Vlie, an act which brought upon the English humiliating revenge planned by De Witt himself.

The Great Plague and the Great Fire of London, with the attendant loss of revenue from customs, excise and hearth tax, completed the ruin of Charles's finances. Even with another subsidy, a further campaign would have been impossible in 1667. Consequently, as soon as it seemed probable that Louis XIV would obtain reasonable terms for him in negotiations at Breda, Charles took the momentous decision to save money by laying up the capital fleet and remaining on the defensive. Although this exposed London to the danger of a blockade of the mouth of the Thames if peace did not come about, this was not necessarily a bad decision in itself, always provided that measures were taken to guard against an attack upon the dockyard at Chatham. There was talk of a fort at Sheerness, but due to the financial situation and the incompetence of the administration, little was done. Clarendon later protested that he did not even know where Sheerness was, so that he could not possibly be responsible. Even so, Charles and his ministers might have got away with it, but for the daring of De Ruyter on his dangerous expedition up the Medway, which a lesser admiral could not have brought off. His subordinate, Captain Brakel, broke the chain across the river, and the Dutch towed away the English flagship, the *Royal Charles*, burned other ships and forced more to escape upstream and strand themselves on shore.[19] There was great panic in London and there was even talk of an attack on the Tower. Pepys arranged for his father and wife to carry £1300 in gold off to the country, where to his dismay they buried it in broad daylight in the front garden, one Sunday morning.

Marvell's satirical *Last Instructions to a Painter*, with praise reserved for the Scots officer who stayed to be burned to death with his ship rather than desert his post without orders, was the greatest possible contrast to Waller's original. Pepys remarked 'that they managed their retreat down this difficult passage, with all their fear, better than we could do ourselves in the main sea ... Thus, in all things, in wisdom, courage, force, knowledge of our own streams, and success, the Dutch have the best of us, and do end the war with victory on their side.' The material damage was not so great as the moral; but there could now be no talk of peace with honour. Charles could consider himself fortunate that he escaped with nothing worse than the Treaty of Breda. He kept New York and the Dutch kept Surinam, which they had captured and, with its sugar plantations, thought more valuable. The Dutch even rather vaguely conceded the right of salute 'in British waters', whatever they might be, as long as there were no practical implications; but, more practically, they gained the right to transport goods from the Rhineland through Holland to England, in an amendment to the Navigation Act.

Charles II did not rest content until he had tried to avenge this disgrace. Yet the second Anglo-Dutch war has been described as the turning-point in Anglo-Dutch relations,[20] for there were already that hostility to the French was growing greater than hostility to the Dutch, as Louis's ambassadors reported in 1665. The government of France was absolutist, Catholic, protectionist, and overbearing, and the Dutch Republic was none of these things. It was Frenchmen, rather than the Dutch, who were popularly suspected of responsibility for the Fire of London. Even among Charles's ministers there were some, like Arlington (Sir Henry Bennet, who had a Dutch wife) and his protégé Sir William Temple, who thought it preferable to divide England's enemies by an approach to the States-General rather than an approach to France. Popular fury after the Medway disaster was directed at the incompetence and waste of the government rather than at the Dutch; and it was commented that there had been English pilots on De Ruyter's ships. Pepys's informant 'did hear many Englishmen on board the Dutch ships speaking to one another in English; and that they did cry and say "We did heretofore fight for tickets; now we fight for dollars!" and did ask how such a one and such a one did...'. There were reported, with some exaggeration, to be as many as 3000 English and Scots seamen on the Dutch fleet.[21] Some no doubt were there simply to earn a living; others were persecuted Nonconformists who had sought refuge in Holland and had relatives in England.

On the Dutch side, as we shall see in chapter six, the Orangist party looked to Charles II as a possible source of advancement for his nephew, the Prince of Orange, and of peace by means of this connection. But De Witt, too, detected a community of interest between England and the States-General over the fate of Flanders, which simply had to be preserved from absorption by Louis XIV. By this time it was abundantly clear that Spain was much weaker than it had once been, while the France of Louis XIV was far stronger and more dangerous. By the Peace of the Pyrenees (1659) Louis had already absorbed the province of Artois from the Spanish Netherlands, and it was obvious that his ambitions did not stop there; if the Spanish Netherlands were conquered he would be a formidable neighbour. The Pensionary had raised the subject in conversation with Downing even before the war, and fear of 'the growing greatness of France' in the Republic had been stimulated by dissatisfaction with the aid rendered by France during it. Louis's invasion of the Spanish Netherlands in 1667 had been one reason for De Witt's consent to a relatively lenient peace at Breda. Fears that in a second campaign he would carry his frontier up to that of the Dutch led De Witt to fall in with the offer of an English alliance to induce Louis to desist.

The Triple Alliance of 1668 (with Sweden) was a landmark in the history of the two peoples.[22] Negotiated within five days, a fact demonstrating the new-found community of interest, it was remarkable because, only seven months after the Medway, it was greeted with genuine and very general rejoicing in both capitals. This seemed justified when Louis desisted from his advance. There were many at the time who thought, as Burnet did in retrospect (in his *History of My Own Time*), that this 'was certainly the masterpiece of King Charles's life; and, if he had stuck to it, it would have been both the strength and the glory of his reign'. The Anglo-Dutch collaboration of 1689 could have begun twenty years earlier.

But Charles did not stick to it. The outbreak of the third Anglo-Dutch war in 1672 was largely the King's personal doing, whereas in the war of 1665-7 he had responded to widespread pressure. There is no need to explain here why Charles hankered after a friendship with the most powerful monarch in Europe, and had indeed only authorized Temple to make the Triple Alliance when private negotiations with Louis broke down.[23] However, it is necessary to note that an essential part of his plans was a renewal of the struggle with the States-General, this time with Louis XIV as his ally in a land attack, to wipe out the humiliation of his previous failure. By the Treaty of Dover of 1670 his share of the spoils was to be in Zeeland – namely Goeree, Walcheren, Sluis and Cadzand, which control the mouths of the estuaries. There were politicians like Clifford and Downing who were inveterate enemies of the Dutch, and others like Arlington who would fall in with Charles's wishes. There were also grievances which could be fomented into pretexts for war, such as problems over a marine treaty which would govern navigation in the East Indies; problems over the evacuation of English settlers from the plantations of Surinam; and medals struck in Holland which could be interpreted as insults to Charles. The crowning insult was the failure of the Dutch fleet to make the full salute demanded when a yacht carrying Lady Temple sailed through the middle of it. These had some effect on English public opinion, and yet it was not worked up to anything like the same extent as in 1664. Pamphlets like Josiah Child's *Brief Observations concerning Trade and Interest of Money* (1668), Roger Coke's *Reasons of the Increase of the Dutch Trade* (1671), and the anonymous *Royal Fishing Revised* (1670) were primarily concerned, until war had broken out, with rehearsing the causes of Dutch success for emulation, rather than with reciting grievances. Thus the first two of these dwelt upon the low Dutch rates of interest, for which the Dutch could be praised but hardly blamed, as the *causa causans* of their prosperity in order to influence debates on these in Parliament. The East India Company had to be prodded into making demands, since it could profit in areas other than the Spice Islands; and almost nothing was heard from the Royal Africa Company.

Most significant of all was the fact that in order to finance the campaign of 1672, Charles relied on French subsidies and on the (much larger) proceeds of the moratorium on the repayment of his debts. He did this rather than risk an appeal to the House of Commons which, it was feared, might have preferred to uphold the policy of the Triple Alliance. One of the motives of the Declaration of Indulgence which accompanied the declaration of war was to remove a grievance of the Nonconformist friends of the Dutch. The envoys of the States-General were kept incommunicado and sent home as hastily as possible lest they made trouble. Yet reluctance to fight, where it existed, rested more on hatred of the French than cordiality to the Dutch. Naturally, it tended to be swept away when actual hostilities began, though a Yarmouth correspondent of the Secretary of State declared of the first Dutch land disasters at the hands of the French: 'We are so Dutchified here that a Dutchman cannot be more dejected than generally our people are here for the sad condition we understand the Hollanders to be in, which I attribute to the constant trade we have with them in times of peace.'[24]

The war came close to success when Louis's armies marched into the centre of the Republic. Panic brought about the fall and lynching of De Witt and Dutch offers of terms to Louis. The subordination of the Republic to him would have entailed enormous consequences for Holland, for the whole of north-western Europe, and probably for England. It was therefore vital for all that William III held out behind the impassable barrier of the flooded Dutch countryside in the 'water line', so that the Republic and England could, twenty years later, form their coalition against France. It was also important that the 'water line' should not be taken in the rear by an English landing. This was effectively ruled out when De Ruyter again sought out the English fleet under Sandwich and the Duke of York off the English coast. The Battle of Sole Bay (May 1672) saw one of the most dramatic episodes of all these wars when the magazine of Sandwich's flagship was hit by Dutch fire. Sandwich was killed by the explosion, and the *Royal James* suffered a worse but more heroic fate than the *Royal Charles*. The fighting may have been more even, but the strategic advantage certainly lay with the Dutch. The English had to give up plans for an invasion, and storms prevented their fleet, when it re-emerged from port, from capturing the returning East India fleet. As a result the number of prizes captured was smaller than in either of the two previous wars.

There was nothing for it but to appeal to the House of Commons for the money to finance a second campaign in 1673. At the beginning of the session the Lord Chancellor, Shaftesbury, made his celebrated comparison with the Punic Wars against Carthage which the Roman Republic had fought to a finish in ancient times. 'You judged aright, that at any rate *delenda est Carthago*; that government is to be brought down. And therefore the king may well say to you, it is your war. He took his measures from you, and they were just and right ones;

and he expects a suitable assistance to so necessary and expensive an action....'[25] This was not a piece of rhetorical vehemence as is sometimes supposed. Rather, it was a tactical argument to remind his hearers that the House of Commons had first seen English and Dutch interests as irreconcilable in 1664, and pressed for war then; therefore they ought logically to vote money now to destroy their eternal enemy, the modern Carthage. It was not exactly successful in inflaming the patriotic fervour of members, but they did not question the rightness of the war, and they did vote for supplies in return for the withdrawal of the hated Declaration of Indulgence.

The enmity of the new Rome and Carthage was, in fact, so far from being eternal that Dutch propaganda, combined with the realization that the heir to the throne, James, Duke of York, was a Catholic, turned the scales in the next few months.[26] The pamphlet *England's Appeal from the Private Cabal at Whitehall to the Great Council of the nation, the Lords and Commons in Parliament assembled* (1673) was smuggled into the country in large numbers. This was probably written, with the help of advice from others, by Pierre Du Moulin, a Huguenot who had fled from the English service to enter that of William III. It argued that there was a sinister connection between the French alliance and the policies of Charles's ministers, whose excuses for the reversal of the Triple Alliance and the Dutch war were merely pretexts. The effect upon English opinion of this and other pamphlets was such that, after the end of the war, Charles did not rest until Du Moulin was dismissed from William's service.

The battles of 1673 were less dramatic than Sole Bay, and no more successful. The reconciled De Ruyter and Tromp's son Cornelis were equal to all that the English could do at the battles of Schoneveld and Texel (Kijkduin), and the English were indignant at the performance of the allied French squadron which should have given them the advantage of superior numbers. The Dutch propaganda had been so effective that there could be no question of the House of Commons voting money for another campaign in 1674. Charles had no option but to admit failure and to withdraw from the war with the Treaty of Westminster. He gained no Dutch territory, and rested content with another acknowledgment of the right of salute as a mark of respect (without any mention of his claim to sovereignty over the seas) and with a reference to Surinam. The problems of the East Indies and the obnoxious medals were not even mentioned. As a sweetener the States-General promised to pay the sum of 800,000 patacoons, but since Charles owed money to his nephew the Prince of Orange, he made no real gain even from this.

There was no question of a fourth war to destroy 'Carthage' in the seventeenth century. On the contrary, Englishmen came to regard the States-General, and William of Orange in particular, as their bulwark once more in the common cause against the dominant continental power. Jealousies there might be, but for a century they were not of the type likely to lead to war, and then in 1780 only as part of a very different struggle. For the present the wars subsided with each party having a very healthy respect for the other.

CHAPTER FIVE

Some Seventeenth-Century
English Views of the Dutch

The great Dutch historian Huizinga once commented on the number of uncomplimentary references to the Dutch in proverbial expressions in the English language – 'Dutch courage', 'Dutch treat', 'Dutch uncle', 'Dutch feast' and so on. He pointed out that such expressions were much more numerous than similar references to the French and Spaniards, and that they antedated the period of the bitterest hostility during the Anglo-Dutch wars. In part the confusion between 'Dutch' and 'German', to which reference was made in chapter one, may have contributed to this stereotype. Huizinga noted that the usual diminutive of the name Johannes used by Englishmen was Hans, whereas a true Netherlander would naturally have been called Jan, and cited a 'Hollander' in Dekker's *Northward Ho* who talks of Augsburg as 'the city of his parents'.[1] It is also true that jibes about the Dutch may contain no deeper animosity than those used by the inhabitants of one part of the British Isles about those of another.

Nevertheless, the real surprise is in the way in which, except in the cruder wartime productions, Englishmen tended to intersperse critical comments on the Dutch with compliments in a way which they would never have done when discussing the French or the Spaniards. The number of compliments was remarkable, when European observers often remarked on the Englishman's usual dislike of foreigners. Even people generally hostile to the Dutch were capable of seeing their good qualities. Thus Sir William Monson (writing in about the year 1624) described them as 'people that desire rather to live without virtue than to die without money', but went on to praise their frugality, public spirit, and laboriousness: 'they are industrious ... just in contracts, holding a conscience, in the little religion that they have, not to defraud any man. They are inventors of arts, which, to their praise, they have enriched the world with.'[2] More generally, criticisms of their alleged avarice were balanced with praise for their charity to the poor, attacks on their covetousness were mixed with acknowledgements of their love of painting and flowers. At all times their industry, and the cleanliness and neatness of their towns and houses, were praised by people who felt that their English countrymen emerged poorly from a comparison. On the whole, as one might expect, those who lived most among them respected them most and held them up for imitation. Whatever their station in life, their comments were those of observers from a largely aristocratic, landed and monarchical society upon a predominantly commercial, urbanized and pluralist one.

War inevitably brought crudities from authors who had probably never seen the Netherlands. In the first war, in the middle of the 'Puritan Revolution', the humour of the lavatory found its way into print in *The Dutchmen's Pedigree or a Relation, Showing how they were first Bred and Descended from a Horse-Turd, which was enclosed in a Butter-Box* (1653). This may be regarded as a coarse rejoinder to the belief professed by Dutchmen that Englishmen were born with tails. The second war produced *The Dutch Boar [Boer] Dissected, or a description of HOGGLAND* (1664), which declared that 'A Dutchman is a lusty, fat, two legged Cheeseworm: or a Creature that is so addicted to eating butter, drinking fat drink, and sliding [skating] that all the World knows him for a slippery Fellow.' Abuse of the low-lying, marshy territory on which the poor Dutch were unfortunately condemned to live was common. Owen Felltham, after 'three weeks' observation of the vices and virtues of the inhabitants', wrote of 'the great bog of Europe', 'a green cheese in pickle', with 'spiders as big as shrimps'.[3] The Dutch were often described as 'frogs': Charles II was said to have 'endeavoured by kindnesses to charm these swarming frogs, who are now ready to become an Egyptian plague, by croaking against him in his own waters'.[4] Another ingenious wit argued that because the Low Countries were so low, their inhabitants were nearest to the devil. The most high-class exponent of this sort of thing was the poet Andrew Marvell, who (having spent some time in Holland) wrote his propagandist 'Character of Holland' in 1653. It began:

> Holland, that scarce deserves the name of land,
> As but th'Offscouring of the British Sand.
> And so much Earth as was contributed
> By English Pilots when they heav'd the lead;
> Or what by th'Oceans slow alluvion fall;
> This undigested vomit of the Sea
> Fell to the Dutch by just Propriety.

Naturally there was little reply that the Dutch could make to this line of argument. Their most effective counter was in the form of woodcuts, which could overleap the language barrier and make an immediate visual impact upon the English reader. Before the end of 1663 Charles II had been shown 'with his pockets turned the wrong side outward, hanging out empty – another, with two courtiers picking of his pocket – and a third, leading of two ladies, while others abuse him'; and later it was said that he had been pictured 'with his hand in his pockets, as an idle spectator, looking on his ships as they burned at Chatham'.[5]

In peace time, Englishmen could admit the advantages to the Dutch of being 'water devils at sea being all seamen born ... and like frogs can live both of land and water; not a Vriester [*vrijster*, or young woman] but can handle an oar, steer a boat, raise a mast, and bear you out in the roughest straits you come in'.[6] Sir William Petty converted this into the language of the political scientist when he put the cost of water carriage at one-fifteenth or one-twentieth of that of land carriage, and argued that this was one means by which a small country with few people might be equivalent in wealth and strength to a far larger people and territory.[7] Those responsible for navigational improvements and the construction of canals in eighteenth-century England were simply acknowledging the Dutch perception of the advantages of water transport.

If the Dutch were described as 'frogs able to live both on land and sea', they were also described as 'the Pismires' (or ants) of the world. All writers on aspects of trade policy would have acknowledged some justice in Van Meteren's claim that his countrymen were more industrious than the English. They also commented on the absence of beggars, 'nor scarce an idle person among them: whereas in England multitudes of idle persons and beggars for want of employment everywhere swarm....' 'Provision is made for their necessitous people, but none for the idle, who must work there or they shall not eat....'[8] In addition to the industry of the Dutch, Englishmen recognized their technical inventiveness, particularly in labour-saving devices. Many examples were to be found on Dutch ships, in Dutch looms, and in other ways. Pepys, when the second Anglo-Dutch war was imminent, reported a conversation with some Dutchmen 'with whom we had good discourse touching stoveing and making of cables. But to see how despicably they speak of us for our using so many hands more to do anything than they do, they closing a cable with 20 that we use 60 men upon.'[9] The technical expertise of Dutchmen was for obvious reasons seen to be greatest in matters of drainage. In the 1580s Humphrey Bradley, an Englishman by name, but 'the Brabanter of Bergen-op-Zoom', brought specialized craftsmen to work on harbour construction at Dover, and then prepared a scheme for the draining of the Fens. Half a century later the great Cornelis Vermuyden actually added 400,000 acres to the total of English agricultural land, with the aid of Dutch workmen, Dutch capital and English sponsorship.[10] One inventor who spent most of his life in England was Cornelis Drebbel, who was reported to have made the first submarine on the Thames in about the year 1621. In the middle of the next century the engineer John Smeaton still thought it worthwhile to add to his engineering experience by visiting the Netherlands, and he left an account of what he had seen there.[11]

Some Englishmen connected Dutch commercial success with the fact that they 'generally breed their youth *of both sexes* (my italics) more in the studies of Geometry and Numbers especially than the English do'. Thus English economic backwardness was early put down to deficiencies in education. Coke added that Dutch merchants *and their wives* were more conversant in trade than the English. Whereas Van Meteren had described England as a paradise for married women, partly because of their opportunities for idleness, Englishmen commented on the part played by Dutch women in their husbands' businesses. Josiah Child gave as one reason for Dutch success 'the education of their children, as well daughters as sons; all which, be they of never so great quality or estate, they always take care to bring up to write perfect good hands, and to have full knowledge and use of arithmetic and merchants' accompts ... the women are as knowing [in commerce] as the men ...' and the knowledge of arithmetic encouraged thrift. Sometimes the admiration was tinged with amusement: 'Both within doors and without, they govern all, which considering the natural desire of women to bear rule, maketh them too imperious and burdensome', wrote one male chauvinist. Fynes Moryson seriously detected a dominance of women over men which he ascribed to the wives' privilege of disposing of their goods by their own last will and testament, 'and by the contracts in respect of their dowry (which to the same end use to be warily drawn), they keep their husbands in a kind of awe, and almost alone, without their husbands intermeddling, not only keep their shops at home, but exercise traffic abroad. Nothing is more frequent than for little girls to insult over their brothers much bigger than they, reproving their doings, and calling them great lubbers, whereof when I talked with some scholars my companions, as a fashion seeming strange to me, they were so far from wondering thereat, as they told me, it was a common thing for wives to drive their husbands and their friends out of the doors with scolding, as if they consumed the goods wherein they had a property with their husbands. I should be too credulous, if I should think all families to be sick of this disease; and I must confess, that in few other nations all families are altogether free from like accidents: but I may boldly say that the women of these parts are above all other truly taxed with this unnatural domineering over their husbands.' 'In their families', one observer added, 'they are all equals, and you have no way to know the master and mistress, but by taking them in bed together....'[12]

At the beginning of the seventeenth century, though rather less so at the end of it, the unaristocratic virtue of frugality was seen as an essential ingredient of Dutch commercial success. Fynes Moryson, writing in the second decade, said that 'the men use modest attire of grave colours, and little beautified with lace or other ornament'. The paintings of Frans Hals would hardly bear out the absence of lace, and Moryson himself agreed that 'the Hollanders ... do by little and little admit luxury, and their sons apply themselves both to the apparel and manners of the English and French ... as well men as women for their bodies and for all uses of the family use very fine linen; and I think that no clowns in the world wear such fine shirts as they in Holland do'. Others, like James Howell, writing in 1619, claimed that 'the wealth doth diffuse itself here in a strange kind of equality, not one of the burghers being exceeding rich or exceeding poor'. This too became less and less true as the century proceeded, and some statements about Dutch frugality by writers on Dutch commercial success may have been as much designed to point a moral to their readers as to comment with absolute accuracy. Yet it was still possible for a hostile author, like Owen Felltham, to say that 'they are frugal to the saving of eggshells, and maintain it for a maxim that a thing lasts longer mended than new'. Even at the end of the century it was almost axiomatic to comment on the 'great frugality and order in their expenses', and the thrift which gave them capital and enabled them to support a high level of taxation. Sir William Temple wrote about the Dutch in 1672 when Terborch and the painters of *pronkstilleven* (showy still lifes) depicted on their canvases costlier garments and more expensive ornaments. Though he could see the steady infiltration of French styles, he still saw a relative contrast between the styles of life of the Dutch regent and the English aristocrat. He could still speak of 'the great simplicity and modesty in the common port or living of their chiefest ministers'. His famous picture of De Witt, with his 'one man, who performed all the menial service of his house at home', and 'seen usually in the streets on foot and alone, like the commonest burgher of the town,' needs to be seen with his comment that this 'was the general fashion or mode among the magistrates of the state'. Englishmen might reasonably suppose, and even see in the streets of Dutch towns, that this style survived longer among those below the patrician.[13]

Another feature of Dutch society which many English observers believed to be conducive to their commercial success was religious toleration. This was used as an argument for a similar toleration in England after the Restoration. For more spiritual reasons Puritans and sectaries welcomed the greater freedom which they saw, and often enjoyed, in the United Provinces, even though they might criticize the inadequate Sunday observance. Less dogmatically inclined observers like Temple approved of a state in which refusal to employ 'forcible courses' avoided the kind of dissensions which marred English history in the mid seventeenth century. Others who accepted the view that there was one religion to which everyone should conform were more scornful, and saw toleration as a sign of irreligion, and as placing a higher value upon opportunities for making wealth than upon devotion to the true faith. John Hall, speaking of Amsterdam where there was the greatest diversity of faiths, said '... you may be what devil you will there, so you be but peaceable: for Amsterdam is an university of all religions, which grow there (like stocks in a nursery) without either order or pruning. If you be unsettled in your religion, you may here try all, and take at last what you like best. If you fancy more, you have a pattern to follow of them that would be church to themselves: it's the fair of all the sects, where all the pedlars of religion have leave to vend their toys, their ribbands and phanatique rattles; their republic is more to them than heaven, and God may be more safely offended there than the States-General.' Sir William Monson wrote derisively: 'They debar no man, be he Turk, Jew, or Christian, the freedom of religion, which made one truly say that the true religion was professed in Amsterdam. For all sects, be they never so diabolical, are there allowed and maintained by some or other.' Some Presbyterians as well as Anglicans thought in this way about a people without an all-inclusive national church, among them, ironically, the poet Marvell, shortly before becoming Cromwell's secretary:

> Sure when Religion did itself imbark,
> And from the East would Westward steer its Ark,
> It struck, and splitting on this unknown ground,
> Each one thence pillag'd the first piece he found;

> Hence Amsterdam, Turk-Christian-Pagan-Jew,
> Staple of Sects and Mint of Schisme grew;
> That Bank of Conscience, where not one so strange
> Opinion but finds Credit, and Exchange.[14]

The toleration given to Jews seems to have particularly intrigued many Englishmen. Many sightseers visited the synagogues to be found in Holland. In the words of one writer in the second decade of the century, 'Their religion hath the shew of a reformed church, and their public services make a good face and presence of a Christian congregation; but otherwise they are receptacle both of Jew and Gentile: all sects and schisms are as freely there as the religion publicly professed by the state, and a man may live there all his life-time, and be of no congregation, with impunity: for as there is no distinction of parishes, so every man may address himself to what church they list, or may stay at home. It was in deliberation at Rotterdam, whether they should admit the building of a synagogue; the Jew children at Amsterdam going to the common schools, do so confidently blaspheme in the presence and hearing of their school-fellows, the burgher children, as if they were in a synagogue among their own nation; which liberty, as it begetteth a confluence of all sorts of people ... so it portendeth destruction and confusion....'[15] From Amsterdam, Manasseh ben Israel, the well-known rabbi and scholar whom Rembrandt painted, sought to take advantage of the Commonwealth's interest in the fulfilment of Biblical prophecy through the Jews to call for their readmission to England. Amongst his influential supporters in England was Hugh Peters, by virtue of his experience of the toleration of Jews in Holland. During a stay of nearly two years in London, Manasseh printed *Humble Addresses* to the Protector and Commonwealth, and presented copies to the Council of State. 'In the Low Countries also,' he declared, 'the Jews are received with great charity and benevolency, and especially in this most renowned city of Amsterdam, where there are no less than 400 families; and how great a trading and negotiation they draw to that city experience doth sufficiently witness. They have there no less than three hundred houses of their own, enjoy a good part of the West and East India Companies....' Unfortunately this was a double-edged argument, and fear of commercial competition may have been one reason why, after conferences at Whitehall and some goodwill from Cromwell, the Jews had to rest content with practical indulgence, not official toleration.[16]

On the practical indulgence shown to Catholics in the United Provinces, English observers had surprisingly little comment to make, in comparison with their interest in the position of sectaries and Jews. Sir William Temple defined the position as one of connivance in Catholic worship in return for payment. There were numerous Catholics both among the peasants and in the towns, who were 'not admitted to any public charges; yet they seem to be a sound piece of the state, and fast jointed in with the rest; and have neither given any disturbance to the government, nor expressed any inclination to exchange, or to any foreign power.' His general conclusion about the religious diversity he observed was that in the Dutch Republic it made for internal peace, not division and civil war as much conventional thinking had it. 'It is hardly to be imagined, how all the violence and sharpness, which accompanies the differences of religion in other countries, seems to be appeased or softened here, by the general freedom which all men enjoy, either by allowance or connivance.... No man can here complain of pressure in his conscience: of being forced to any public profession of his private faith; of being restrained from his own manner of worship in his house or obliged to any other abroad ... religion may possibly do more good in other places, but it does less hurt here; and wherever the invisible effects of it are greatest and most advantageous, I am sure the visible are so in this country, by the continual and undisturbed civil peace of their government for so long a course of years....' The contrast beween British and Dutch religious history, at any rate since the Synod of Dort, was obvious. Temple's views, often reprinted and quoted, were those which were to predominate in the England of the Age of Enlightenment.[17]

Whether Englishmen thought of this religious indulgence as a sign of irreligion, indifference, or enlightenment, and whether they praised the accumulation of money as a sign of thrift or abhorred it as a sign of avarice they united in admiration of the generous provision which the Dutch made for the poor and unfortunate.

William Carr, for some years English consul, described 'the acts of charity of Amsterdam, the which is so extraordinary that they surpass all other cities in the world, for they are daily and hourly giving to the poor.' There were poor-boxes in the home, poor-boxes to accompany commercial transactions, house-to-house collections by deacons, ministers and elders and 'men belonging to the hospitals', almsmen at the door of the booths of ropedancers, puppetplayers and 'that sort of unnecessary vermin which frequent fairs' to see that the poor were not cheated of the third penny which was their share. In 1672 when the French were threatening to seize and plunder the city, Charles II 'said he was of opinion that God would preserve Amsterdam from being destroyed if it were only for the great charity they have for the poor'.

Much of the proceeds was spent on almshouses. These were particularly admired by English visitors, not simply by reason of their number but because they 'look more like princes' palaces than lodgings for poor people'. There were houses for poor old men and women, and houses for orphans and foundlings. Carr noted that the children were carefully given two doits every Sunday to put into the deacons' sack when they took the church collection for the poor, and that they were allowed to travel free on the *trekschuits* which plied on the waterways between the cities. There was a house for mad people, 'so stately that one would take it to be the house of some lord'. Evelyn was especially interested in the hospital 'for their lame and decrepit soldiers, it being for state, order and accommodation one of the worthiest things that I think the world can show of that nature'. This was probably the same hospital for soldiers and sick women to whom, Fynes Moryson noted with curiosity, 'they gave clean sheets, a good diet, and necessary clothes, with great cleanliness, and allow them physicians and surgeons to cure them' at a time when there was no such provision in England. Not less praiseworthy to English visitors was that 'there are houses where common beggars and gamesters and frequenters of taphouses are kept hard at work'. There was also the Rasphuis where 'petty thieves and such as slash one another with knives,' and confidence tricksters were given tasks such as scraping dyewood; and 'a house where whores are kept to work, as also disobedient children who live idle and take no course to maintain themselves, likewise women commonly drinking themselves drunk, and scolds'. All these inadequates were Dutch too, as was the combination of welfare with social discipline. 'All these sorts of hospitals and almshouses are stately buildings richly adorned with pictures, and their lodgings very neat and clean;' and, said Carr, 'It is very observable that the women govern their women hospitals better than the men do theirs.'[18]

Seventeenth-century Englishmen, like tourists in later ages, also agreed in praising the Dutch virtues of cleanliness and neatness, though Owen Felltham rudely remarked that 'their houses they keep cleaner than their bodies, and their bodies than their souls'.[19] Conversely, Dutch visitors to England commented on the dirt which degraded public buildings like St Paul's and Westminster Abbey, but without saying that English bodies and souls were cleaner.[20] It must be confessed that the English sometimes found the Dutch obsession with cleanliness rather odd and quite inexplicable. Thus Sir William Temple found to his surprise that 'Dining one day at Monsieur Hooft's, and having a great cold, I observed, every time I spit, a tight handsome wench (that stood in the room with a clean cloth in her hand) was presently down to wipe it up, and rub the board clean: somebody at table speaking of my cold, I said, the most trouble it gave me was to see the poor wench take so much pains about it.' Temple, courtier, baronet and ambassador though he was, thought this reaction to what he saw as the perfectly natural action of spitting so strange as to be worthy of inclusion in his memoirs. After adding that Hooft told him that if his wife had been at home she would have turned him out of the house, he went on to tell the story of what happened when he retold the anecdote elsewhere. 'Many stories were told of the strange and curious cleanliness so general in that city [Amsterdam]; and some so extravagant that my sister took them for jest.' Another guest capped them by pointing out the house where a visitor 'knocking at the door, a strapping North Holland lass came and opened it; he asked whether her mistress was at home? She said, yes; and with that he offered to go in; but the wench, marking his shoes were not very clean, took him by both arms, threw him upon her back, carried him across two rooms, set him down at the bottom of the stairs, pulled off his shoes, put him on a pair of slippers that stood there, and all this without saying a word; but, when she had done, told him, he might go up to her mistress, who was in her chamber.'[21]

These stories may stand for many remarks about the house-proud Dutch – and implicitly about the dirtiness of the English who found them remarkable. It must be made clear, however, that this zeal for cleanliness did not apply only to the homes of burgomasters like Hooft. John Locke, visiting a farm outside Amsterdam where the people slept in the same room as the cattle, noted that the place was 'much cleaner than one shall see any kitchen, nay most of the finest parlours in England'. Further, the general neatness was observable in the streets and along the *grachten* (canals). Peters, commending the cleaner streets of the Dutch, wanted London streets 'to be paved with such flat foursquare stones as in Holland'. Evelyn painted a picture of the Amsterdam *grachten* with 'a whole navy of merchants and others environed with streets and houses, every particular man's barque or vessel at anchor before his very door, and yet the streets so exactly straight, even and uniform that nothing can be more pleasing, especially being so frequently planted and shaded with the beautiful lime trees, which are set in rows before every man's house, affording a very ravishing prospect'.[22]

One visitor speaks of a butcher's shop in Amsterdam 'which was paved with black and white marble, and the walls lined with white and blue tiles, such as you get in chimneys in England, so as if they had not seen a couple of oxen hanging up in it, they should have taken it for a room belonging to some rich merchant'. Others commented on the way in which relatively ordinary dwellings had contents which would have been thought unusual in comparable places in England. Thus Sir Dudley Carleton spoke of 'the common inn where we dined, which hath divers rooms hung with tapestry, and some furnished with pictures of the best hands'. Another traveller wrote: 'As for the art of painting and the affections of the people to pictures, I think none other goes beyond them, there having been in this country many excellent men in that faculty, some at present as Rembrandt, etc, all in general striving to adorn their houses, especially the outer or street room, with costly pieces, butchers and bakers not much inferior in their shops, which are fairly set forth, yea many times blacksmiths, cobblers, etc, will have some picture or other by their forge and in their stall. Such is the general notion, inclination and delight that these country natives have to paintings. Also their other furniture and ornaments of their dwellings very costly and curious, full of pleasure and home contentment, as rich cupboards, cabinets, etc, imagery, porcelain, costly fine cages with birds, etc, all these commonly in any house of indifferent quality, wonderful neat and clean, as well in their houses and furniture, service, etc within doors as in their streets.'[23]

Evelyn was 'amazed' by the number of pictures ('especially Landscapes and Drolleries, as they call those clownish representations') which he found at the annual fair at Rotterdam in 1641. Some of them he found 'not ill done' and 'carried all Europe over' from these fairs. He even bought some of them (unspecified) and sent them into England. There he would have known nothing similar in his experience; the majority of English paintings in the first half of the seventeenth century were commissioned portraits, not paintings of a variety of subjects for a mass market. Evelyn declared that 'a common farmer' might invest two to three thousand pounds (amended more reasonably to read five to six hundred pounds in the *De Vita Propria* recension of his journal) in paintings of this kind. Farmers' houses were 'full of them', and they might even maintain painters in their houses. Evelyn put this down to the shortage of land in which to invest (as his English counterpart would have done); but whatever the superficial attractiveness of this theory, it must be ruled out. There were many other potential investments, and paintings at this time were exceptionally cheap and not likely to appreciate considerably in value. The Cheshire landowner Sir William Brereton, later a parliamentary commander, bought ten pictures for 64 guilders (a little over six pounds) for which he could have acquired very little land at home.[24]

There are few other indications of contemporary Englishmen buying paintings by Dutch artists to send home. Sir William Temple, a generation after Evelyn's visit, made no reference to Dutch art, and such paintings as he bought were mainly portraits and not by major artists, though he was in the country in all for seven years. The signs are that until a later age English travellers bought fewer paintings in Holland than one might expect. There is plenty of evidence that they regarded love of paintings as a Dutch characteristic, and no one but Evelyn attempted to find over-subtle motives. 'He that hath not bread to eat hath a picture. . . . The lining of their houses is more rich than the outside; not in hangings, but pictures, which even the poorest of boors are there furnished with; not a cobbler but has its toys for ornament. Were the knacks of all their houses set together, there would not be such another Bartholomew fair in Europe.'[25]

A reputation for frugality and these artistic tastes were combined in the minds of English observers with a supposed Dutch liking for drink. At first this was said to be mainly beer; but before the end of the century a taste for gin had become more prominent, and after 1688 it spread to England, until it became the subject of Hogarth's *Gin Lane*. So far as food was concerned, Englishmen who traditionally fed on beef were somewhat scornful of a diet in which butter and cheese played such a large part. Their boxes of butter led to the nickname of 'butter-boxes'. 'Nothing is more ordinary', wrote Fynes Moryson early in the century, 'than for citizens of good accompt and wealth to sit at their doors (even dwelling in the market place) holding in their hands and eating a great lump of bread and butter with a lunchen [*sic*] of cheese. . . .' At this date 'roots' were also said to be popular, 'which the boys of rich men devour raw with a morsel of bread, as they run playing in the streets. . . .' The cloth was laid four times a day 'for very servants, but two of these times they set before them nothing but cheese and butter'. The delicacies were 'mushrooms and the hinder parts of frogs . . . which frogs young men used to catch and present them to their mistresses for dainties'. Oysters were commonplace: 'I have seen a hundreth of oysters in divers cities sold sometimes for eight or 12, yea for twenty or thirty stivers.' Inevitably fish, with sauces made from butter, figured more in their diet than beef: apart from herring and other salt-water fish, the maidservants in Dordrecht were said to have complained that they were given too much salmon. It may well be surmised that by the end of the century meals had become more sophisticated, but Englishmen still described the Dutch as 'butter-boxes' in the traditional way.[26]

Most of these observations were based upon experience of the towns of the province of Holland: Amsterdam, Leiden, The Hague, Rotterdam, Delft, Dordrecht and others, and of journeys between them. Soldiers and others penetrated further into the country, but have left fewer accounts of what they saw. Farmers imitated the systems of crop-rotations practised in the Netherlands, in which root crops featured largely, and also followed Dutch methods of stock rearing and constructed Dutch barns. But only in the eighteenth century, the age of 'improving landlords' *par excellence*, did travellers come to record farming methods in detail in travel journals. The differences which Englishmen saw between Dutch society and their own resulted from the fact that Holland was a land of strong civic communities and fewer hierarchical gradations. The tone set by burgomasters and city council was different from that set by a monarchical Court, great landed magnates (or even an influential gentry) and a Church claiming to possess authority over all its citizens. In a more open and decentralized society, with a relatively wide diffusion of prosperity, in which it was easier to avoid the pressures of authority while combining a generous provision of welfare with a measure of social discipline, the domestic virtues had room to flourish. Englishmen, even jealous Englishmen, found much to envy.

Many of the envious would have liked to import these values into their own country and in particular into its commercial capital. Many Londoners wanted the same commercial success, the same religious freedom (at least for Protestants), the same opportunities to accumulate household goods while still providing for the poor. Many besides Hugh Peters hoped that 'we may so follow as to stand at length upon their shoulders, and go on further'. He would have liked Puritanism in religion and at the same time arrangements for the appointment in every city, town and hundred of able men 'to determine all controversies for debts and strifes ... as in Holland'. The class for which he spoke contained the largest proportion of Dutch sympathizers. Not all would have been so radical as to comment: ' 'tis strange to see in the Low Countries how their boors, or men in country towns, that in many places have power of life and death, will do better justice than learned men in other countries'. But many like Brereton would have commended Dutch arrangements at local level for arbitration by 'friend-makers' to compose differences. Consul Carr praised the Dutch commissioners in the bankruptcy office, commenting that the settlement of debt was much easier than in England, and that very few were in prison for it. Rounding off a prolonged comparison between London and Amsterdam, Peters said that if London magistrates would follow his recommendations, 'there would be no need of any deceitful, base, and Machiavellian courses to keep a commonwealth in peace and obedience, as may be seen in the Low Countries, where no people have more liberty than they, nor pay such great taxations, nor so little state anywhere used to preserve authority; and yet the people of so many nations and religions live in the greatest peace and plenty of the world, merely by good justice, mercy, and religion. . . .'[27]

Assessments of the personal characteristics of men of other nations inevitably vary with the eye of the beholder. English opinions on the Dutch were often cool, or, in war-time, much worse. Ambassador Downing's collaborator in the writing of a discourse in 1672 wrote them off as 'perfidious, ungrateful, bloody and cruel'; but then two years later a Dutch preacher said that the English were second to none at 'slandering, lying, twisting and cheating'. For Felltham they were 'hardy, headstrong, churlish and testy ... you may sooner convert a Jew to Christianity, turn an old bawd Puritan, than convince a Dutchman of reason. . . . Not a man of them but may be a statesman, for they have all this gift not to be too nice conscienced.' Elsewhere they were 'clownish and blunt to men, respecting neither person nor apparel; they gaze at and envy, but never reverence a gentleman'. Much of this simply meant that they could not be bullied into accepting the opposing point of view, expressed with the supposedly superior manners of an English gentleman. *A Late Voyage to Holland* (1691) gave a left-handed and rather condescending compliment in saying that 'they are a race of people ... dull and slow of understanding, and so not dealt with by hasty words, but managed easily by soft and fair; and yielding to plain reason, if you give them time to understand it. . . .'[28]

A more mixed judgment was that 'they are neither much devout, nor much wicked, given all to drink, and eminently to no other vice; hard in bargaining but just, surly and respectless, as in all democracies, thirsty [thrifty?], industrious and cleanly, . . . inventive in manufactures, cunning in traffic. . . .' Taken altogether, these judgments tell us something about seventeenth-century Englishmen as well as of their Dutch neighbours across the sea: grudging in their attitudes to foreigners, patriotically conscious of the superiority of their countrymen to anyone else, yet able to give some credit where it was due. Despite the insults, they gave more credit to the Dutch than to any other people. Those who visited the United Provinces as a place of refuge from an oppressive government, as represented by Peters, admired them most. Those whose admiration grew in the course of co-operation with the Dutch before returning to England may be represented by Sir William Temple. He did more than anyone to explain them to Englishmen as potential allies against Louis XIV, and his judgment was that 'their country is a much better mistress than a wife; and where few persons, who are well at home, would be content to live; but where none that have time to spare, would not for once be willing to travel.' Cool as this may sound at first, he had nothing but praise for the Dutch as 'citizens of the world'; and many to whom this concept would have been quite strange would have agreed that next to their own country the Netherlands was the most civilized in which to live.[29]

The feature of Dutch society which Englishmen found most difficult to understand, even as explained by Temple, was its political institutions, and it is to these and the relationship between the Stuart and Orange houses that we must now turn.

CHAPTER SIX

Orange, Stuart and the Glorious Revolution

E xcept in the period of the Commonwealth, English politicians dealt overwhelmingly with states ruled by one person. Even at Brussels they dealt with a governor-general representing the King of Spain who had his Court, selected his advisers and distributed his patronage. To this the United Provinces were the most important exception. Apart from the Princes of Orange at whose anomalous position we shall look in a moment, and whose offices until 1674 were owed to appointment rather than birth, there was no comparable single person. Moreover, there was no Parliament similar to that in England. The States-General had no upper chamber filled by a hereditary peerage, and it was in no way the result of election. It consisted of seven delegations from the provinces of Holland, Zeeland, Utrecht, Gelderland, Overijssel, Friesland, and Groningen, normally totalling fewer than thirty members, and those delegations had to refer back to their provincial States for instructions on all important matters, and then achieve a decision. The provincial States were similarly composed of delegations. In the most important of them, the States of Holland, there were 18 from the towns and only one from the nobility; and the town councils in turn were the result of co-optation rather than election. The most important statesman, the Advocate or Grand Pensionary, was only the paid official of the States of Holland. The Council of State was an administrative, not a policy-making, body.

It was difficult for Englishmen to know precisely where the decisions were taken; and Temple had to explain that this was not, as at first sight it appeared, 'a popular government', though he did note 'the strange freedom that all men took in boats and inns, and all other common places, of telling openly whatever they thought upon all the public affairs, both of their own state and their neighbours ...'.[1]

In these circumstances British politicians, and especially their monarchs, naturally turned to the Princes of Orange to provide the leadership and the authority which seemed to be both axiomatic in politics and to be lacking in the Dutch Republic. They could at least claim to be princes, even though their principality was not Dutch but in the far south of France (and eventually it was seized by Louis XIV). But they were not sovereigns in the Republic. Nor, in the seventeenth century, were they even stadholders in all seven provinces, for a cadet branch of the family supplied stadholders for Friesland and Groningen. In any case, the stadholderate gave only general authority over law and order, and a commission to reconcile disputes, rather than a formal power to take policy decisions. Stadholders could appoint burgomasters only from a nominal short list submitted by the towns, and their patronage was limited, except in the army. The only really important post held by the Prince of Orange was that of captain-general of the forces of the whole Republic in time of war. When the leading member of the Orange family was a minor, as in 1650–72 and again from 1702, both the stadholderate of the five main provinces and the captain-generalship alike lapsed.

From the beginning of the Revolt, Elizabeth tended to look to William of Orange as the leader with whom she wanted to deal. It was more than the usual princely courtesy when she graciously agreed to be godmother to the latest Orange baby in 1577, with Philip Sidney as her proxy. She did not encourage William to aim at 'sovereignty', any more than she was prepared to accept sovereignty herself, though William might have become Count of Holland had he lived. When he was assassinated in 1584 his eldest son was a prisoner, and the next son, Maurice of Nassau, was only 17. He rapidly became stadholder of Holland and Zeeland in 1585 and added Utrecht, Overijssel and Gelderland (more than his father had held) in 1590, partly as a counterpoise to English influence. However, he was content to concentrate on military matters, leaving diplomacy to Oldenbarnevelt and others until, after 1600, his relations with the Advocate became strained. James I gave Maurice the Garter in 1613, and exerted his influence in support of Maurice against the Arminians. James's ambassador, Sir Dudley Carleton, advised that the Prince's acquisition of sovereignty was the natural solution to the Republic's constitutional problems but the Prince had no consistent interest in the details of diplomacy and no ambitions to acquire sovereignty with its attendant responsibilities. It was not until 1640 that the opportunity for a closer union between Orange and Stuart arose.

By that time, William the Silent's remaining son, Frederick Henry, had been stadholder of five of the seven Dutch provinces for 15 years. He had a reasonably successful military career and had strengthened his political influence by informal means steadily employed over a period. Furthermore, with his ambitious wife, Amalia von Solms, he had built up a cosmopolitan court in their two new palaces at Honselaarsdijk and the Huis ten Bosch. The marriage of his son William (later William II) to Mary, daughter of Charles I, has been seen as the logical next step in an attempt to enable his family to take their place among the dynasties of Europe, irrespective of the Republic's interests. More recently it has been plausibly argued that there was no real conflict between the interests of the Prince, the States-General and the States of Holland. Quite apart from personal considerations, the marriage could be seen as a sensible step to draw England away from its previous stance as a neutral friendly to Spain in the war of independence.[2]

Charles I had no liking for the Dutch, and Queen Henrietta Maria, as a daughter of France, regarded the House of Orange as rather beneath them, taking its title as it did from a small principality on the Rhône. Moreover, the eldest of her daughters was only nine. Yet in the circumstances of 1641 Charles and Henrietta needed all the friends they could get, and particularly friends with the resources of men and munitions which were at the disposal of the Dutch. Negotiations for the marriage of their second daughter to William did not prove satisfactory, but the marriage between William, aged 14, and Mary, aged nine, did take place on 2 May 1641; Van Dyck painted the bridal pair. Ten days later Strafford was executed, and when at last Henrietta Maria took her daughter to the Netherlands the attempted *coup d'état* against the Five Members had failed: Henrietta Maria also had the mission of raising money for the civil war which was now imminent.

For this purpose she could pawn her jewels and raise money in Amsterdam with the aid of the English merchant, John Webster, but she could also appeal to her son-in-law's father, Frederick Henry. To the Dutch the Civil War came as something of an embarrassment, except to those merchants who could profit from selling munitions to both sides, as they had already sold to Royalists and Covenanters in the Bishops' Wars. Thomas Cunningham, Conservator of the Staple at Veere from 1644–60, organized the use of Scots coal as payment for arms purchased in the Low Countries for the Covenanters. Cunninghams were prominent in Veere at this time, intermarrying with the Dutch until Thomas's son Arnold became a long-term member of the town council and ultimately burgomaster in 1673.[3] It has been said that the Covenanters and Royalists shot at one another with Dutch powder and foreign guns; but Henrietta Maria naturally wanted preferential facilities. The States of Holland saw this as a diversion from the main struggle with Spain, and did not want to become involved; many in any case sympathized with the Puritans rather than with the King's cause. Frederick Henry himself was not so well disposed to it as was once represented. Henrietta Maria described him as *une personne malaisée à engager* and in the end had to rest content with a personal loan and some private military help. Her departure came as a relief to Frederick Henry, as well as to many others. Afterwards he was not even tempted by a plan for a second marriage connecting the two families, this time between the Prince of Wales (later Charles II) and Frederick Henry's eldest daughter, in return for political and military help. There is little sign that he would have provided such help even if he had had more complete control of Dutch policy. The presence of incriminating papers on the negotiations in Charles I's cabinet, when it was seized by the Parliamentarians after the battle of Naseby, is more an indication of Charles's desire to obtain foreign help than of Frederick Henry's resolve to supply it.[4]

The marriage of this first William and Mary remained, however, and the fortunes of the two families were inextricably intermingled. When the reckless young man succeeded as William II in 1647 and the long struggle with Spain ended in the following year, the prospects of Orangist support for the restoration of his wife's Stuart relatives became much greater. In the summer of 1648 the Prince of Wales, at 18 some four years younger than William, came to join the Orange Court at The Hague, solacing himself with Lucy Walter. At the same time the English courtiers who had surrounded Mary were further augmented by Cavalier exiles. It was at The Hague that Charles received the news that his father was to be put on trial and, as a result of his appeal, an embassy from the States-General was sent to plead for his father's life. It was politely received but there was no chance that any attention would be paid to its representations. Charles was not recognized as King of England by the Dutch and he was only lent a ship by his brother-in-law when he sailed to claim the throne of Scotland in 1650. Within two months William II arrested his leading opponents in the States of Holland, packed them off to the fortress of Loevestein, and made an attempt to seize Amsterdam. From this crisis he might well have emerged with greater political powers which he could have used to support Charles II. But within three months he was dead of smallpox at the age of 24, and his opponents the 'Loevesteiners' were determined that no Prince of Orange should ever again be in a position to repeat the coup of 1650. It was at this black moment in the fortunes of both families (literally black; the bedroom was draped in mourning) that the posthumous child, William III, was born, burdened with the regents' memory of his father's political sins.

For the next twenty years the positions of the two families were reversed. Instead of the House of Stuart looking to the House of Orange for aid, it was the Orangists who hoped to return to power through the restoration of the Stuarts in England and the employment of their pressure upon the Republic. The baby could not be prevented from inheriting the title of Prince of Orange, though Louis XIV occupied even that principality in 1660, but no position within the Republic was even nominally bestowed upon him. His mother, a widow at 18, may be forgiven for her lack of appreciation of the politics of the Republic in her youth. But she never acquired any, regarding herself always as the Princess Royal of England exiled to a lesser country where her status was insufficiently recognized until her brother was once again king and able to come to her rescue. She surrounded herself with English people, amongst whom there was no one of a competence remotely comparable with that of John De Witt, who became Grand Pensionary in 1653, and quarrelled with the boy's grandmother, Amalia von Solms, and his cousins of the cadet branch of Leeuwarden. As a result, it was impossible to build on the favourable sentiments of the populace and the Calvinist preachers who regarded the Princes of Orange as the heroes of the struggle for independence. Orangist demonstrations among the distresses of wartime in 1653 only led to the Act of Seclusion, by which the States of Holland undertook never to accept a member of the House of Orange as stadholder or to allow his appointment as captain-general of the Union. De Witt's *Deductie* identified him firmly with this standpoint, and nothing seemed left to the House of Orange but their attachment to the Stuart pretender.

In 1660 the great day of the Stuart restoration dawned, and before Charles and his brother James returned home they were feasted at The Hague by the States-General. Entering The Hague in the state procession, William, aged nine, sat on his uncle James's knee in the crowded royal coach; on the beach at Scheveningen Charles embraced and blessed the boy 'as if he were his own son'. Before leaving, Charles commended him to the States-General as a person peculiarly dear to him. Like the head of a Scots clan he accepted a responsibility for his relatives and expected them in return to accept his leadership and his view of the family interest. It was only with time that he had to realize that William would not accept the position of a protégé and follow where Charles led. Immediately, Charles could not do much for the boy, but after Mary had returned at last to England after 18 years of exile, only to die there of smallpox like her husband, Charles accepted the guardianship of his orphaned nephew, along with the boy's grandmother and his uncle by marriage, the Great Elector of Brandenburg.

So William grew up during the 1660s, lonely and without (as he thought) the rightful position owing to a Prince of Orange, but nephew of the King of England. As he grew up, his importance as a prince of the blood steadily grew. Had Charles's large brood of children been legitimate, or had the Duchess of York produced, from her numerous pregnancies, a son who had lived, his position would have been weaker. But by 1670 there were still only James and James's two small girls, Mary and Anne, between him and the succession to the thrones of England, Scotland and Ireland. Apart from his bachelor uncle, Prince Rupert, he was the only British prince of his generation. Moreover, he was serious-minded, not in the least addicted to the youthful dissipations of his father, William II. For the moment, however, he had to accept the tutelage of some not very discreet Orangists in his household, and even these he had tearfully to give up when, by arrangement between his grandmother and the States of Holland, he became a 'child of state' in the spring of 1666.

De Witt's aim in this arrangement was to make sure that William did not become a political pawn of the English. Sir George Downing, during his years as ambassador, had tried to form connections with the Orangists, English and Dutch, in William's household. When the second Anglo-Dutch war broke out and began with a crushing Dutch defeat at Lowestoft, those who wanted peace sought to use the boy's relationship to Charles II to obtain peace terms. There was even talk of sending William, aged 15, as ambassador to London, when it was naïvely supposed that Charles would be lenient to his nephew. There was an incredible comic opera climax in 1666 involving Buat, a captain in William's guards and a very bad conspirator too often in his cups. He handed to De Witt, along with a letter in the authorized correspondence he was known to be carrying on with London, another marked '*Pour vous-même*' (that is, for Buat) which made plain the secret intrigues between Charles's agents and the Orangists. Fortunately William himself was not involved when the comic opera turned to tragedy, and Buat was executed. Another Orangist who was implicated, Kievit, escaped to London. There he was knighted and, typical of his people, produced a splendid project for embanking the Thames with brick, from the Temple to the Tower, like the Keizersgracht in Amsterdam. Evelyn actually visited an ingenious kitchen created by Kievit and his Anglo-Dutch partner, Lord Wotton, in the Fens, 'where I saw fish swim up even to the very chimney hearth, by a small cut derived through the room, and running within a foot of the very fire,' apparently offering themselves up to be cooked.[5]

In this second Anglo-Dutch war Charles had failed to turn to account the presence of an Orangist element at The Hague which looked to him for patronage, but in his preparations for the third war of 1672 a place was designed for his nephew. The secret Treaty of Dover with Louis XIV in 1670 laid down that Charles should make territorial gains in the islands of Zeeland. It was also agreed that, after France had made its own conquests, 'inasmuch as the dissolution of the government of the States-General might involve some prejudice to the Prince of Orange, nephew of the King of Great Britain ... the said lord kings shall do all they can to secure that the said Prince may find his advantage in the continuation and end of the war....'[6] Charles intended that as his protégé William should have some power in the rump of the Dutch Republic which might remain after the two kings had satisfied their greed, and William, who was quite ignorant of the treaty, was invited over to England to be suitably flattered. On this, his first visit, he was aware that through his mother he was an English prince of the blood, a 'grand-child of England'; that his uncle Charles had no legitimate children; and that only Charles's brother James, Duke of York, and the latter's two children, Mary and Anne, stood between him and the succession.[7] He was given precedence accordingly. However, he conceded nothing to Charles's attempts to establish intimacy with him; and there are signs that he and James did not take to one another. Though on one occasion he was plied with too much drink and had to be restrained from breaking into the quarters of the maids of honour, the whole atmosphere of Whitehall was uncongenial to him. His youthful Calvinism was affronted by what he interpreted as Charles's statements of his preference for Catholicism.[8] Reports suggested that William's straight-laced conduct, in contrast with the dissipation of Charles's court, did him no harm with a wider public.

When Charles and Louis attacked the Dutch in 1672, William made private offers to Charles to try to divide his enemies (vainly)[9], but he emphatically refused to play the part of protégé which his uncle had designed for him. William was left to inspire the Dutch national resistance behind the 'water-line' and to secure the with-drawal of England from the war, as a result of the propaganda of Du Moulin (see chapter four), at the Treaty of Westminster in 1674. William became Stadholder of five provinces and Captain-General for life without owing these promotions to his uncle. His period as Charles's pawn was now over. Indeed it was now Charles's turn to be wary of William's connection (through Du Moulin) with the parliamentary opposition, and he did not rest until Du Moulin had left William's service. Charles still regarded his nephew as a junior who ought to look to him as guardian of the family interests but who was in fact a self-willed young man who would not follow his advice.

Yet Charles and William soon discovered that, small as their liking might be, they needed each other. With Holland saved, the war merged into a French attack on the Spanish Netherlands, and William found that he could make no headway unless he could gain the support of neutral England. Charles, on the other hand, found that he needed to secure an end to the war in order to escape from parliamentary pressure to intervene on behalf of the traditional English and Protestant interests in Flanders against France. This was the background to the marriage between William and Mary in 1677.[10]

For many the cousins' marriage was a natural outcome, but William knew that such a proposal might be unwelcome both to the regents and his allies. The regents might recall the consequences of the marriage of his parents, William and Mary, in 1641, while his allies might regard it as a 'sell-out' to the King of England whom they did not trust. By 1677 Mary was 15, an age when girls were in their prime at Charles's court and marriageable, so that an approach could not be delayed, but William could only afford to make it as part of an agreement which would bring him England's political support. Yet, interestingly in an age when all princely marriages were political, he was not indifferent to the personal implications. He made use of his friendship with the Temples, in whose embassy he spent more and more time, to get Lady Temple to report on Mary's suitability for a man who knew that he 'might, perhaps, not be very easy for a wife to live with': temperament, and a devotion to war, politics and hunting as his favourite occupations did not make him a ladies' man.[11] Charles at first refused to allow him to come to England, but when satisfied that the parliamentary pressure upon him to save Flanders would not cease, he accepted the advice of his minister, the Earl of Danby. Overbearing his brother James, the Catholic father of the bride, Charles consented to the marriage and the Anglo-Dutch treaty of January 1678, which followed it. The general rejoicing at the marriage was marred only by those who regarded it as going over to the establishment. On the great Protestant occasion of Queen Elizabeth's birthday, they hung round the neck of the papal effigy which was to be burnt the inscription: 'What the great Duke of Alva could not do [that is, subdue the Dutch heretics] will be done by the skirts of a woman', an interpretation of the marriage as popish which would baffle later Ulstermen.

The marriage did not begin well. Mary is said to have cried for a day and a half on being told that she was to marry a Dutchman who did not exactly exude charm. She was further disappointed when William consoled himself with the more intelligent company – the relationship was not primarily physical – of her maid of honour, Elizabeth Villiers, who was nearer his age. Rumours of pregnancies soon disappeared, and with them the possibility of a permanent Anglo-Dutch dynastic union which would have affected the histories of both countries. Instead it followed the abortive offers of union under Elizabeth and Cromwell into the 'might-have-beens' of history. Yet Mary soon became devoted to her husband, attached herself to his interests rather than her father's, and did not adopt the faintest hint of an independent line in the great crisis of 1688–9. William's frantic grief when Mary died in 1694 contrasted with Mary's tears when they married. Had her attitude been otherwise, the story of the Glorious Revolution would have been very different.

The immediate sequel to the marriage disappointed William's hopes of bringing England into an anti-French coalition. The Anglo-Dutch defensive alliance of 1678 remained officially in force for a century, but after six months of intense complications, the European war ended with the signing of the Treaty of Nijmegen without Charles having to intervene. Further, the Exclusion Crisis which followed, with the attempt of the Whigs to secure the exclusion of William's Catholic father-in-law, James, Duke of York, from the succession, was an embarrassment to William as well as to Charles. On the one hand, except for a few months in 1677–8, James had been regarded for at least a decade as being pro-French and anti-Dutch, and his exclusion would eliminate an obstacle to William's dream of an anti-French coalition which included England. On the other hand, if James did succeed, William's wife was the next in line – always provided that the Duchess of York still had no sons. The triumph of the Exclusionists might mean the legitimizing of Charles's bastard son Monmouth or restrictions on the royal prerogative, even if they were more favourably disposed to the anti-French cause. So William hesitated, and though he almost came to England to look after his interests at the end of 1680, he made no positive intervention, and was left with virtually no influence upon Charles in the Stuart reaction which followed the dissolution of his last Parliament in 1681.

A further complication was that in these years Monmouth took refuge in Holland. William and Mary, knowing both that he was the figurehead of the Whigs and that, in spite of everything, he remained Charles's favourite, gave him warm hospitality, with balls and festivities in his honour. When James II succeeded as king and head of the family in 1685, he called upon William to follow his policy lead and to have no further dealings with Monmouth. Authoritarian himself, he overestimated William's authority over the States-General and over the town of Amsterdam, and clearly blamed him when Monmouth was allowed to leave on his expedition, with the aid only of such resources as he could raise from English refugees. It is natural to suspect that William may not have tried too hard to prevent Monmouth from sailing. But the responsibility was not his, and as Captain-General he accepted James's right to recall English and Scots regiments in the service of the States-General to assist in putting down the rebellion. Some of the troops may have disliked the mission – a few Scots were shot for drinking Monmouth's health and 'engaging in some other unseemly talk' – but the rebellion did not last long enough for their services to be required. A popular revolt relying on hopes that some royal troops would desert was not enough. Within a few months of shining in the balls at The Hague, Monmouth met his death under the axe of Jack Ketch.

From now on, those who were dissatisfied with James's rule could look only to William and Mary, whether they hoped for Mary's peaceful succession or for William's active intervention. James and William kept up cool relations: neither of them was a natural letter-writer and neither could conceal that he had little to say, other than to exchange notes about some wretched stag he had hunted across the countryside. James, characteristically unoriginal, had some difficulty in finding a formula with which to end his letters, and instead of saying 'hope this finds you as it leaves me at present' would conclude by saying to William either 'Be assured that I shall be as kind to you as you desire,' or 'Be assured that I shall be as kind to you as you can expect.' His use of these two different formulae serves as a barometer of their relationship, and as time went on the latter came to predominate. More and more Englishmen visited The Hague, wrote letters, or received William's envoys, Dyckvelt and Zuylestein: they could hardly be prevented from keeping in touch with a prince of the blood, husband to the heir to the throne. Dissatisfaction grew. The only Parliament called between 1681 and 1689 was that needed to renew taxation at the beginning of the reign, and when there was talk of another one it was accompanied by manipulations of the borough electorates and candidacies. The standing army was built up, and was believed to be intended to enforce Catholicism upon the nation. So too was James's use of the power he claimed to dispense individuals from the laws preventing non-Anglicans from holding office. Later, he was to arouse suspicions even further by suspending those laws altogether. The Declaration of Indulgence was ostensibly designed to relieve both Catholics and Dissenters, but it was widely believed to be in the interests of the former. Consequently it was thought worthy of comment when Fagel, Grand Pensionary of the States of Holland and very much William's man, wrote and distributed a *Letter* saying that William and Mary were prepared to tolerate Dissenters and Catholics, but not to repeal the Test Acts. Indulgence, without the right of Catholics to hold office, represented the position in the United Provinces.

Before the end of 1687 it was officially announced that the Queen was pregnant, and it is remarkable how quickly it was assumed that this pregnancy (unlike previous ones) would produce a healthy boy, who would exclude Mary from the succession and ensure the perpetuation of James's régime. It is impossible to be sure how early William took the decision to intervene. But it was certainly before the birth of the Old Pretender on 10 June 1688, and the invention of the famous myth of the 'warming pan' in which a child, who was not the Queen's, was conveyed into the Queen's bedroom. Mary is more likely than William to have believed in this attempt to deprive her fraudulently of her rights to the succession, but his personal decision to invade (assuming the consent of the States-General) must have been taken earlier. The States-General's consent was essential because William could not mount an invasion on the basis of his own resources and his authority as stadholder and Captain-General. Monmouth's failure had shown that a handful of volunteers would not be sufficient; a full-scale expedition would be necessary, backed by the resources of the Dutch state. The States-General later sent in a bill to England for £600,000 as the cost of the expedition by the forces in their service. The consent of the States-General involved the previous consent of the States of Holland, which in turn implied the consent of the city of Amsterdam. All this could not be taken for granted, for in the past decade William's relations with Amsterdam in particular had not been harmonious. As a result, it was particularly important that influential Dutch opinion should put its weight behind the expedition. This it did, swayed as it was by the influx of Huguenot refugees after the Revocation of the Edict of Nantes, by Louis XIV's renewed tariff measures, and above all by the likelihood of a general European war in 1689 in which James could well figure on Louis's side. For the success of the Revolution, England owes a debt to the Dutch, rather than just to William. In their turn the Dutch certainly gained from the Revolution's success, for it meant that England was now incorporated into the ranks of those opposed to Louis's aggressions in north-western Europe.

The apparent ease of the Revolution should not lead to the assumption that the result was a foregone conclusion. The 'Immortal Seven' of the Earls of Danby, Devonshire, and Shrewsbury, Lord Lumley, Bishop Compton of London, Henry Sidney and Edward Russell, sent the invitation, as requested by William, for him to come to the rescue of their religion, liberties and properties on 30 June (three weeks after the birth of the Old Pretender). However, the expedition could not be mounted until the autumn. The States of Holland gave their formal consent only in September, when there was no longer a danger that their frontiers would be attacked by the French armies in William's absence. An expedition at that time of year carried with it formidable risks. Over 200 ships were required to transport the 15,000 troops, 4000 horses and 21 guns, together with hay, a smithy, a portable bridge, a printing press and other paraphernalia. Even though convoyed by over fifty ships of the Dutch navy, these small ships, each carrying about 200 men, would be terribly exposed both to storms and to an encounter with James's fleet. As it was, when William's ships first sailed, storms forced them back to port, and the panic which had reigned at James's Court, leading to a promise at last to call Parliament, gave way to relief. If William managed to make a successful landing in November, when the usual campaigning season was over, he would be faced by an army more than twice the size of his own. He also knew that Monmouth's hopes of desertions from James's professional troops had been ill-founded.

William's departing words, *Aut nunc, aut nunquam* [now or never] show that he was well aware of the risks. In the words of a later Jacobite pamphlet,

> And for a speedy Parl'ment
> He [James] doth forthwith declare;
> The surly brute [William] not minding this
> Does to our coast repair,
> With several thousand Belgic Boars,
> All chosen rogues for spight,
> Joined with some rebels who from hence
> And Justice had ta'en flight.[12]

William may or may not have been aware that, according to the imperial ambassador in London, English sailors were avoiding service in their own ships in order to avoid having to fight against their 'friends'. The majority of the captains were Dutch, but some English pilots certainly sailed with him, including a masterpilot of Hull. The fleet sailed north as though to go to the mouth of the Humber, like Bolingbroke and Edward IV, and there to link up with risings organized by Danby, Devonshire and others. At sea, however, a council of war was followed by a change of course which took them to a landing in Devon. It has sometimes been suggested that this was to ensure that William would not owe his success to his political allies in the north. However, it would have been quixotic in the extreme if William had set out to land, apparently without contacts, at the opposite end of the country from the area where support was planned, to operate against a force over twice the size of his own, unless there was an immediate strategic advantage to be gained. As it was, the unusual easterly winds confined James's fleet under Dartmouth to their station at the Gunfleet, and enabled William to sail along the Channel, avoiding what would have been a very risky battle. He then made an unopposed landing, ironically in the very county from which Dartmouth took his title.[13]

The landing at Brixham is commonly described as a Dutch invasion, but many of the troops were not in fact Dutchmen, though they were all in Dutch pay. Indeed, William tactfully placed in the forefront at the landing, and later at the entry into Exeter, the three English and three Scots regiments which had been in the Dutch service since the Elizabethan wars. In the previous winter James had tried to recall these forces, as being his subjects, under the terms of the defensive alliance of 1678, but the States-General had given officers only the option of returning if they wished to do so, and not many had availed themselves of the opportunity. As a result, according to the calculation of the historians of the Dutch army, of 11,212 foot 3960 were British. The rest were Dutch, Huguenots, or Dutch mercenaries – German, Swiss and Swedes. Also among those who marched for English religion, liberties and property, were Suri-namers, and even Laplanders (in hired Scandinavian regiments):

> Since these Switzers and Dutchmen
> Come to stand by our churchmen
> With hardy grim fellows from Finland.[14]

Having safely crossed the 'herring pond', a phrase applied in 1688 to the North Sea where it could be said to be literally correct, they marched, as William's secretary noted, past people who called 'God bless you' and gave apples and mead. These welcoming people included old women with pipes of tobacco in their mouths, 'smoking without shame', as did lads of 13 and 14. Between Exeter and Honiton they were still lining the roads in pouring rain as the army marched by. But James's proclamation that all who helped them were traitors inevitably gave pause to those who remembered the bodies of Monmouth's rebels, hanging tarred and quartered outside the villages after the Bloody Assize. The Bishop and Dean of Exeter fled from the 'Switzers and Dutchmen' who had come to stand by them, and gentlemen were slow to commit themselves openly. William was observed to be unusually irritable as the crisis approached. But it would be untrue to say that they marched through an apathetic countryside. None realized his own isolation more than James. He had hastily countermanded some of his policies on hearing that an invasion was imminent, and as some officers, including his favourite John Churchill, and even his younger daughter Anne deserted him, he knew that he could rely on no one, and his nerve failed him. He did not dare put it to the test in battle, even with a nominally superior army, and William entered the capital on 18 December, six weeks after the landing. He proceeded to St James's through cheers from crowds with orange favours in their hats and oranges on sticks.[15]

Yet even now James was not finally defeated. Many of those who welcomed William's intervention wanted to secure, through his protection, the reversal of James's policies, the recall of a free Parliament, and some form of guarantee for the future, but they did not necessarily want James's deposition. Tories especially, having voted against Exclusion in 1678–81, were bound to regard him as the legal ruler. In not following Monmouth's example and proclaiming himself and Mary King and Queen after landing, William had carefully taken those feelings into account. Had James stood his ground, there could well have been a reaction in his favour. There was an early dislike of the Dutch guards who replaced the Coldstreams at Whitehall. All sorts of views were possible about the course of action to be taken for the future. It is conceivable that James could not have been deposed without another civil war in which William's Dutch troops took part. But James was demoralized and had no heart for the manoeuvring which this would have entailed. When he tried to escape to France and failed, William obligingly provided him with another opportunity. After James's departure to the court of Louis XIV, to whom most Englishmen were hostile, his supporters were hopelessly handicapped.

Thus a Revolution, peaceful in England, was carried out by means of William and his Dutch troops. In the Convention Parliament of 1689 there were still those who would have preferred a regency or the succession of Mary alone, but these solutions failed for lack of encouragement from Mary and because William would not consider being 'his wife's gentleman usher'. The imminence of war with France also meant that the disputes in the Convention had to be cut short. The joint kingship which resulted was not so unusual as is sometimes imagined, for Philip and Mary Tudor had reigned in the previous century. But William intended to have much more effective control than had been allowed to Philip. From 13 February 1689 the King of England was a Dutchman, albeit the son of one Stuart princess and the husband of another, who became at the same time Mary II. The House of Orange had effectively ousted the family which had once patronized it.

With the offer of the crown went the Declaration of Rights. The wording of the claims of the Convention (afterwards enshrined in the Bill of Rights) was very unspecific and would have presented serious difficulties had it ever been questioned in the courts; but it served its purpose by setting out in general terms the policies against which England had set its face. William could afford to regard the rights as liberties which he had restored rather than as innovations. Without children to whom he could expect to pass on his prerogatives, he could afford to regard them as much less important than the all-consuming struggle against Louis XIV, to which he could now bring English resources. In the course of the war against France the liberties granted by 'Dutch William' were strengthened and confirmed. The Bill of Rights declared, *inter alia*, that the power to suspend laws without the consent of a freely-elected Parliament, as claimed by James, was illegal; that a standing army without parliamentary consent was illegal, and that 'Parliaments ought to be held frequently'. In fact the needs of the war ensured that Parliament should meet annually and since William's landing there has never been a year without one. The Toleration Act gave parliamentary sanction for freedom of worship for Dissenters; the best that Catholics could expect was a practical indulgence, as in the United Provinces. Catholic public worship was only legalized after another century, while both Dissenters and Catholics were legally excluded from office and Parliament until the reign of George IV. A more bigoted Protestant than William, with his Dutch experience, might have stimulated more anti-Catholic measures after the popery of James II. England now had a king who shared the Protestantism of most of his subjects without persecuting those who did not share it.

These were considerable gains, made possible by the intervention of William, with Dutch backing, in English affairs. Had he not crossed the North Sea they might perhaps have been achieved in some other way, but this can only be surmise; if there had been a domestic rebellion without William's troops it would probably have been accompanied by bloodshed. Certainly as events turned out Englishmen owed a great deal to William and the Dutch, though some Tories and Anglicans retained uneasy memories of their previous oaths of allegiance to James.[16]

If Englishmen owed much to William so too, indirectly, did Scotsmen, even though he never set foot in their country. The Claim of Right (1689) was the counterpart of the Bill of Rights, and indeed went into more detail. Not only were parliamentary rights affirmed, but there was some parliamentary reform. The Stuarts had ruled Parliament through the management of a committee known as the Lords of the Articles, which was now abolished, so that Parliament became freer. Ironically, in the next reign this led to the ending of an independent Scots Parliament by the Union of 1707. Presbyterianism was restored in accordance with the wishes of most lowland Scots, and it was certainly not William's intention that the re-establishment of the kirk should be accompanied by the 'rabbling' of the Episcopalian clergy who had been imposed upon the parishes in Charles II's reign. But, contrary to the course of events in England, the new settlement was not applied to the highlands without bloodshed. A regiment from the Scots Brigade, now diluted by other Scots, took part in the operation against the Jacobites. Oddly, at the battle of Killiecrankie both commanders had seen service under William in the Low Countries: the Jacobite, Claverhouse, had survived at Seneffe in 1675 to meet his death at Killiecrankie (and be succeeded by Cannon, who had also served in the Netherlands) whereas Hugh Mackay survived at Killiecrankie, only to be killed at Steenkirk after a long career in the Scots Brigade.

Ireland, of course, was quite a different story, best treated as part of the ensuing war against France, for this was essentially the light in which William regarded his campaigns in that country. From 1689 Dutch and English fought side by side in the great coalitions against Louis XIV.

CHAPTER SEVEN

Allies against France

'It is interest that governs kingdoms. Nations do not fall in love with one another as particular persons do for their beauty.'[1] These remarks are particularly apt in relation to the English and Dutch when they were allied against France between 1689 and 1713, as they had been allied against Spain between 1585 and 1604. They had obvious common interests in preventing Louis XIV from extending his influence over Flanders, which he might use as a base for the invasion of the United Provinces or Britain. They had wider interests in preventing Louis from dominating the Spanish Empire and building up his naval, colonial and protectionist control. And these interests carried with them the implication that both must prevent Louis from putting James back on the English throne, and preserve the Protestant succession against a Jacobite restoration.

Yet there were also reasons for friction, and not simply the inevitable differences of emphasis between allies over objectives, the means of reaching them, and the post-war power position. Nor was the trouble simply the continuation of old jealousies over fishing, commercial, colonial and naval rivalry and the carrying trade. Pamphleteers returned to those traditional themes, and wrote once more of Amboina and other old grievances, and it would be absurd to say that they carried no weight. But this time it was the moneyed and commercial men of the City (and the Dissenting element among them) who most favoured the policy of a land war and therefore a

Dutch alliance, and it was the Tory, landed and Anglican groups which had most reservations about them. 'If you wish to discover a concealed Tory, Jacobite or Papist, speak but of the Dutch': attitudes to them were the touchstone of domestic political and religious divisions. Opponents of William III and his ministers were likely to transfer their hostility to the Dutch; and the same was true of the opponents of Marlborough and the Whigs in the latter stages of the War of the Spanish Succession.

A suitably business-like note was struck from the very beginning when the Dutch claimed and received £600,000 for the cost of William's expedition (the expenses of sending Dutch troops on the later campaign of the Battle of the Boyne were not recouped until 1721). Dutch hopes that they would be rewarded with the repeal of the Navigation Act were not taken seriously by either side, and they noticed ruefully that to satisfy the patriotic prejudices of his new subjects William was as rigid in requiring the right of salute to his ships as his predecessors. The needs of the imminent war against France made it impossible to object.

Whereas the Triple Alliance of 1668 and the defensive treaty of 1678 had provided for equal naval contributions, it was agreed in May 1689 that the English should provide fifty ships and the Dutch thirty, under permanent English command, with ten more English ships for trade protection. But the Dutch admiralties failed to have even this smaller number ready on the dates stipulated. The Dutch navy was now definitely the weaker of the two, and though they built more ships than their ally in 1689–90, the shallower waters round the Dutch coasts made it difficult for them to employ ships of the same size as the English and French. In return for a smaller naval contribution the Dutch were to provide a greater one to William's armies, in the same proportion of five to three. This suited William's personal preference for action on the battlefield, his awareness of the greater military experience of his Dutch army officers, and everyone's realization that the Dutch frontiers were in more immediate danger from the proximity of Louis's troops. No attempt was made to institutionalize the co-operation. In the Dutch Republic William ruled with the aid of the long-serving Grand Pensionary, Heinsius, through the traditional bodies, but with a stricter control. On the English side he had the services of a secretary at war, William Blathwayt, who travelled with him and acted almost as a third secretary of state. The politicians carried on in London when he was on campaign, while he kept a close control over diplomatic policy. The link between the two countries was simply the personal influence of the king-stadholder, with the treaty of 1689 for combined action against France.

There were inevitably difficulties, for instance over the late arrival of Dutch ships for joint expeditions, and once again the problem of trade with the enemy reared its head. The English preferred a total ban, but Dutch merchants supplied munitions in spite of resolutions from the States-General. The English also feared that the continuation of postal services concealed the extensive remittance of money by bills of exchange from Amsterdam. But these seemed minor matters in comparison with the Dutch contribution at the Battle of Beachy Head (1690) where, as a result of the mismanagement of Admiral Torrington, the Dutch vanguard had to bear the brunt of the attacks by Tourville's ships. Queen Mary's apology for the lack of English support, which has been described as 'one of the most humiliating addresses ever delivered to a foreign government', assured the Dutch that their sick and wounded would be cared for, that their ships would be repaired at English expense, and that those responsible for the defeat would be punished. The comment of *A Satyr on the Sea Officers* on remarks about 'Dutch courage' was:

> The Dutch were drunk, you barbarously say,
> Pray, next, do you be drunk too, so you stay.
> For 'twas your sober fighting lost the day.[2]

There was some reaction by sympathizers with the English navy at the time of Torrington's trial, and unfortunately at the time of the triumph of Barfleur (La Hogue) in 1692, where there were 63 English ships to 36 Dutch, the Dutch had little opportunity to shine.

At the Battle of the Boyne (fought on the day after Beachy Head) there was a contingent of William's Dutch Blue Guards, who were significantly said by those ill-disposed to them to be in better health than the English because they had the best of everything: all the best doctors, and tents at the edge of camp where they had more fresh air. In fact, they had the experience to know what was best.[3] Dutchmen did not, however, form a large proportion of William's army, and William himself was there not because of the intrinsic value of Ireland (though afterwards he rewarded his friends from confiscated land), but because the core of the opposing army was French rather than Irish. James had brought a French force with him to Ireland in 1689 and, apart from the preference of his English subjects, William had to prevent the country from becoming a base for a French-backed invasion of England. Though he was a convinced Calvinist, his Dutch background prevented him from being an extreme anti-Catholic bigot, as did his allies at Vienna and Madrid, not to mention Rome, where the Pope celebrated the news of the victory at the Boyne with a Te Deum. His desire was to liquidate the struggle in Ireland and return to his central preoccupation with the campaigns in Flanders as quickly as possible, rather than to take measures of exceptional severity against the Irish. Accordingly, within two months he returned to England, leaving the Dutchman Ginkel to win the battle of Aughrim and the title of Earl of Athlone. It was not William's fault that the not ungenerously drafted Articles of Limerick were attenuated, in letter and in spirit, by others.

From now on William spent his summers on campaign in the Low Countries, and his winters in London wrestling with a variegated crew of politicians and parliamentarians whom he could reconcile neither to one another nor to his policies. In the Spanish Netherlands he won some important successes, frustrating the armies of Louis XIV and recapturing the great citadel of Namur (1695) at the price of antagonizing English officers. They felt that in terms of promotions they were unfairly treated in comparison with William's fellow-Dutchmen. In England he was never liked after the first few months, and was even less popular after the death of Mary, until the assassination plot of 1696 reminded Englishmen how much they depended upon him. Those who were not comfortable with the idea of James II's deposition, whether or not they would have welcomed his return, had never been positively disposed towards William. They were reinforced by many who disliked him as non-Anglican and identified him with ministers, policies and taxation of which they disapproved. The unpopularity of the king was transferred to the nation from which he came: 'The names of Whig and Tory', it was predicted in 1691, 'will at last change into English and Dutch'.[4]

How little William was able to do to counteract this swell of opinion is evident from Bishop Burnet, himself no enemy of the Dutch since he had come over with the expedition of 1688, leaving behind a Dutch wife. According to Burnet, 'The King was thought to love the Dutch more than the English, to trust them more, and to admit them to more freedom with him. He gave too much occasion to a general disgust, which was agreed both among the English officers and the nobility. He took little pains to gain the affections of the nation, nor did he constrain himself enough to render his government more acceptable; he was shut up all the day long, and his silence, when he admitted any to audience, distasted them as much as if they had been denied it.... And the strain of all the nation almost was that the English were overlooked, and the Dutch were the only persons favoured or trusted. This was national: and the English [said the Scotsman] being too apt to despise other nations ... grew to express a contempt and an aversion for them.... It is true, the Dutch behaved themselves so well and so regularly in their quarters, and paid for everything so punctually, whereas the English [troops] were apt to be rude and exacting ... so that the common people were generally better pleased with the Dutch soldiers than with their own countrymen; but it was not the same as to the officers.'[5]

William had no more liking for them than they for him, and he always preferred the state in which he was stadholder to the one in which he was king. He told one of his Dutch friends, 'I can see that this people was not made for me nor I for them.' He found little to enjoy in the English style of life, and ridiculed 'those silly old Popish ceremonies' in 'that farce of a coronation'.[6] At one point he threatened to abdicate, and was restrained by the needs of his obsessive struggle with Louis, rather than by positive feelings for England.

Already in 1690 *Min Heer T van C's answer to Min Heer H van L's Letter of the 15th of March, 1689[/90], representing the true interests of Holland, and what they have already gained by our losses* purported to demonstrate that the Revolution had been for the benefit of the Dutch, not the English. Another Jacobite, complaining of Dutch advantages in the matter of convoys, declared: 'They have been always our rivals, and are now our masters.... Do we think they will ever let us get up again, or re-enter into that universal trade which they have occupied during our cessation?' It was said that 'we may soon have not only Dutch bishops, Dutch presbyters and Dutch lords, Dutch commons and Dutch everything; and Lord Dutch may become as formidable to us as Lord Dane was to our ancestors'.[7] An exaggerated responsibility was attributed to William's old friend Bentinck (Earl of Portland), who in return told a compatriot that he intended to take his son out of England as soon as he was 12 'that he might not learn debauchery in that country', and quoted others to the effect that 'it was a devil of a country, so dirty, and so wicked'.[8] This did not prevent him, the younger favourite Keppel (Earl of Albemarle), Elizabeth Villiers and other friends from benefiting from grants of titles and lands. Ferguson 'the Plotter', who had served William in 1688 and turned against him later, referred to 'the rapacity and covetousness of his beloved Dutch'. Two-fifths of the confiscated Irish land went to Dutchmen, or about 300,000 acres, and after a parliamentary storm excited by the Tories, an Act of Resumption was passed in 1700.

Sir John Knight concluded an attack on a Naturalization Bill in the House of Commons in 1694: 'Let us first kick the bill out of the House, and then foreigners out of the Kingdom.'[9] Most obnoxious of all, because most visible, were the Dutch guards at Whitehall, the *Lijfgarden* or Lifeguards (the Dutch word *lijf* means body). The opportunity to get rid of them, together with most of the hated standing army, came after the Peace of Ryswick (1697), the second of the three great European treaties signed on Dutch territory (with Nijmegen [1678] and Utrecht [1713]). To William's great reluctance they had to leave the country. According to Ned Ward, Londoners were freed from the smell of herring-bones in the park after breakfast; 'the nostrils of our squeamish ladies' were no longer offended by the smell of Orinoco tobacco, and these same ladies could go for a walk without shrinking back at a 'terrible pair of Dutch whiskers'. Defoe, on the other hand, talked of the Dutch:

> How they came here our freedom to maintain,
> Were paid and cursed, and hurried home again![10]

Within two years Dutch help was needed once more. The Partition Treaties between William and Louis were followed by Louis's acceptance of the will by which Charles II of Spain unexpectedly bequeathed the whole of his empire to the French claimant, Louis XIV's grandson, Philip, Duke of Anjou, rather than to the Austrian claimant, the Archduke Charles. At first it seemed that public opinion in both England and Holland, unenthusiastic about supporting William in another war, would accept the French claimant as Philip V of Spain, but it veered strongly when it became clear that Louis aimed at controlling Spanish policy in French interests. His troops marched unopposed into the critical Barrier fortresses, which were on the border between the Spanish Netherlands and France and which the recent treaty gave the Dutch the right to garrison. The Spanish Netherlands would no longer be a buffer between France and the Dutch Republic. It also seemed likely that French merchants would be in a position to monopolize trade with Spain and the Spanish Empire, and that the Maritime Powers' trade with the Mediterranean would be endangered. Furthermore, Louis recognized the Old Pretender as James III, with the prospect that Flanders might be a base for foreign invasion in his interests. Before the end of 1701 a Grand Alliance was again in being.

This time there was no stadholder-king to fight the war that followed, and to keep together the motley collection of opponents of France. William III died in 1702, leaving no adult successor and bringing to an end the short period when the two dynasties were under the same head. The war was carried on by Marlborough for Queen Anne, with Heinsius leading the Dutch administration; their partnership was enshrined in a long and confidential correspondence.[11] The British became more and more clearly the predominant partner, with complaints about the Dutch falling behind in their quotas and being late in arrival, especially as the British devoted more attention to the war in Spain. The Dutch capital ships decreased in numbers from 55 in 1702 to 40 in 1711. The ships of Almonde and Callenberg co-operated at Vigo, in the capture of Gibraltar and at the battle of Malaga, but on the last occasion there were only 12 of them and thereafter the naval war was fought mainly by privateers.

The States-General once again supplied more than half the troops in the Low Countries, either Dutchmen or mercenaries in Dutch pay. At their peak there were some 120,000 of them and Ouwerkerk in particular distinguished himself. The difficulty was that in return for accepting Marlborough's command the States-General called upon him to accept field deputies, led by Goslinga, who restrained his willingness to deliver battle. They knew how little William III's battles had achieved and how difficult it would be to replace a decimated army. Marlborough was only able to make his famous march to the Danube on the Blenheim campaign by means of a deception. Though Marlborough praised the Dutch for their contribution at the battle, public opinion did not give sufficient credit for the fact that there were more Dutch than British troops there. Already in 1705 there were those who complained that:

> Mechanics, base Republicans control
> The vast designs of Marlborough's thoughtful soul.
> See now, they doubt and stop the conquering hand
> That gave them victory at his wife's command.[12]

Such complaints were not brought to an end by the battle of Ramillies (1706), in which the Dutch bore the brunt of the action that recovered almost the whole of the southern Netherlands for the Archduke Charles. The irony was that the fears of the Dutch deputies were justified in the last of Marlborough's great victories, at Malplaquet in 1709. The losses of the Dutch troops led by the young Prince of Orange (from the cadet branch of the family) were frightful, especially in one half-hour of dreadful carnage. On this occasion Goslinga's gallantry was much admired and he did not reproach Marlborough for the casualties the army incurred, which amounted to almost half their strength.

The complaints of the British against the Dutch field deputies were by no means their only grievances. In the early years of the war it was again believed that the French armies were being paid by means of bills of exchange through Amsterdam, and under Tory pressure a ban was imposed on postal services and trade with the enemy. As a result the Dutch lost much of their carrying trade to the neutral Swedes and Danes, but the ban was not renewed, nor was there much English demand for it after 1705.[13] Too much should not be made of this friction. Even the restraints of the deputies and the unpunctuality of the Dutch and their failure to keep to their quotas could be forgiven so long as the war was proceeding successfully. Moreover, Tories who might have objected to the nation from which King William had come were held back by their loyalty to Marlborough and the Queen. There were complaints that the Dutch were 'a people who will expect a pennyworth for their penny,' and they were believed to be accumulating vast wealth from the war; but in any study of international relations the historian has to beware of 'a tendency to emphasize disagreement and dissension, and to ignore the less easily detected areas of agreement. Tension is much more spectacular than détente.'[14] If the war had come to an end in 1709 it would have done so without any serious division between the allies.

By that date the Whigs were dominant among the Queen's ministers, and their fear was not so much that British opinion would refuse backing for the war as that the Dutch might defect. Before the Treaties of Nijmegen and Ryswick the French had sought to draw diplomatic profit from concessions to the merchants of Amsterdam and elsewhere who wanted a return to peaceful trading conditions, and the same might happen again. After the Battle of Ramillies and the reconquest of the Spanish Netherlands in 1706 the Dutch no longer had reason to fear the proximity of France to their frontiers. Consequently, they were not as insistent as the Whigs upon making the deposition of Philip V an indispensable condition of peace, provided that they had commercial access to Spain and its empire. After the possibility of a French and Jacobite invasion in 1708, moreover, the Whigs wanted a guarantee of Dutch support for the Protestant succession of the Hanoverian descendants of James I in Britain after Queen Anne's death. Accordingly they negotiated the Barrier Treaty of 1709. The States-General pledged themselves to maintain the Protestant succession as ordained by Parliament and to make no peace with France until Louis had acknowledged it and expelled the Pretender from his dominions. In return, Britain promised to obtain for the Dutch the right to garrison a line of barrier forts, including Lille and further conquests from France, along the frontier between France and the southern Netherlands (now to be Austrian). There would also be an inner line of communicating towns, and the Dutch would receive an annual revenue with which to maintain their garrisons, and the important commercial right to import goods for them free of duty. Moreover, any commercial privileges given to the British in any part of the Spanish dominions, including the important *asiento* contract to supply slaves to the New World, would apply equally to the subjects of the States-General.[15]

As a result, the Dutch became the most convinced supporters of the war in its concluding stages in order to obtain the concessions which had been guaranteed to them. However, in Britain the war-supporting Whigs were overborne by a swing of public opinion and their rival Harley's skill in winning the Queen's favour, which together meant the triumph of the Tories at the parliamentary elections of 1710. The peace movement was partly the result of war-weariness and the burden of taxation, especially the land-tax under which the Tory gentry suffered while (as they saw it) the moneyed interest in the City, including Dutch stock-jobbers, made enormous profits. The army officers who flourished (apart from those who met their deaths) in the land-war in the Low Countries were no more popular when the early glories ceased to impress. And Anglican clergy fostered a sincere, if greatly exaggerated, belief that 'the Church was in danger' from Dissenters, who were linked with sectaries in the Dutch Republic.

The Dutch were especially vulnerable to this turn of opinion as convinced backers of the land-war, of Republicanism in politics and free thought in religion, and they could be represented as profiting most from the war. Sacheverell's famous sermon, by reviving old ideas of divine right and Jacobite dislike of revolution and King William, also brought unpopularity upon the heads of William's nation. Tory propaganda played upon these feelings, and soon the Dutch were once more 'the crab-lice of Europe', the 'undermining, You-tricking Dutch', while Swift's *Examiner* asked 'Is there a mongrel sect in Christendom, which does not croak, and spawn, and flourish, in their bogs?'[16]

Government propagandists revived the abuses of the Anglo-Dutch wars in order to justify the desire of Lord Treasurer Harley (Earl of

Oxford) and Secretary of State St John (Viscount Bolingbroke) to default on Britain's treaty obligations to their allies. The most distinguished of them was Jonathan Swift who, ironically, in the 1690s had been the secretary of Sir William Temple. As such he had had the responsibility of seeing through the press the edition of Temple's *Letters* in which he illustrated his long efforts to bring into existence an Anglo-Dutch coalition against France. Indeed, Temple's *Letters* and *Memoirs*, the first such publications by an English statesman, reprinted and translated, did as much as any book to develop the idea that this was Britain's true interest in foreign policy. We know little of the reasons why the ex-secretary of an admirer of the Dutch became a hater of them. But it may be that he had never fully shared his master's approval of the Dutch religious system, as expressed in the passages of the *Observations on the United Provinces* mentioned in chapter five, and that he reacted to the cry of 'The Church in danger' which carried with it the implication that a similar régime was developing in England. At all events the change seems to have taken place in those same years 1708–9 when Sacheverell came to the forefront.

Swift's most famous pamphlet (though more often referred to than read) was *The Conduct of the Allies*, published in 1711.[17] In this he went back to the war of William III, and argued that it was fought in the Dutch, rather than the English, interest, 'and the greatest part of six millions annually employed to enlarge the frontier of the Dutch. For [William] although King of England, was a native of Holland.' Forgetting what Temple had told him of the English interest in preventing the French from absorbing Flanders, he declared that 'the grounds of their quarrel with France are such as only affect themselves, or at least more immediately than any other prince or state,' such as the seizure of the Spanish Netherlands by French troops. At the cost of millions the British had conquered a noble territory for the States, whose manufactures, 'added to their skill, industry and parsimony, will enable them to undersell us in every market of the world'. By the Barrier Treaty the Dutch would 'in effect be entire masters of all the Low Countries,' and he held out the alarming prospect that, with this accretion of resources, the Dutch would become not merely the carriers, but 'the original possessors of those commodities with which the greatest part of the trade of the world is now carried on'. He complained, like many Englishmen, about the effects of the war-time Anglo-Dutch condominium over the southern Netherlands in the name of the Austrian claimant. In doing so, he pointed out that, by extending the old system in operation on the Scheldt, all Flemish ports would be made subject to similar duties, so that English traders would effectively be shut out. The Dutch failure to supply their quotas in the treaty of alliance was raked up, and on the other hand, 'when our armies take a town in Flanders, the Dutch are immediately put into possession, and we at home make bonfires.'

This pamphlet at least distributed blame over all the allies, including Austria, whereas, as the title indicates, *Some Remarks on the Barrier Treaty between Her Majesty and the States-General* (1712)[18] concentrated entirely on the Dutch and was correspondingly more severe. A Chinese not acquainted with British politics, he said, might imagine from the Treaty that Britain was a minor tributary of the Dutch. Only two of 22 articles related to Britain, and they only gave the British what was guaranteed by the Grand Alliance. They were worse off than in the time of Charles II of Spain, by virtue of the 'double duties' on goods going to the 'new conquests' made since the Barrier Treaty. But the same treaty gave the Dutch a share in all British advantages: 'This is Dutch partnership, to share in all our beneficial obligations, and exclude us wholly from theirs, even from those we have got for them. . . . We see the whole nation groaning under excessive taxes of all sorts. . . . Let us look upon the reverse of the medal, we shall see our neighbours, who in their utmost distress called for our assistance, become by this treaty, even in time of peace, masters of a more considerable country than their own; in a condition to strike terror into us, with 50,000 veterans ready to invade us, from that country which we have conquered for them. . . .'

Much of this was hopelessly unrealistic. There was not the remotest chance that 50,000 Dutch veterans, even bolstered by Belgian resources, would invade England. In short, there is no sign of any realization of the way in which the balance of resources had changed. The United Provinces not only had fewer resources in population and ships, but they had been crushed by a burden of taxation which required them to pay more per head than the British. Like many eighteenth-century British commentators, Swift supposed Dutch wealth to be limitless. He gave no credit to the Dutch for their part in the successes Britain had won, and scarcely acknowledged what Britain had gained, nor that the Barrier Treaty had been made very much under British pressure. Above all, he did not discuss the obligations which one ally has to another after a freely signed treaty between them.

Harley and St John had little regard for any such obligation either, and the latter has even been accused of 'a pathological hatred of the Dutch'. The peace settlement was made essentially by private Anglo-French negotiations, and the Dutch were dragooned into acceptance. There was even talk of war if the Dutch did not fall in, and the *Examiner* quoted from the old *Delenda est Carthago* speech. Defoe's *The Justice and Necessity of a War with Holland, in Case the Dutch do not give in to Her Majesty's Measures, Stated and Expressed* appeared nine days after the news of the Dutch defeat at Denain. The notorious 'Restraining Orders', communicated to the French but not the Dutch, had prevented Ormonde, Marlborough's successor, from fighting, and many Germans in British pay had had to be taken into that of the Dutch.

The Dutch were now helpless, and the Earl of Strafford was sent over, as Swift wrote in his *Journal to Stella*, to 'let them know what we have been doing; and then there will be the devil and all to pay, but we'll make them swallow it with a pox'. 'Those scoundrels the Dutch' would have no choice in the matter. 'Though they kick and flounce like wild beasts caught in a toil, yet the cords are too strong for them to break: they will soon tire with struggling, and when they are tired grow tame.' They could vent their frustration only by throwing stones at Strafford's windows, breaking Bolingbroke's effigy on the wheel in the streets, and writing poems declaring that England's 'white cliffs for noble shame were blushing'.[19]

Yet even Bolingbroke, much as he hated the Dutch, could not simply leave them at France's mercy. 'We shall not dare leave them behind us ... some of our best friends among the Tories would, in such cases, join to condemn us.' Along with the Treaty of Utrecht (1713) the Dutch were granted a second Barrier Treaty, by which they were to receive a reduced number of barrier fortresses, severely limited in number but better than that given at Ryswick in 1697, with the right to send duty-free materials for their garrisons. However, there was no reference to trade with Spain or the *asiento*. 'I continue still to think', wrote Strafford condescendingly, 'that the way to treat these people is with a mixture of authority and kindness;'[20] but not as equal partners.

The Dutch, however, still had warmer friends among the Whigs. John Withers wrote *The Dutch better friends than the French to the Monarchy, Church and Trade of England (1703)*, which included the points that the Dutch had had more soldiers and heavier taxes; that the defence of the southern Netherlands was as much an English interest as a Dutch; that French patriotism was more serious than Dutch rivalry; and that it was doubtful whether the English merchants at Amboina were innocent. Relying on their knowledge of the past support of the Whigs for the Barrier Treaty, Dutchmen hoped for better treatment when, after the death of Anne, George I brought them back into power, but there was no return to the Treaty of 1709. The third Barrier Treaty ceded Venlo and other places to the States-General, but Mons, Ghent and Charleroi were omitted from the fortresses mentioned in 1713.[21]

Yet in spite of the Dutch disappointment, the fact remained that both peoples had gained greatly from co-operation over more than twenty years. Louis XIV, like Philip II, had been frustrated, and the Low Countries were again preserved from domination by an authoritarian ruler. Both maritime powers were safe from invasion for the next thirty years, and with the assistance of the Dutch, Britain had been saved from the risk of French support for a Jacobite restoration. After the trauma of 1672 the Dutch were able to relapse into relative somnolence, and for Britain the Treaty of Utrecht was the basis for overseas expansion and for naval supremacy.

CHAPTER EIGHT

Economic Exchange: Goods and Investments

In the words of Charles Wilson's book, the years 1603–1763 were those of *England's Apprenticeship*[1] in economic matters to the Dutch. By the middle of that period most of the apprenticeship in trade and industry had been served, and what had still to be learned were the techniques of the 'financial revolution', the Bank of England and the development of the National Debt.

One sign of the changing times was the ending of the Merchant Adventurers' legal monopoly (often evaded in recent years) of the great English export trade in cloth. They tried to redeem their Puritan past by celebrating Charles II's restoration and then his coronation in 1661. The inhabitants of Dort were supplied with plenty of excise-free wine and an exhibition of burning tar-barrels and a crown full of fireworks. There were also 'countless' rockets which came down on to the market-place to the terror of those assembled there. But in 1668 there was no protest from Charles II when the States did not renew their privileges and an Act of 1689 officially opened the trade to all English merchants.[2] They now had sufficient experience of the commercial interchange not to need to channel it through a chartered company with its irksome regulations, though the Fellowship remained in existence until 1751, when the last sur-vivors were granted exemptions from taxation which were to expire with their deaths. The Scots Staple at Veere retained its official status for longer, until 1799, but by the 1690s it was already in obvious decay: the coal which had become the principal export from the Firth of Forth was more easily marketable at Rotterdam for the nearby breweries.[3]

By the end of the seventeenth century a change had begun in the nature of English cloth exports, for they no longer consisted mainly of unfinished cloth as at the time of the Cockayne project. The Dutch techniques had been learned, and this, together with the lack of native sources of raw wool and a high level of wages, led to the decline of the Leiden cloth industry. At the same time a new form of English cloth developed. Most of the inhabitants of Exeter and Tiverton were employed in the making of serge, which went to London and to Holland, whence German linens bleached in Haarlem came in return. When William III came to Exeter in 1688 the bishop and dean might not be there to receive him, but he could expect a welcome from those associated with the Dutch in commercial enterprise and not least from a colony of Dutch merchants themselves. These merchants' houses can still be seen in the outport of Topsham from which the serges were exported.

Anglo-Dutch trade was also carried on in other commodities besides textiles. Corn and malt were sent from the ports of East Anglia, with clover, coleseed and turnips coming back across the North Sea. English exports predominated over imports, and included increasing re-exports of raw sugar and tobacco from the plantations. In 1680, indeed, the complaint was made that 'the Dutch coming to be furnished with our sugars and dyeing stuffs, much cheaper than the English (as being charged not with half the customs) have been by that means able to set up and beat us out of the foreign trade of baked sugars, of which they bake and vend above twenty times the quantity the English do.'[4] In the same way the Dutch led in treated (as opposed to leaf) tobacco, and in 1706 were supplying it to the English navy. But their technical lead was not permanent, especially when the industries dealt, as they generally did, in raw or partly finished materials from other states like England which could cut them off or impose protective tariffs in the interest of their own products. Using the 'Dutch loom' as it was called in Lancashire, it was claimed that one man could do the work of four, and London weavers were still rioting against it in 1675, but by the 1680s it was a common sight in Manchester. The loom had really ceased to be 'Dutch', and the eighteenth-century technological inventions in the textile industries were English.[5] At first England imported earthenware made in Holland from English china clay; but in 1676 Temple patronized a Dutch potter, John Ariens van Hamme, who came to England in return for privileges for 'the art of making tiles, porcelain, and other earthenware after the way practised in Holland'. At the time of the Revolution the brothers Elers from Amsterdam introduced the method of salt-glazing, and made their red ware near Burslem. Though they probably later moved to Chelsea, it is from this period that the Staffordshire potteries date, and once the industry had been established the native supplies of china clay gave it an advantage.[6]

Gradually the English also freed themselves from their earlier dependence on Dutch shipping (though in 1714 Mandeville, author of the *Fable of the Bees* and himself a native of Dort, wrote that the Dutch had more shipping than the English and in 1721 it was still said that most trade with France was carried on in Dutch ships). By about 1676 the purchase of foreign ships for the timber trade (in spite of the principle laid down in the Navigation Acts) came to an end, and in 1698 Davenant, another writer on commercial affairs, said that English ships were being built on the Humber and Trent as cheaply as the Dutch. Increasing quantities of coal went from Newcastle and Sunderland to Holland, and the imposition of an extra duty on the export of coal in foreign ships gave native shipowners a big advantage over their foreign competitors. So too did the stipulation that an export bounty on corn would be paid only if it was shipped in British vessels. This and the steady pressure of the Navigation Acts, especially in the trade to and from the plantations, inevitably had their effects. As late as 1778 there were still more Dutch ships entering the Sound than British, but it could no longer be said that generally British shipping cut a poor figure beside the Dutch.[7]

Complaints about the Dutch fishing industry were also much more muted after the reign of Queen Anne. It had in any case suffered severely from the depredations of the French privateers in the wars of 1689–97 and 1702–13, and it never reached the old level again.

Dutchmen and Danes were apparently recruited in some numbers to sail on British fishing-boats, and there was no urgent financial stringency leading the British government to call upon their allies to pay for a licence to fish. As for whaling, in the eighteenth century the large British ships were able to penetrate further into Arctic waters than ships built for the shallower waters round the Dutch coast; and they used mechanical harpoons.[8]

For seventeenth-century Scotland the trade with the United Provinces was relatively even more important than the Anglo-Dutch trade was for England. In the early part of the century half the shipping from Leith alone went to Holland, and in addition there was the trade from Fife to Amsterdam in coal, salt and building stone from Longannet quarry. In the later part of the century more shipping out of the Firth of Forth still went to Holland than anywhere else, even England; and a special clause in the Act of Union was needed to cope with the number of Scottish ships (overestimated by the English) owned or part-owned by Dutchmen. In return for their products the Scots received a miscellany of goods, from church bells and luxury textiles, to bricks, pantiles and 'groceries' like raisins and onions.[9]

At the end of the seventeenth century the United Provinces were still England's principal export market, taking goods valued at about £1,500,000 out of total English exports valued at about £3,500,000. They were no longer responsible for England's principal imports, providing goods valued only at £500,000 out of £3,500,000, but this was because Dutch goods had been passed by cargoes coming across the Atlantic from the plantations. They remained England's trading partners in Europe, but now Englishmen were on much better trading terms. In many cases the connection was a personal one: younger sons or brothers of the head of the firm in one country visited the other. One partner might visit Amsterdam when the linens were received from the Haarlem bleacheries, to do a year's buying; Dutch firms sent brokers to the East India Company's sales in London. Some English merchants, and the Scotsman Andrew Russell, settled in Rotterdam to carry on trade there; Amsterdam merchants set up branches of the firm in London (where the possibility of evading the Navigation Acts was an additional incentive) and settled in London or Exeter. An intimate correspondence was carried on between merchants on the two sides of the North Sea, and in many cases English merchants wrote in Dutch. Presents were exchanged. The De Neufvilles of Amsterdam traded with more than fifty export houses in London.[10]

As the eighteenth century proceeded, Anglo-Dutch trade declined, both relatively and to a certain extent even in absolute terms. On the eve of the War of American Independence British exports to the United Provinces were valued only at a million, out of total exports of £14,800,000, while imports were now £400,000 out of £11,400,000. To these figures, it is true, something must be added to cover smuggling, another kind of co-operative enterprise which spread greatly in the period, particularly in tea; but this does not much alter the picture of the proportions involved. In part the decline was simply due to the great expansion of British trade to other destinations, but this in itself partly signified, for instance, direct British shipments of cloth to Germany and Spain, without using the Dutch as middle-men. Similarly, colonial goods were re-exported directly. Just as English cloth no longer needed dyeing in Holland, so the rise of bleaching industries in northern Germany meant that linens could come direct from Hamburg and Bremen instead of coming by way of Haarlem. At the same time the linen industry began to grow in Ulster, with the encouragement of William III himself through the agency of Louis Crommelin, a Huguenot who came by way of Holland where he had seen the bleacheries of Haarlem. As a result, fashionable gentlemen ceased to choose the linen of Holland for their shirts.[11] For such reasons as these, Dutch firms and the Dutch colony in London transferred their attention more and more from profits made from the exchange of goods to those possible from investments, particularly in the British public funds. By the middle of the eighteenth century these investments totalled several times more than the total annual value of British exports to, and imports from, the United Provinces together.

The import of Dutch capital was not new. The first joint stock of the English East India Company included the large sum of £4,000 (equivalent to over a million today) from an Amsterdammer. Dutchmen, including prominent men like Reynier Pauw and Jacob

Cats, invested in the drainage of Hatfield Level and the Fens, knowing from experience at home what profits could be made from such schemes. In 1668 a single Dutchman invested £13,000 in the draining of the Isle of Axholme. In the middle of the century Thomas Violet put the foreign capital in England, which must have been largely Dutch, at £3,000,000. In 1669 a parliamentary committee on the decay of trade was told, more reasonably, that four London goldsmiths, including one with the Dutch-sounding name of Vandeput, had £400,000 of Dutch money in their hands, and lent it out at rates exceeding those current in Holland. It is not possible to tell how accurate these estimates were, but even if they were exaggerated, the very fact that they seemed credible to contemporaries is significant.[12]

English pamphleteers also pointed out the advantages to their Dutch competitors of the Bank of Amsterdam, emphasized the low rates of interest which resulted, and clamoured for the establishment of a bank in England. During the Protectorate Samuel Lambe argued that the bank 'brings down their interest of money to 3 or 4 l. per cent, at which rate I know at present many thousand pounds there let out, in a parcel, in ready money, which the Dutch do often deliver by exchange for London, and there the same takers at interest out of the banks may let it out again in England at 6 l. per cent, formerly at 8 per cent....' Money from the banks, he suggested, made it possible for Dutch merchants, through their agents in England, to buy up commodities at the times of year when they were cheapest.[13] Others who made the same point about banks and low interest were Benjamin Worsley (in *The Advocate*), Henry Robinson, Francis Cradock and Josiah Child, much of whose *Brief Observations concerning Trade and Interest of Money* (1688) made the low interest from Dutch banks into the *causa causans* of Dutch commercial success. Governments were not indifferent to the successes of Dutch financial techniques (and the excise tax which contributed so much to parliamentary success in the Civil War was probably imitated from the Dutch). They had the Bank of Amsterdam, which was founded on the municipal credit of that city, as an example to follow. But between the outbreak of the Civil War and the Revolution circumstances made public credit so poor that there was no possibility of founding a bank upon it. In 1665 Sir George Downing's scheme to encourage lending to the state, as deposits in the Bank of Amsterdam made possible loans to the government of the Dutch Republic, foundered on the collapse of Charles II's finances at the end of the decade.

It was the Revolution of 1688 and the long and expensive French wars which followed it that made a 'financial revolution'[14] both necessary and possible, with Dutch aid. William III's armies had to be paid, fed, clothed and transported on a scale greater than ever before, and much of this had to be done through the agency of people he had already employed in the Low Countries. He had already used the services of one Sephardic Jew in the Republic, Francisco Lopez Suasso, who made a crucial loan of two million guilders for the Glorious Revolution. When in the 1690s William crossed to and from the mainland (that is, twice a year) the Suasso household had a place in the first following boat. Antonio Alvarez Machado and Isaac Pereira were responsible for provisions, both in the Low Countries and in Ireland. Machado, who accompanied William to Ireland and was still an army contractor in the time of the War of the Spanish Succession, was connected with the family of Medina and sons. This was the family to which Sir Solomon Medina, the first Jew to receive a knighthood (from William III), had belonged: he too had helped in the financing of the Revolution.[15]

To the Dutch merchants in London, clustered round Austin Friars, was therefore added a group of Sephardic Jews from Amsterdam whose synagogue was at Bevis Marks from 1702.[16] From these two communities came many merchants and contractors, and from them and their connections in the United Provinces eventually came many investments in the public funds. Though Parliament was more generous in supporting the French wars than at any previous time, loans were needed and the foundation of the Bank of England in 1694 effectively converted what had been a royal into a national debt, secured by parliament. The Bank at last met the needs which had been satisfied in the Dutch Republic by the Bank of Amsterdam, and its existence encouraged the development of a similar market in securities, stock-jobbing and speculation, using techniques worked out in Amsterdam, from which the Stock Exchange eventually developed. At the same time the depredations of French privateers in two wars encouraged the English, following the Dutch lead, to develop marine insurance.

Down to the present century a chair of Divinity at Utrecht University still included original Bank stock amongst its endowments.[17] But after an initial spurt it appears that Dutch investment in Bank stock declined for some years, perhaps in part because there was an element of risk in it as long as the Hanoverian succession was not assured. Dutch investors and their London attorneys at first preferred life annuities (themselves based on Dutch example), lotteries and short-term speculation. However, it has been estimated that by 1700 credits backed by the States-General totalled about one million pounds, in addition to which there were private credits and contracts with Dutch financial houses and victualling firms. In the increased need for advances of money in the War of the Spanish Succession and the enhanced speculation which resulted, the unpopular 'moneyed interest' included Dutchmen like Joost or Sir Justus Beck. The latter became Director of the Bank of England in 1710, and was an agent for Dutch investors and a dealer in Bank stock.[18]

The establishment of the Protestant succession and the failure of the Jacobite rebellion of 1715 further encouraged Dutch investors. And the emergence of an international money market did indeed make the South Sea Bubble crisis in 1720 a Dutch as well as a British one. In London the secretary of the South Sea Company, Conrad de Gols, was a Dutch immigrant. In Amsterdam too there was a wave of company promotions, some serious (for instance in insurance) and others frivolous: Englishmen and Scots appeared in the subscription lists. It was important for dealers in the Kalverstraat to know how London prices were faring, and by July 1720 there was a regular 12-hour relay of messages between Harwich and Hellevoetsluis. It was said that some fishing-smacks left Dutch ports and disappeared over the horizon, only to return immediately with false stories to influence prices. The inevitable crash affected speculators in both countries. In London, Sir Justus Beck was amongst those bankrupted, with debts to the value of £347,000; and Sir Theodore Janssen (born in France but of Dutch stock), a director of the South Sea Company who had been knighted for his services to William III, was an obvious scapegoat by virtue of his surname. He was expelled from the House of Commons and allowed to keep a mere pittance of £50,000 from his fortune of £243,000. One of his large family, Stephen Theodore Janssen, nevertheless built up his own fortune, became Lord Mayor in 1754, was bankrupted in 1756, and survived to become City Chamberlain. It was not always an age of stability for individuals. In Amsterdam 'the fall of their stocks has ruined many of their former merchants; and stopping of payment there hath been as much in fashion as with us'. As a result, Moses Haasverberg's English coffee house, where Englishmen read the London papers over 'English elixir' (Epsom salts) and other British drinks, was sacked and burned.[19]

Yet the crash did not bring about a severe loss of confidence among Dutch investors, as did the contemporary failure of Law's Mississippi Company in France. On the contrary, Dutch investments in British government securities had for the first time become really substantial by 1723-4, and they went on increasing for the next fifty years. An important factor in this growth must have been the number of agents and attorneys in the Dutch community in London, who could give accurate and speedy information about the financial situation to encourage investors in the United Provinces. Indeed, this may have been the reason why Dutch investors in English stock seem to have acted prudently and cautiously in the Bubble year.

The outstanding Dutch financiers in London were Sir Matthew Decker (Governor of the East India Company, member of parliament, and Sheriff of Surrey), and above all the brothers Gerard and Joshua van Neck, the sons of the paymaster of the Republic's land forces who had settled in England (leaving four other brothers in the United Provinces: an attorney-general, a town pensionary, a professor and a burgomaster). Of all the Dutch financiers, the Van Necks were the most successful in making the transition into British society. Joshua's daughter married a Walpole, and he passed a large country estate at Heveningham to a younger Joshua, who became the owner of a most un-Dutchlike country house, and Lord Huntingfield in the Irish peerage in 1796. The elder Joshua was the largest underwriter for the government's loan of eight million pounds in the *annus mirabilis* of 1759, in which a series of successes against France included the capture of Canada. He undertook to raise one million of the funds required. The noted financier Sampson Gideon made similar use of his connection with Dutch Jewish brokers. Two other important families were the Vansittarts, who after moving to Danzig came to England in about 1670, and the Barings, whose family originated with a Lutheran pastor at Bremen, and moved to England by way of Groningen in connection with the West Country cloth trade.

These, however, were only the most prominent names. Numbers of attorneys carried on a living by making investments for Dutchmen of different backgrounds. A sample of 200 Dutch stockholders had 56 agents with powers of attorney, 12 of them specialists and many Dutch. A majority of investors were merchants, but they also included clergymen, doctors, and public officials, as well as women, schools, orphanages, universities and churches, all seeking a safe investment with a return which was rather more than Dutch rates. The extra yield was not as great as it had been in the previous century; on the other hand, the profits from investments in the British funds, unlike those in the Dutch, were not liable to tax. Between 1694 and 1726 there were 102 Dutch Jewish investors in Bank stock, and there was also a significant number of Dutch Huguenot investors.[20]

The question remains how great Dutch investment was in proportion to the whole of the National Debt. Not surprisingly, contemporaries over-estimated it. Two estimates of 1723 and 1737 put Dutch investments in the funds at £10,000,000 and in 1776 (after two expensive wars) another estimate, attributed to Lord North, put them at £59,000,000 out of a total of £143,000,000 or about three-sevenths of the whole. This is likely to be too high. The most reliable calculation is probably that of Dickson for the year 1750. Of the nominal capital of £35,336,605 covering Bank stock, East India stock, and South Sea annuities old and new, or about half the National Debt, he calculates Dutch holdings at £5,391,645 or 15 per cent. (Taking Bank stock alone, the proportion of Dutch holdings is much higher – £3,263,044 out of £10,780,000, or about 30 per cent.) The Dutch contribution to the other half of the National Debt is likely to have been smaller, and Dr Dickson's final conclusion is that an estimate of 12 per cent of the whole of the National Debt is nearer the mark. Of course there were other private speculations as well. Contemporaries supposed that there were large Dutch investments in mortgages and in various enterprises, but it is impossible to quantify this.[21]

Many British people at the time looked askance on this Dutch involvement. The National Debt was not popular in any case, and the fact that some of it was held by Dutchmen, even if it was not as much as popularly believed, was an extra inducement to adopt a device like a sinking fund in order to liquidate it. More modern financial opinion has tended to minimize the sums leaving the country in interest paid to foreigners. Instead it has emphasized the part played by Dutch capital in the superior credit which gave the British such an advantage over the French in the wars of 1739–48 and 1756–63. The financial connection between London and Amsterdam was obviously also important in the remitting of subsidies to allies in Austria and Prussia, and in the payment of the British forces in Germany. If the total Dutch contribution to the National Debt were 12 per cent, or £8,500,000 out of £70,000,000, this is still a far from negligible sum. It represents not only a far higher amount than the total value of British exports to and imports from Holland (less than £2,000,000) but an amount which the ministers of Louis XV would have coveted. The importance of Dutch money to the development of British industry, by releasing funds which would otherwise have been needed for government loans, cannot easily be estimated.

For the Dutch, too, the connection was important. It made it possible for investors, and therefore to some extent those dependent upon them, to have a more comfortable lifestyle than they would otherwise have had in a time of declining revenue from industry and trade, until the outbreak of the Fourth Anglo-Dutch War in 1780 led to the undermining of their prosperity. On the other hand it has been said that investment in the public funds of Great Britain brought in safe and steady returns instead of being available for riskier enterprises which might have brought more growth. This is possible, but in a world of increasingly protectionist states, and without the assistance of any native resources except butter and cheese, as one pamphleteer expressed it, Dutch industry and trade were in any case likely to be in some difficulties. It is by no means clear that extra supplies of capital, even if investors had been prepared to supply it, would have solved the root problem.

If Dutch agents and financiers operated on the London money market, it was also true that both Englishmen and Scots operated in the United Provinces. By the 1750s a third of the names of depositors in the Bank of Rotterdam were English, Scots or Irish.[22] In Amsterdam two banking firms in particular may be mentioned. The Cliffords originated from a Lincolnshire vicar; their firm collapsed resoundingly in 1772–3. The Hopes had a longer career. The precise connection between the bankers and the Scots earls of Hopetoun is not clear, but they addressed one another as cousin. Archibald, the father of the two brothers who were the real founders of the banking firm, was christened in the Scots church at Rotterdam in 1664 and became a member of the thriving Scots community. Like many Dutchmen, the Hopes found financial operations more profitable than trade in the middle of the eighteenth century. The two financial crises at Amsterdam in 1763 and 1772–3, like the South Sea Bubble crisis of 1720, illustrate the interlinking of the two money markets. In 1763 London bankers, including the Bank of England, went to the rescue of their Dutch correspondents, and in 1772, although the Cliffords had been insolvent for some time, their fall was caused by ill-calculated speculations in British East India stock. The crisis in Amsterdam was preceded by one in England and Scotland; Anglo-Dutch trade was paralyzed and six big London houses suspended payment. The crisis was solved not by any action in Amsterdam but by the action of the Bank of England in permitting the withdrawal of large amounts of specie for sending to Holland: its new regulation on discount at the same time was much criticized there.[23]

Anglo-Dutch commerce and finance did not recover from the fourth war between the two countries in 1780–4. Dutch investors preferred investments in the United States, and Britain was by now able to stand on its own feet without the same need for financial assistance. The invasion which made the Dutch Republic a dependency of France after 1795 only completed the process. By the years 1807–10 it seems that only about £20,000,000 out of an inflated

National Debt of well over £500,000,000 was in foreign ownership. This was quite a different order of importance from that previously occupied by Dutch investment.[24] The Hopes had fled back to England before the French armies in 1794, and two years later 'Thomas Hope of Amsterdam' was painted wielding a most unlikely-looking cricket bat. Though the firm resumed operations after the Treaty of Amiens, it was to deal with loans to governments other than the British.

In the same way, even before the French revolutionary wars, Anglo-Dutch trade had shrunk to occupy a relatively far smaller place than in its heyday. It was no longer indispensable to Britain, though its interruption under Napoleon's Continental System, which banned British goods, was a severe blow to the Dutch. Even the lead in technical invention which had belonged to the Dutch had passed to the British by 1776. The brothers Thompson from Matlock in Derbyshire, in association with Pieter Hohenpijl who had connections with the English colony at Rotterdam, tried to introduce machinery for spinning into Holland within ten years of Arkwright's discovery of the water-frame. Both Newcomen's and Watt's steam engines were introduced for drainage in a reversal of what had been a Dutch speciality. However, none of these British inventions was taken into general use at this time.[25] Whether the process of mechanization would have gone further in Holland had political developments not broken the connection we cannot be sure. What is certain is that after the Industrial Revolution economic relations between the two states, one of them much larger and with far greater industrial resources than the other, had to be built upon a quite different footing from before.

CHAPTER NINE

The Exchange of Ideas: Religion, Free Thought and Science

For English scholars of the seventeenth century, the Dutch Republic was where the best maps and uncensored books (including their own, either in the original or in translation) were published in larger numbers than in their own country. It was the home of a great European university, Leiden, as well as Utrecht and others of lesser fame (for each province wanted its own); at these there were many theologians and Latin scholars who were well known in their day. It was in particular the native country of four authors of European-wide reputation or notoriety – Erasmus, Arminius, Grotius and Spinoza – but not of poets, playwrights or writers of literature in the vernacular who were much known outside Dutch frontiers. It was the home of lenses and microscopes, of four well-known individual scientists – Simon Stevin, Christiaan Huygens, Leeuwenhoek and Swammerdam – (but not of any equivalent of the Royal Society or the Académie des Sciences) and of one great man, Boerhaave, whose writings were in chemistry and botany but whose fame was as a teacher of medicine. It was a place of refuge for scholars and others whose ideas made them out of favour with the English government. It was the home of correspondents with whom the latest ideas and news about books could be exchanged, and from the 1680s of journals in which they were reviewed. It was the second home of Locke, Furley and the philosopher Earl of Shaftesbury, as it was of Bayle and Le Clerc, and for all these it provided the freest atmosphere to be found. For the Scots too the Republic was all of these things; but their theological contacts were much more with orthodox Calvinists than with the Arminians whom some of the English preferred. Scots students carried Boerhaave's medical training back to found the Edinburgh medical school, and others went to Utrecht for education in Roman law. For the Scots the United Provinces were pre-eminently their window on to the culture of the Continent.

For Dutch scholars England did not have the same advantages. They did not need a place of publication for their books in the same way, nor, after the Revolt, did they have to escape from an illiberal political or ecclesiastical authority. Even after the Synod of Dort, Arminians did not come to England in any large numbers, probably realizing that they could not expect preferment from James I, and from the 1630s they were indulged in the United Provinces themselves. Dutch students did not go to Oxford and Cambridge in the same numbers as English students went to Leiden, though some prominent Calvinists did visit William Perkins, the best-known Puritan theologian at the beginning of the century; Arminius's opponent Gomarus visited both universities. From the Restoration the attraction which took Nonconformists to Leiden had no counterpart to bring Dutchmen to an Anglican and episcopalian university. Though British scholars were invited to chairs at Leiden and Utrecht in the early years of those universities there was little movement in the other direction. Yet devotional literature in English had much to offer, and books were translated into Dutch, from *Religio Medici* to *Pilgrim's Progress* and beyond. The approach of the group of scholars generally known as the Cambridge Platonists to religion had much in common with that of the Remonstrants (or Arminians). English literature seems at first to have been not much better known to Dutchmen than Dutch literature was to the English. However, a knowledge of the English language spread more quickly amongst the Dutch than the Dutch language amongst the English, and from the end of the century the United Provinces was the channel through which a knowledge of Shakespeare and Milton, as well as Locke and Newton, spread to the Continent. As for Scotland, in spite of its ancient universities it was too remote to be of much interest to

Dutchmen, though Scots professors, usually of Calvinist theology, were encouraged to come to them.

Of these themes, it is appropriate to begin with maps, for just as the Dutch tended to monopolize the carrying trade and put so much energy into voyages across the seas to the East Indies and other destinations, so they led the way in maps and charts. After the Plantins' move northwards from Antwerp to escape from the Spaniards, there was a great succession of producers of maps. The two best known were Blaeu and Hondius, whose shop in Amsterdam Evelyn went out of his way to visit, and whose collections included maps of English counties. Two Dutchmen engraved the maps of Camden, Saxton and Speed. But the maps of greatest utilitarian value were the 'rutters' and 'waggoners' upon which seamen relied for navigation. The 'waggoners' were so-called by the English after Lucas Wagenaer, whose *Spieghel der Zeevaert*, first published by Christopher Plantin in 1584–5, consisted of charts of the coasts of Europe. Its value was so quickly appreciated in England that a translation, made by Anthony Ashley, Clerk to the Privy Council, appeared within four years, and 'waggoners', suitably brought up to date, remained the basic charts for two centuries.

If Dutch maps attracted connoisseurs like Evelyn as well as sailors and merchants, books were indispensable to scholars. Whereas printing in England in the early modern period was confined to London and the two university cities of Oxford and Cambridge, in the United Provinces there were booksellers and printers in all the large towns. There were said to be some 200 in 1675; a little later there were 273 in Amsterdam. Whereas in England (apart from the Civil War period) books had first to be submitted to a censor in the government or church establishment until the Licensing Act was allowed to lapse in 1695, there was no comparable censor in the United Provinces. On comparatively rare occasions material which was particularly obnoxious, and which usually related to foreign governments, might get printers into trouble with the authorities. However, penalties were light and easily evaded, as we have seen in chapter three. An excellent paper industry (which England, as usual, had to copy) gave plentiful supplies of good and cheap paper. There was no language problem, since in the seventeenth century Latin was still the *lingua franca* of scholarship, though the steadily increasing numbers of books appearing in Dutch included many translations of Puritan devotional books, as well as James I's collected works. Such printers as the Elseviers led the way in providing good, clear type, and not merely of the Roman kind which became orthodox: the special type devised to suit Leiden University's interest in oriental languages was bought up by the Oxford University Press in the eighteenth century. Until then English printers acknowledged the superiority of Dutch presses, Dutch type-foundries, and Dutch ink.

Among the early printers there was one notable Englishman, Thomas Basson, who arrived in Leiden in 1584 and enjoyed Leicester's patronage before settling down to a long career of publications for a university clientele. His work included translations and an Anglo-Dutch textbook.[1] With the exception of the Elseviers, individual Dutch printers were less important than the fact that somewhere a printer could always be found for anything, however unorthodox. The historian of Unitarianism, in a chapter entitled 'Holland, the gateway for Socinianism into England', has described how these ideas were spread partly by personal contacts (Bartholomew Legate, the last heretic to be burned at Smithfield in 1612, visited Holland in the course of his business as a cloth merchant) and partly by imbibing ideas in print there. At Leiden many English souls were said to take 'a cup too much of Belgic wine, whereby their heads have not only grown dizzy in matters of less moment, but their whole bodies stagger in the fundamentals of their religion'.[2] The most notoriously heterodox English thinker of the century, Thomas Hobbes, had his *De Cive* (previously privately printed in a limited edition at Paris) published by the Elseviers in Amsterdam. It sold out rapidly, with hundreds of copies still required, and a French translation was published by Blaeu in 1649. When Hobbes found it impossible to get a licence for printing his Latin works in England after the Restoration, he reverted to Blaeu, and his *Opera* (1668) included the first Latin translation of *Leviathan*. It is right to add that Hobbes was denounced by the ecclesiastical and municipal authorities in Holland, and that the Dutch translation was banned by the States of Holland in 1674. The great Dutch philosopher Spinoza did not think it wise to publish his heretical works under his own name. But it is not easy to be sure that such unorthodoxies could have been published elsewhere in Europe, and official bans did not prevent the books from being read, by English as well as Dutch scholars.[3]

Apart from the controversies around the doctrines of Arminius, the seventeenth-century Dutch authors most read in England were certainly Grotius and Spinoza. The former's *Mare Liberum*, in defence of the freedom of the seas, was read in order to contradict it rather than because it was persuasive. His *De Jure Belli et Pacis*, which was to have a longer fame and to earn for him the title of 'the founder of international law', was written while he was in exile for political reasons, but betrays all the signs of his Dutch background. The same could be said of his *De Veritate Religionis Christianae*, which is less well known now, but was translated several times and much read by the Englishmen who shared its liberal and rational outlook in the late seventeenth century. Spinoza, on the other hand, was at first regarded as objectionable for his Christology and his view of the Scriptures; he was regarded as an extreme Hobbist and was opposed, for instance, by the Cambridge Platonists. It was only gradually that his rationalist metaphysics became more acceptable, but even then few identified themselves with him. Other well-known authors were the Latinist, poet and critic, Daniel Heinsius, and 'the Pope of Utrecht', Gisbertus Voetius. Heinsius's theories on poetry and tragedy may have been known to Ben Jonson and Milton and were certainly read by Dryden, only to be rejected at length in his *Essay of Dramatic Poesy*.[4] Voetius promulgated an ultra-Calvinist orthodoxy from his chair of theology at Utrecht which made him an authority to many Puritans.

All the above wrote in Latin. Englishmen paid little attention to poets who wrote in Dutch and the greatest of them, Vondel, was largely unnoticed. About a century ago, however, the theory was put forward by Pattison, Sir Edmund Gosse and the historian Edmundson that Vondel may have influenced Milton. His epic *Lucifer* (to which Calvinist preachers were hostile) was published in 1654, and it is known that Milton had learned Dutch from Roger Williams, who was in London from 1651 to 1654, and that he had friends who could have kept him informed about current controversies in the United Provinces. (In his *Ready Way to establish a free Commonwealth* (1660) Milton praised the system of 'a standing senate' in Dutch city councils.) Edmundson listed parallel passages in *Paradise Lost* and in *Lucifer*, as also in *Paradise Regained* and *Adam in Ballingschap* (1664), and in *Samson Agonistes* and *Samson* (1660). Most recent Dutch critical opinion has been that the resemblance is simply due to the fact that both men had tackled a subject, the fall of man, which was of obvious interest to many in the controversies over predestination in the seventeenth century. Grotius, whom Milton had met in Paris in 1638, was himself writing a Latin drama, *Adamus Exul*, around that time.[5]

If books were the most obvious means of scholarly interchange, universities came next. British students went to sit at the feet of Voetius in Utrecht and Ames in Franeker, but most of all they went to Leiden, described by Milton as 'that famous university and renowned commonwealth, which has been as it were a sanctuary of liberty'. Founded in 1575, within a year of the raising of the siege by the Spaniards, the university knew how to attract good professors and students. Professors had good salaries and facilities, and students were able to register without having to swear any oath of allegiance to any official religion, Protestant or Catholic. The inner man was attended to by eighty measures of wine and six barrels of beer annually for a guilder and a quarter, without excise duty. English-speaking students were the most numerous of the foreigners who went there before 1800, although the lectures were in Latin rather than English. It was the fact that they were in Latin which made attendance possible, for few knew Dutch. For obvious reasons, the number of English matriculations was especially high during the decade of the Civil War, when there were 300. Not all who matriculated remained to graduate; Evelyn moved on after only four days, and many went from one university to another in the course of their education. Conversely, after studying at Montpellier and Padua, Sir Thomas Browne spent a term or more at Leiden before gaining a Leiden degree.

Some Englishmen contrasted the university unfavourably with Oxford, because, being non-collegiate and having nothing comparable with Christ Church, it had 'scarce the face of an university', and because 'a small time and less learning will suffice to make one a graduate; nor are those formalities of habits and other decencies here', as they were in England.[6] What this meant in practice was that the curriculum was less traditional, the minimum period of study shorter, and life less regulated. But these were not disadvantages to many students, and amongst those who admired what they saw was the English ambassador, Sir Thomas Bodley, who may perhaps have taken the title Curator to apply to the librarian of his new foundation at Oxford.

Obviously most students went to study theology, but the repute of Daniel Heinsius has already been mentioned. The university's Hortus Botanicus was founded in 1587, the first in northern Europe. (Oxford's dates only from 1621 when it was founded by Sir Henry Danvers, later Earl of Danby, who had served under Maurice of Nassau and must have seen the garden at Leiden.) Leiden was also prominent in the study of oriental languages, Arabic, Chaldean, Syriac and Hebrew. Here there was an interchange with Oxford, though Jan van den Driessche, who became Regius Professor of Hebrew at Oxford, had actually been educated at Louvain. An unkind legend has it that the first Regius Professor of Hebrew at Glasgow, having no students, was sent to Holland to learn the language, and that when thereafter a Scots youth appeared to learn Hebrew, Chaldean or Syriac he was asked if he was a Scottish professor.[7] A far more popular subject, medicine, will be treated later, since Leiden reached the height of its fame for this in the early eighteenth century.

Though Leiden had lectures in botany and an astronomical observatory, when neither English university had one, the most important scientific contacts were outside the universities. The work of Christiaan Huygens (1629–95) in mathematics, physics and astronomy was much esteemed by Englishmen in the same fields, including Thomas Hobbes, though he disagreed with Newton on the subject of optics. In addition to his exchanges with some of the early luminaries of the Royal Society he (like his father) came to England three times. Though he compared London unfavourably with Paris (to which he had been attracted by Colbert) and found the English, as well as being reluctant to recognize the merits of foreigners, 'melancholic, the gentlefolk polite enough but not very sociable, the women very little conversable and not by any means so witty or so lively as in France', he was impressed by the Royal Society group. On his first visit his telescope was set up in the garden behind Whitehall and the Duke and Duchess of York came to look at the moon and stars.[8] The Dutch skill in lenses, this time in microscopy, was also admired in the work of Leeuwenhoek and Swammerdam. The former, like Huygens, published many of the papers communicating his discoveries in the *Philosophical Translations* of the Royal Society, and was eventually made a Fellow.

From 1662 English Nonconformists had a powerful additional reason for studying at Leiden University. The restoration of Charles II to the English throne was followed by a renewed attempt to impose Anglican conformity upon the Church, and the universities of Oxford and Cambridge, whose primary function was to train the clergy, did not escape the general pressure. The Act of Uniformity of 1662 not only made the use of the Book of Common Prayer compulsory, but it effectively excluded non-Anglicans from the universities. As a result, the English Secretary of State was told in 1670 that accommodation in Leiden was over-taxed by the influx of Nonconformist students. In Scotland, too, the replacement of the presbyterian kirk by an episcopalian church had a similar effect in encouraging a stream of students to Dutch universities.

There were good reasons for many others to take refuge in the Dutch Republic. By doing so, they could avoid the effects of acts of 1664 and 1670 forbidding religious meetings not in accordance with the Book of Common Prayer. They could also escape from the effects of the Licensing Act of 1662 which reimposed a censorship. Those whose political past in the Cromwellian period made them particularly obnoxious to the new government of Charles II had a specially urgent reason for flight. Except for three regicides, they benefited from the protection or the careful neglect of the authorities. An example of this was when the magistrates of Rotterdam allowed Colonel Joyce, who had taken Charles I into his custody in 1647, to evade the official request of the English ambassador for his extradition in 1668. After the failure of the Whigs to secure James's exclusion from the succession in the crisis of 1678–81, a further stream of refugees sought to escape the reaction which followed. In old age, the author of the *Delenda est Carthago* speech, the first Earl of Shaftesbury, was one of the fugitives to Amsterdam and was received, it is said, with the words *Carthago nondum deleta*. The editor, theologian and publicist Le Clerc, praised Amsterdam for its hospitality: 'May this town ever remain a safe sanctuary to the innocent.' But the greatest English scholar who took advantage of Dutch freedom was undoubtedly Shaftesbury's former secretary, John Locke, who fled there to join the Whig plotters against the Stuarts, to study and to bring out his first publications. It was Le Clerc who persuaded Locke to contribute to his journal, the *Bibliothèque Universelle*, and it was in Gouda that his *Epistola de Tolerantia* was published in 1689; his ideas must have originated before he came to Holland, but they must have equally been fostered by his stay there.[9]

At various times there were coteries of English and Dutch scholars who met or corresponded with one another. The first of these was at Leiden in the earliest years of the Republic, when those literary humanistic circles round Janus Dousa (Jan van der Does, hero of the defence of the city against the Spaniards and a curator of the university) and the followers of Sir Philip Sidney, who gave his life for the rebel cause, came together in an association of political sympathizers with literary interests.[10] The correspondence of Grotius with bishops Lancelot Andrewes and John Overall was also one of men of a similar intellectual outlook, who had the opportunity to meet when Grotius was in London. Heinsius too exchanged letters with a number of Englishmen. A further correspondence was that between the Cambridge Platonists, More and Cudworth, and Arminius's Remonstrant successors, particularly Philippus van Limborch, Professor of Theology at the Remonstrant Seminary in Amsterdam, over the period 1667–87. Their liberal theologies had obvious affinities.[11] Van Limborch also kept up an important and life-long correspondence with Locke after the two men had met in Holland. As the editor of Arminius's successor, Episcopius, he shared Locke's hatred of religious persecution. Their letters to each other contain the same dislike of oppressive religious establishments, whether Anglican, Catholic or Calvinist, and the same belief in free thought, as well as what might be called senior common room gossip about books.

Others in the same circle were Le Clerc (minister in a Remonstrant church and later professor at the seminary, who knew English, dedicated books to Englishmen, and corresponded with many, including Bishop Berkeley) and Benjamin Furley, a Rotterdam merchant and Quaker.[12] As a young man Furley first went to Rotterdam in connection with the family linen business at Colchester (where Anglo-Dutch co-operation went back to Elizabethan times). Not only was he active in writing, translating and distributing Quaker pamphlets, but he built up a splendid library of 4400 scholarly works with a point of view which greatly appealed to John Locke, who resided frequently in his house in 1687–8. Another unorthodox thinker who lived for a time with Furley was the grandson of Locke's old master, best known by his later title of the third Earl of Shaftesbury, for whom the Dutch were 'that mother nation of liberty'. For the many radicals and free thinkers who visited Furley, however, the 'Republic of Letters' was also the present protectress of all those who tried to work out rational and liberal solutions to religious problems. It is not surprising that the scepticism of some contributed to the growth of eighteenth-century deism. For all, the possibilities of discussion and controversy were increased by the journals which freely reviewed scholarly books: Le Clerc's *Bibliothèque Universelle et Historique* (1686–97), the *Bibliothèque Choisie* (1703–13), the *Bibliothèque Ancienne et Moderne* (1714–27) and the *Boekzaal van Europe* (*1692–1702*), followed by *De Boekzaal van de geleerde wereld*. Another refugee who deserves mention – the States-General actually refused James's request for his surrender – was Gilbert Burnet, later Bishop of Salisbury. His preference was for The Hague, where he could be consulted on political questions by William, rather than Rotterdam or the other colonies of exiled plotters; but he too corresponded with Van Limborch and Le Clerc. In his case Dutch and Remonstrant influence contributed to his latitudinarianism rather than deism; and as someone protected by the descendants of rebels against Spain, it must have been difficult for him to believe in the doctrine of non-resistance to authority as he had once done. He found something to admire in rationalist Socinians, mystical Labadists and Cartesian philosophers, and his earlier sympathies with Arminianism were confirmed by his attraction to Van Limborch. 'One thing I drank in. I saw men of all persuasions ... so truly religious that I never think the worse of a man for his opinions.' He naturalized himself as a Dutch citizen, and took as his second wife a Dutch heiress of Scots descent before returning to England with the expedition of 1688. He sent his sons to be educated at Leiden.[13]

Burnet was the most famous Scotsman to visit the United Provinces in the seventeenth century, but there were many others, religious refugees and students. William Carstares was another famous refugee from the brutal political régime of Charles II's minister in Scotland, Lauderdale. He was much consulted by William III on Scots affairs both before and after the Revolution, and ended as Principal of Edinburgh University. Scots Covenanters could still find the English-speaking churches founded some generations earlier in Dutch cities, though there were now not as many as there had been. There was in fact a growing tendency for many even of the English churches, like the English Reformed Church of Amsterdam, to look to Scots Presbyterians for their clergy. Many, like the earlier English Puritans, criticized Dutch laxity over the Sabbath, publishing treatises *De causa Dei contra Anti-sabbaticos* to enlighten their hosts, and they disapproved of the dreadful Dutch practice of using organs, which even crept into the English Reformed Church at Amsterdam. Most returned to Scotland after 1689, but there were some who remained, and like many soldiers became gradually assimilated into Dutch society.[14]

For Scots Calvinists and students of theology, however, the United Provinces were not only a refuge in times of persecution but a means of contact with continental Calvinism over a much longer period. 'The manse of Veere became a theological clearing-house as well as the Scottish depot for continental merchandise,' and, as in commercial matters, Scotsmen soon looked further north. Although they read Van Limborch, they were attracted more to the theologians of the official Calvinist church than to the more liberal writers who appealed to Locke and his fellows. Some were 'Marrowmen', so-called because they studied at Leiden under Marckius, whose book was the *Medulla* or Marrow; others preferred Witsius of Utrecht. The influence of these theologians upon Scots Calvinism (as upon English Dissenting academies) persisted long after students of theology ceased to attend Dutch universities in any large numbers. Translations of Witsius continued to appear in the nineteenth century, and he still earned an entry in the eleventh edition of the *Encyclopaedia Britannica* (1911), though he is now largely forgotten. Even in the eighteenth century, however, many students who had to endure 'Dutch divinity' found it heavy, pedantic, and unrefreshed by new currents of thought – 'dull, Dutch and prolix' in the words of one of them.[15]

Scots also went to the United Provinces, and especially to Utrecht, to study Roman law. Amongst them were Boswell's father and Boswell himself, and although this was partly due to a family connection, they were following a well-established tradition. The early eighteenth century was also the period when students of medicine flocked to Boerhaave, in Leiden, in large numbers. These naturally included many English as well as Scots, but Boerhaave was of particular importance to the Scots because of the part played by his pupils in the foundation of the Edinburgh Medical School.

A century before Boerhaave, Leiden was already second only to Padua for would-be physicians. Many besides Sir Thomas Browne pursued their studies for some time there, including the Scots professor of philosophy at Leiden, Gilbert Jack, who both became an MD and wrote on epilepsy there. Englishmen had a particular incentive, for at Oxford and Cambridge it was necessary to read for a degree in arts before going on to study for one in medicine. In all a doctorate in medicine, following a bachelor's degree, would take 13 years. In Leiden it was possible to graduate more quickly, with more intensive teaching: a course might last between one and two years. It was also the case that from 1662 non-Anglicans (including Scots Presbyterians as well as Dissenters) were excluded from Oxford and Cambridge, and impelled towards Leiden and other foreign universities.

But it was also true that Leiden provided much better facilities. The Hortus Botanicus provided the means of studying the medicinal properties of plants. For twenty years Boerhaave was Professor of Botany (1709–29) and director of the botanical garden as well as Professor of Medicine. He published a catalogue of plants, and lectured systematically in the garden every morning from seven to nine o'clock, from February to July. The university also had a long tradition of anatomical teaching, based on the annual dissection of the corpse of a criminal in the anatomical theatre, at a time when this was by no means the usual European practice. The dissections would be held in December or January, the most suitable time of the year when there was no refrigeration. They lasted several days, during which lectures were discontinued, and they were public occasions to which the magistrates and members of the Surgeons' Guild were invited, and others could attend for a small fee. At other times skeletons of men and animals were exhibited.

Boerhaave's fame was built on this foundation. Evidently he was a truly great teacher. His lectures were popular with students who paid people to go early and reserve a place; they were published (sometimes in pirated editions) in the Latin in which they were delivered. But he was most famed for his clinical teaching. This form of teaching had been inaugurated in Padua, and the example was followed at Utrecht in 1636 and at Leiden in 1637 before it was part of the medical courses in any other country. However, it was in decline when Boerhaave took over and reinvigorated the practice. He was Professor of Clinical Medicine (in addition to his chairs in botany and chemistry) from 1714, and taught twice a week in St Cecilia's Hospital, half a century before there was a hospital at either Oxford or Cambridge.

It is not surprising that the number of English-speaking students doubled after Boerhaave's appointment as professor. There were 746 who matriculated at Leiden between 1700 and Boerhaave's death in 1738. Not all of these went on to graduate, and conversely some were people who already possessed medical degrees from elsewhere and were in search of additional experience. But it is remarkable that no fewer than 45 of Boerhaave's English-speaking pupils have entries in the *Dictionary of National Biography*. Most notable are those who founded the Edinburgh Medical School in 1726. John Monro, from whom it really derived, belonged to the pre-Boerhaave days at Leiden, but 'of the nine men ... following John Monro [including his son Alexander] all without exception had studied at Leiden under Boerhaave, though only one actually took his degree at Leiden.... There must be very few – if any – other examples in the history of medicine where *all* the members of a newly-founded faculty of medicine had been pupils of the same teacher.' Several presidents of the Royal College of Physicians of London, many of the early Glasgow physicians, and those connected with the College of Physicians of Dublin and Ireland, were also Leiden people. As in other spheres, Holland was noted for its splendid editions of medical books.[16]

Such contacts lost their importance with remarkable suddenness. Boerhaave had no outstanding successor, and the number of English-speaking students attracted to Leiden rapidly declined. One Scots visitor found only 22 British students (including John Wilkes) in Leiden in 1745. Nine years later Goldsmith complained that in 'all Leiden there are but four British students, all necessaries being so extremely dear and the professors so very lazy . . . that we don't much care to come hither'; and in another nine years Boswell found himself the only British student at Utrecht. In 1761 the Leiden magistrates resolved to end the English church they had supported there on the death of the current minister (who in fact lived for 47 more years!) because 'no English students any longer attend Leiden university, nor are there any English families'.[17] Yet Dissenters were still excluded from Oxford and Cambridge, although Dissenting academies were now well established. The decline in numbers may possibly have resulted from a decline in the use of Latin as the medium of instruction, combined with the absence of a leading figure like Boerhaave who might have induced people to overcome the problem of language. Underlying this trend was the fact that, just as the Dutch were ceasing to perform a vital function in the world of commerce, so they were losing their position in other ways. Just as the Irish were building up their own industry with the aid of a Dutch-trained immigrant, so the Scots were building up Edinburgh University to provide the education they needed in law and (with the aid of Leiden-trained doctors) in medicine. The British had exhausted what they could learn from the Dutch, and in the age of the Enlightenment were preferring to establish direct contact with the French.

It remains to be considered what the Dutch learned from the British, and what they contributed, as middlemen in ideas as well as commerce, to the diffusion of British culture on the Continent.

Dutch scholars visited England, as Voetius did, to meet fellow

Calvinist theologians, or like Grotius and Constantijn Huygens on diplomatic missions, but they did not (after the early refugees from Spain) reside there for long periods. Gomarus studied at both English universities, and in the 1630s some Dutchmen went to sit at the feet of Prideaux, the leading anti-Laudian and Professor of Divinity at Exeter College, Oxford. But on the whole there were fewer Dutch students at English universities than Englishmen in Holland, and presumably they were excluded altogether by the terms of the Act of Uniformity of 1662. Round 1600 there was some scholarly connection with Aberdeen. To take an example, the influential preacher and writer Willem Teellinck (1579–1629) visited St Andrews as a law student in 1600 before spending six months at Banbury and in London in 1604. He married an English wife, and expressed his gratitude to his British friends by helping in the building of a Reformed church at Middelburg, where he was pastor. It is difficult to weigh the significance of such scattered contacts as these, but it is certain that, for Dutchmen, contacts with English and Scots, either in the United Provinces or through correspondence, were more important. So, too, were translations of English books.

Amsterdam was generally regarded as the home of the sects *par excellence*. In view of this and its easy connection with London – not to mention the freedom of the press in the Republic – it might naturally be expected that the great outpouring of unorthodox ideas in England between 1640 and 1660 would have had its impact upon the Dutch as well. This subject needs fuller exploration and it remains possible that more influences would be shown up if a systematic account of the religious connections with Holland over the whole century were written. One new English sect, the Quakers, did regard the United Provinces as a mission-field, and the story of their reception in Holland is of some interest.

In 1655, and thus only a few years after the appearance of George Fox's movement, one of his followers, William Caton, arrived in Middelburg, where he was soon in trouble with the English Reformed congregation for interrupting their services. When it came to addressing the Dutch, there were immediate language problems, and at Rotterdam he was even obliged to speak in Latin, which was then rendered into Dutch. 'Alas how did we suffer for want of a good

William I, 'the Silent', leader of the Revolt of the Netherlands against Spain in the mid sixteenth century. Painting by A. Key.

Marriage of William, later William II, and Princess Mary, 1641, by Van Dyck.

William III, Prince of Orange and King of England, by Schalcken.

View of the bleaching greens at Haarlem in the second half of the seventeenth century, by Jacob van Ruisdael. Linen was bleached here for the important export trade to England.

(*Above left*) Kew Palace, dated 1631, showing the influence of Dutch style.

(*Below left*) Heveningham Hall, Suffolk, built in the classical English style in 1777 for the Anglo-Dutch financier, Sir Joshua Vanneck.

(*Right*) A chair in the style of Marot, the Huguenot architect and interior designer who worked for William III.

(*Below*) Two Dutch tiles from a set of four, showing oriental influences.

(*Above left*) The anatomical theatre, Leiden University, in 1610 in a print by J. C. Woudanus. Used to show the dissection of human corpses, it was the scene for the display of animal skeletons at other times.

(*Below left*) The philosopher John Locke (1632–1704), in a drawing by S. Brownover. Locke was much influenced by his stay in Holland.

(*Above*) The library at Leiden University in 1610, in a print by J. C. Woudanus.

A carving by Grinling Gibbons, the English woodcarver born in Rotterdam in 1648, from Lyme Park, Cheshire.

The device of the printer R. Schilders, showing a sixteenth-century press and printer at work.

interpreter,' he lamented on one occasion. At Middelburg, however, he was assisted by a young man rejoicing in the name of Humble Thatcher who knew Dutch. They found that there were, after all, limits to Dutch tolerance. Their attacks on paid clergy naturally made enemies, and when, perhaps under pressure from the English, disturbances led to their being taken before the magistrates, there were the usual disputes over their failure to pay respect by taking off their hats. The news that a fellow-Quaker, James Naylor, had entered Bristol on an ass like the Messiah did not help matters. Both Caton and Humble Thatcher were imprisoned, a colleague was sent to the house of correction for two years, and the Quaker William Ames (not to be confused with the earlier Puritan theologian of that name) was confined to Bedlam.

Yet this hostility to the Quakers gradually subsided. There were no difficulties in the United Provinces about the non-payment of tithes or non-attendance at the parish church to exacerbate matters. Converts were made, with the aid of the Dutch wives of English Quakers who interpreted for their husbands. Most of them came from the Mennonite Baptists (like Jacob Sewell, the son of a Kidderminster Brownist, and his wife, the parents of the Quaker historian and journalist of that name) or the unorthodox group of Collegiants. This group said that though they did not usually allow women to address them, they would make an exception in Mrs Sewell's case – until there was a bitter pamphlet warfare and a complete break between them and the Quakers in 1660. By 1677, when William Penn, the well-known Quaker founder of Pennsylvania, came over (himself the son, according to Pepys, of a 'fat, short, old Dutch-woman, but one that hath been heretofore pretty handsome') he spoke of well-attended meetings at Furley's house. There was evidently widespread interest in the sect and no hint of persecution.[18]

Far more influential for the development of Dutch pietism were English books. They included not only scholarly works written in Latin but translations into Dutch, which were much more numerous than translations from Dutch into English. Of 650 titles of new translations in a seventeenth-century checklist, some 75 to 80 per cent were religious writing, to which must be added ecclesiastical history, topical religious matter, and *Pilgrim's Progress* (of which there were nine editions between 1682 and 1699). Most of these books were devotional rather than dogmatic in character, but they ranged from the works of Perkins (26 editions over the whole of the century) to those of the Puritan Baxter, Archbishop Tillotson and Burnet. There were complaints of plagiarism by Dutch authors, who, according to an Anglican bishop 'in some of their theological treatises, have been as bold with the English sermons as with our fishing, and their robberies have been so manifest, that our Church ought to have reprisals against them as well as our merchants'. In the next century Watts, Doddridge, Whitefield and many others, including deists as well as opponents of deism, followed.[19]

Works in English on other than religious subjects were little known in the United Provinces, or for that matter on the Continent as a whole. There were educated Dutchmen who learned the language, notably the poet and scholar (and secretary to successive Princes of Orange) Constantijn Huygens, who translated Donne and whose library contained numbers of English books on a variety of subjects. Other such libraries are known; it has been said that 'the considerable influence of English literary fashions (in the sonnet and metaphysical poetry) upon the Dutch throughout the period is itself evidence of the interest in English among the educated'. English theatrical companies performed in English, and it was said that 'many young virgins fell in love with some of the players, and followed them from city to city, till the magistrates were forced to forbid them to play any more'.[20] On the other hand, when Charles, Prince of Wales, addressed the States-General to plead for his father's life in 1649 he could not be understood.

In so far as Dutchmen learned English before 1688, therefore, it was mostly for commercial and practical reasons and less frequently than French. The editors of the new journals at the end of the century wrote mainly in French, and it was possible for the editor of the *Nouvelles de la République des Lettres* to write: 'Who has heard of Spenser, Milton, Ben Jonson, Shakespeare?' Another reviewer drew up a long list of names, including Donne, Jonson, Milton, Rochester, Shakespeare, Spenser, Suckling and Waller, whom he described as 'English poets who do not touch us Dutchmen very much'.[21] Such gaps were not filled by translations or adaptations, as in the case of religious books. One play by Shakespeare was translated, in 1654. It was *The Taming of the Shrew*, rather curious in view of the supposed Dutch attitudes to women. Milton was known not for his poems but for his political controversy with Salmasius at Leiden over the execution of Charles I (conducted in Latin), and Van Limborch himself advised a publisher against bringing out the *De Doctrina Christiana* because of its supposed Arianism; there was no copy in Huygens's library.[22]

William III's acquisition of the English throne in 1689 was, however, the prelude to a change in the cultural as well as the political relationship between the two peoples. At the same time as the Dutch became increasingly subordinated to the political power of the English, and were equalled or later surpassed in economic strength, the passing of the Toleration Act (1689) and the lapsing of censorship (1695) meant that by degrees the Dutch no longer filled the same position in English intellectual life. Simultaneously, however, the Dutch developed an interest in everything to do with the affairs and the culture of their ally. This was reflected in the books published, translated and reviewed in the journals which occupied such an important place in the European scholarly world of this generation – Le Clerc's *Bibliothèque Universelle*, Sewell's *Boekzaal* and others. In this way knowledge of England was spread to Dutch and thence to European readers. Sewell, the historian of the Quakers, for instance, translated not only Penn but Sir Thomas Browne, Boyle, Burnet, Congreve, occasional poems by Prior, and Temple. There were 36 titles and 14 reprints of translations of 'speculative and philosophical prose', including Locke, between 1680 and 1700, and in the same period there were more works on travel, and on topical, historical and political subjects, than in the whole of the previous part of the century. There were also more and more reviews and announcements of books in the original English. Sewell was responsible not only for translations, but for a dictionary, too.[23]

In March 1715 an extraordinary embassy arrived in London which included two remarkable men who both became fellows of the Royal Society in the following months. The secretary was the scientist, 's Gravesande, who was as much responsible as any individual for the spread of Newtonian ideas to the Continent (Boerhaave was also a great admirer of his). The under-secretary to the embassy was Justus van Effen, who, it has been claimed, deserves to be regarded as the equal of Montesquieu and Voltaire 'as an active and able participator in the great movement of the eighteenth century which spread literature, and especially English literature, beyond national boundaries'. He translated Swift's *Tale of a Tub* and did much for the reputation of Addison (who had himself stayed in Holland); but it was the periodicals for which he was responsible that were most important. *Le Misanthrope*, which advertised English books, was the first periodical akin to the *Tatler* and *Spectator* on the Continent, published by Johnson, a bookseller of English descent at The Hague, and from 1731 to 1735 the *Hollandsche Spectator* followed, based on its obvious English model. In 1717 his *Dissertation sur la Poésie Anglaise* devoted ten critical pages to Shakespeare but acknowledged him as the Vondel of the English and for the first time gave eight pages to *Paradise Lost*. There were also many intriguing comments on the English and their manners, complaining of the same taciturnity of which Englishmen have accused the Dutch. He concluded that 'however much it (the English language) has been abused by foreigners as the scum of all languages, it remains a fact that provided it be well handled, it has no equal for expressing all subjects concisely'.[24]

As indicated by van Effen's own use of it, French became the dominant language of the Age of Enlightenment, but Samuel Richardson and Laurence Sterne were popular with Dutch readers, the latter so much so that there were 'Sterne clubs' whose members called one another by the names of characters in Sterne's books.[25]

It is clear that the Dutch influenced the British through scholarly and literary contacts. As we shall see in the next chapter, they also influenced them in other ways, particularly in their impact on British homes and gardens, and the paintings, furniture and plants which they contained.

CHAPTER TEN

The Exchange of Tastes: Houses, Gardens and their Contents

The simplest example of Dutch influence on English architecture is the Dutch gable, topping the façade of a brick building and concealing a steeply pitched and often pantiled roof. This style was originally devised to suit narrow frontages in Dutch towns, in a country where brick was a more plentiful and cheaper building material than stone (which had to be imported for the new Amsterdam town hall, now the palace on the Dam, from Longannet quarry in Fife). It was not primarily intended for royal palaces or for magnates' country mansions in acres of parkland. The so-called Kew Palace was built for the merchant Samuel Fortrey in 1631 and, rather less than palatial, passed a century later to Frederick Prince of Wales; it was used afterwards by the exiled stadholder William V. At places like Blickling and Raynham Hall in Norfolk, and Wollaton Hall in Nottinghamshire, the Dutch signs are unmistakeable; but landowners with pretensions in the eighteenth century usually preferred to stucco over the brick or to rebuild in the classical style. Even the Vannecks, the great Anglo-Dutch financiers, built Heveningham Hall in a Georgian style and on a scale very remote from those to which their Dutch forebears would have been accustomed. Yet one of the earliest and most influential textbooks of Italian architecture, Serlio's *Reguli generali di architettura*, was first translated from Italian into Dutch,[1] and then from Dutch into English; and some features such as sash windows were known earlier in the Nether-lands than in England.

There was indeed a new and more classical Dutch style which must have been familiar to many Cavaliers from the 1640s, for the Mauritshuis, built between 1639 and 1645 in a position on the Vijver in The Hague, stood near to both the stadholder's rooms and those of the States-General, where no observer could possibly miss it. It employed both brick and stone in a style which much influenced the architecture of country houses after the Restoration. One example was Eltham Lodge (Blackheath), which was built in 1664 for the rich vintner Sir John Shaw by Hugh May, who had lived in Holland for some time. The architect of the Customs House at King's Lynn appears to have been influenced by the Dutch architect van Campen, designer of the Mauritshuis. Yet the Dutch features that remain most evident are the old-fashioned gables and brickwork which survive in more modest houses, usually in areas like East Anglia where Dutch-men came to live, and to which Dutch bricks came in cargos or as ballast. They can be seen in gabled houses at Fen Drayton, at Beccles and Topsham, and also in the inn at Schole in Suffolk. But they can also be seen in buildings in areas more remote from the Netherlands, for instance in Scotland, especially in all the towns on the east coast from Dundee to Leith with which the Dutch traded.[2]

Into all seventeenth-century houses, whatever their size and style, came the products of craftsmen from the Dutch Republic. Oddly enough, the greatest of these was an Englishman, Grinling Gibbons, who was born at Rotterdam in 1648, and began his training in Holland, though he was in England at least by 1670, with apparently only a limited command of English. His wood-carvings of flowers, fruit and game may have been influenced by Dutch paintings, but it is more likely that he was influenced by the naturalistic carvings in marble of Artus Quellin and his team in the cases round the doors in the new Town Hall of Amsterdam. The carvings were of all sorts of objects, including flowers, fruit and shells, and were worked on at about the time that Gibbons was trained. Quellin's etchings were in any case published.[3]

In the same period as Grinling Gibbons, the works of many cabinet-makers entered England from the United Provinces: the craftsmen included not only Dutchmen but Huguenots who had taken refuge there.[4] In 1662 Johannes Fromanteel, a Dutchman living in London, made the first long case, or grandfather, clock and a little later the Lauderdales, Charles II's minister and his wife, bought furniture in Amsterdam for their refurbished Ham House. Through the Dutch East India Company's trade with Japan the first japanned chests came to Europe. Dutch craftsmen produced a native lacquer to compete with those of the Orient and English cabinet makers copied them.

The upholstered chairs and cabriole legs of the William and Mary period are commonly associated with the name of Daniel Marot (1661–1752). Marot was a French Huguenot who as a young man in 1685 brought from Paris to Holland many of the styles he had learned in the France of Louis XIV. He extended them in the course of a long career as architect and designer spent mostly in the United Provinces.[5] Since William and Mary were responsible for bringing him to England his name may fairly be discussed in the context of Dutch influence upon this country, but it is far from clear exactly how long he spent here. When he married (in Amsterdam) in 1694 he was described as being 'of London', and two children were baptised there in 1695 and 1696, but he was in Amsterdam again in 1697. He may not have been in England many years, and it is not easy to be sure for what specific objects he was directly responsible. But in his prints he proudly described himself as being architect by appointment to their Britannic Majesties, and in any case these prints show styles much imitated in England, and not only relating to furniture. Some depict a coach made in The Hague in 1698, much like the Speaker's coach: this may have originally been a state coach, to which further detail from the mid eighteenth century was added before it was reallocated to the Speaker.

Among the furniture that he designed were porcelain cabinets for delftware, a taste which he can hardly have acquired in his youth in Paris. He is indeed thought to have designed tulip-vases and blue and white tiles. Queen Mary II developed a craze for these during her stay in the Dutch Republic, and was widely credited with introducing an expensive fashion for porcelain into England. Some of the tulip-vases and other ornaments with which she filled Hampton

Court and Kensington Palace can still be seen, though the dairy which she created on the Dutch model and the Water Gallery at Hampton Court do not survive. Defoe talked of people copying her by 'piling their china upon the tops of cabinets, scrutores, and every chimney, to the tops of the ceilings, and even setting up shelves for their china-ware where they wanted such places, till it became a grievance in the expense of it, and even injurious to their families and estates . . .'.[6] This accords well with Marot's designs, but though Mary undoubtedly fostered the fashion, it is not quite correct to say that she first introduced it. Certainly this is even less true of tiles, for they were used for lining fireplaces before the Civil War. Sir William Brereton had bought some during his stay in Amsterdam in 1634–5, which probably bore designs of soldiers like those by Jacob de Gheyn. Pepys had fireplaces 'done with Dutch tiles', and tiled fireplaces dating from the 1670s survive at Ham House.

Inevitably the coming of Dutch delftware was followed by imitation English delftware at Chelsea, Lambeth, Bristol, Liverpool, Lowestoft and other places, and naturally this spread into a taste for more refined types of china in the eighteenth century. More importantly, a similar process took place in the paintings with which gentlemen filled their country houses; Dutch paintings were collected, Dutch artists were introduced and native English artists were encouraged and influenced by their example.

Before the Civil War, though a few English connoisseurs bought Italian works in Holland, they seem to have bought relatively few works by the greatest contemporary Dutch artists there. Prince Henry owned paintings, some of them presented by the States-General. The Earl of Arundel owned several Breughels and a painting and drawing by Rembrandt, but none, for example, by Hals, though the inventory of the Earl's paintings ran to some 600 items. Charles I owned a youthful *Self-Portrait* by Rembrandt and the *Portrait of his Mother* which is still in the royal collection, but there is nothing to show that he put a high value on them in comparison with the Titians and others of which he was passionately fond. For Englishmen in Elizabethan and early Stuart times, indeed, the United Provinces were primarily the home of portrait painters who might be brought over to England and employed to paint members of the family. One of the things that the Dutch did, for Englishmen as for Europe, in the course of the century was greatly to widen the range of subjects open to the artist and then to the collector. The very words 'landscape' and 'still life', like the word 'easel', were derived from the Dutch; English visitors began to note and to buy what they called 'drolleries', presumably peasant scenes like those by Brouwer and Steen. Then there were flower-pieces and seascapes. Dutch paintings from Lely's collection were sold in 1682. Once again Defoe ascribed the introduction of the love of painting to the royal example, in this case that of William III, and with the same inaccuracy. William bought paintings and cartoons, and may have encouraged a vogue for the work of Dutch artists, but he also took back some works from the English royal collection for his palace at Het Loo. They included a painting by Dou (valued at a specially high price at that time) which sounds like the one presented to Charles II by the States-General in 1660. Blathwayt, William's secretary-at-war, who spent much time in the Low Countries, bought minor Dutch paintings (as well as tulip-vases and Dutch leather) for his new house at Dyrham Park. Dutch paintings began to be collected really extensively in the early eighteenth century. Even then it is curious to find that there are some yawning gaps in the notebooks of the engraver and antiquary Vertue, and Horace Walpole's journals of visits to country seats recorded only a few Rembrandts, an occasional Francis Halls (*sic*) and not many others.[7] Even so, the growing taste for pictures, and not merely portrait galleries, brought with it a taste for Dutch painting which celebrated the beauties of objects, materials and scenes of everyday life in a naturalistic fashion, though it is unlikely that many appreciated the emblematic significance of genre paintings.

From the reign of Elizabeth to the age of Kneller, patrons who wanted portraits imported painters born or trained in the Netherlands. However, the greatest of them, Van Dyck, came from Antwerp, and his portraits breathe a very different atmosphere from those based on Holland. Several of the early painters, including Mytens, derived their style of portraiture from the school of Miereveld at The Hague, though Cornelius Johnson, or Janssen, of Netherlands stock, was born in London in 1593 and baptised in the Dutch Church there. Mytens was discovered by the Earl of Arundel and brought to England, where between 1618 and 1632 he enjoyed a pension and painted both Buckingham and Charles I. His portraits are far from negligible, but obviously come from the society of the Dutch regents rather than the aristocratic and strongly royalist milieu to which Van Dyck appealed during the years of the Personal Government of Charles I. This is still more true of Hendrik Pot's portrait, now in the Louvre, in which a diminutive king can scarcely be reconciled with an assertion of royal authority. Lely was actually born in Westphalia, but his family were Dutch and owned property in The Hague. His father served in the Dutch army and he was trained at Haarlem. He was in England by at least the age of 28, and all his surviving paintings were done there, including those of the 'flag-officers' who fought against his Dutch countrymen at sea. Even Kneller, whose origins and early career were German, spent some time at Amsterdam as a pupil of Ferdinand Bol. In the nature of things William III was also painted by Dutch artists, and they included Wissing who was sent back to the United Provinces for the purpose after some years in England, and Schalcken, who was in London between 1692 and 1697.[8]

Other Dutch artists paid shorter visits, amongst them Hoogstraten, who was in London between 1662 and 1667 and whose 'piece of perspective', a *trompe-l'oeil*, Pepys much admired. He was equally appreciative of a flower-piece by Verelst, and for the same sort of reason: 'a little flower-pot of his doing, the finest thing that ever I saw in my life – the drops of dew hanging on the leaves, so as I was forced again and again to put my finger on it to feel whether my eyes were deceived or no. He doth ask 70L for it; I had the vanity to bid him 20L – but a better picture I never saw in my whole life, and it is worth going twenty miles to see.'[9] The artists employed by the Lauderdales have their place in the history of English landscape painting. But the greatest artists whom Charles II imported – and in whose invitation he played a direct part – were the Van de Veldes. Porcellis and Vroom had figured in Charles I's collection without beginning a tradition of English marine painting as they did. The elder William van de Velde had been the official Dutch war artist in 1652 in the first Anglo-Dutch war; twenty years later, in the middle of the third, he changed sides and, with his son, came to

London to become one of those rare war artists who have worked in turn for each side. Both Van de Veldes were given official appointments and encouraged to make sketches of sea-fights. But the younger man in particular was much more than a painter of sea-fights with careful attention to the detail of rigging and an account of such dramatic incidents as the blowing up of Sandwich's flagship at Sole Bay. He painted the sea for its own sake, and was regularly taken out on the Thames 'a-skying', or studying the appearances of the sky in all weathers, fair or foul, in the best Dutch tradition of combining sea and cloud effects with the accurate rendering of ships.[10]

In many ways English artists followed in the traditions developed by their Dutch predecessors. The satires of Hogarth were surely influenced by the works of Brouwer, Steen and van Heemskerk. Most important probably was the influence of the Dutch landscape painters, such as the Ruisdaels, Cuyp and Hobbema, upon English artists, both in oils and in water-colours. Many of the English landscape painters came from East Anglia, where the surroundings of land, sea, light and cloud were not too dissimilar from those in the United Provinces. In his early career Gainsborough copied the works of Dutch painters whenever he could, and restored them for dealers in London.[11] The affinities are pronounced in the case of Cotman, Crome and the Norwich school and attention has recently been drawn to the impact of Dutch masters upon a much greater painter in Turner.[12]

The works of Dutch artists, like those of Dutch craftsmen, thus became acceptable to a more aristocratic and well-to-do public than those Dutchmen who had bought them in the early seventeenth century. Other examples could be multiplied – gilt-framed mirrors, marquetry and leatherwork. Rather oddly, because the Dutch Republic was not renowned for sculpture, two sculptors, Bernard and Geraert Janssen, who possibly were brothers, worked in England in the reign of James I. They worked mainly on tombs, but Geraert executed the portrait bust of Shakespeare in the church at Stratford on Avon.[13] They may have been pupils of Hendrick de Keyser, the Amsterdam sculptor of the tomb of William the Silent at Delft. The leading English tomb-maker of the period, Nicholas Stone, certainly trained under him between 1606 and 1613, and married his daughter.[14] In the next century, in contrast, Jan van Nost was a noted maker of lead statuary, particularly for gardens, as at Melbourne Hall.

Dutch gardens were as distinctive in style as Dutch brick houses and gables. Though there were larger examples attached to William III's palaces at Het Loo and at Hampton Court, most were of moderate size, on one level, and without fountains or extensive vistas. In the words of the engineer John Smeaton there was 'much neatness without the least nature'.[15] They were gardens of carefully designed parterres and well-clipped box and yew. By the beginning of the eighteenth century the topiary had become more and more elaborate, with hedges trained to resemble birds, animals, and even ships. How many of the so-called 'Dutch gardens' actually had Dutch gardeners must remain uncertain: Beaumont, the gardener of the well-known 'Dutch garden' at Levens Hall, was in fact French.

It was generally thought that though a liking for topiary had existed before the Revolution it, like other fashions, was stimulated by the coming of the Dutch stadholder; and that the same was true of the plants grown. Just as Defoe ascribed to Mary a taste for East Indian calicoes and for chinaware, so he ascribed to William a love of painting, and a love of gardening. Although evergreens had put in an appearance since the Restoration, William apparently had a special liking for them as 'preserving the figure of the place, even in the roughest part of an inclement and tempestuous winter'. His changes at Hampton Court and Kensington were followed by other gentlemen, 'with such a gust that the alteration is indeed wonderful through the whole kingdom', especially in the counties near the capital. Landowners like Sir William Temple (whose zeal for his garden was itself stimulated by his years in Holland) also introduced evergreens – not only laurels but also oranges, lemons and myrtles which could be housed in sheds (or 'greenhouses') in winter and brought out in earthenware or terracotta pots at the appropriate season: Temple stood his oranges in pots on Portland stone pedestals against a wall and 'not in any particular square'. Though William took a personal interest in his garden it was his favourite, Bentinck, Earl of Portland and Superintendent of the Royal Gardens, who was responsible for importing large numbers of plants from his country seat at Soestdijk. Dutch trade with the Far East made many new specimens available, and in 1690 Charles Hatton at Hampton Court saw 400 rare plants, new to England, which were 'very wonderful and scarcely credible'. A catalogue of Queen Mary's plants apparently includes the crystal rose, the music tree, the apples of love, the perfuming cherry of Arabia, and the silver lotus. Flowers with less exotic names range from the familiar tulip and the cabbage rose to the humble lobelia. The latter was named after Matthias de l'Obel, or Lobelius, who, having been born in the Netherlands, was put in charge of the royal gardens under Elizabeth and James I.[16]

If the flower-garden benefited from contacts with the Netherlands, the same is also true of the vegetable garden. Paradoxically the nation primarily responsible for the importation of the spices with which Europeans had seasoned their food was also responsible for developing the fresh vegetables with which they varied their diet. There is a legend that in the sixteenth century a cabbage from Holland was thought to be an acceptable present, and according to Evelyn, the same Anthony Ashley who translated the Latin edition of Wagenaer's collection of sea-charts was the first to grow cabbages in England. Aubrey recorded a talk with an old lady who claimed to remember 'when all the cabbages came from Holland'. Other vegetables developed by the Dutch with their aptitude for market-gardening were 'carrets', asparagus, artichokes and water-cress, though it is impossible to make a clear distinction between imports from Flanders and those from the northern Netherlands. In any case it is probable that these vegetables were grown in England in small quantities before the arrival of the refugees from the Low Countries in Alva's time. As for turnips and other root crops, these will be mentioned shortly in a different context.

First, however, since reference has been made to these literal 'tastes', it may be appropriate to include a word about drink. As we have seen, the Dutch had a reputation for drunkenness, and until the mid seventeenth century this was based mainly on beer (apart from their import of wine). When Temple encountered gin in 1666 it was unknown to him; it was not until after the Revolution and the arrival of William's Dutchmen that the vogue for it spread until cheap gin became the great social evil of Hogarth's day. However, it is also true that tea seems to have been first introduced into Europe by the Dutch East India Company in about 1610, and to have spread to England from China via Holland in about 1658. In Hanoverian times both East India Companies imported it and no doubt smuggling from Holland to avoid the customs duty kept prices down slightly.

The contribution of the Dutch to the Englishman's food also manifested itself in the boost to productivity on the farm given by methods imported from the Low Countries. New systems of crop rotation and new root crops meant that less land had to be left fallow and that animals did not have to be slaughtered at the onset of winter for lack of fodder. Once again it is impossible to make a clear distinction between ideas imported from the northern and the southern Netherlands, in both of which intensive cultivation was necessary to feed urban populations, just as the people of London had to be fed. Sir Richard Weston called his very influential treatise, which went through several editions, *A Discourse of husbandry used in Brabant and Flanders*, and as late as 1700, 192 cwt of clover seed were imported from Flanders against 153 cwt from Holland, although the latter's supplies increased in the eighteenth century. What is certain is that the new crops spread first in Suffolk and Norfolk, the English counties closest to the Low Countries, in areas where refugees from Alva settled, and in the large and fertile lands in the Fens drained by Vermuyden and his Dutch workmen. The cultivation of orchard fruit, for instance Kentish cherries, has also been attributed to the Low Countries, and Leonard Mascall's treatise (1582) on the management of orchards used Dutch practice.

The crops grown for fodder included rape seed and sainfoin as well as clover, but most important was the turnip. It is traditionally associated with the name of 'Turnip' Townshend, who had served in the Dutch Republic, and who on his retirement to his Norfolk estate at Raynham as an improving landlord made the turnip 'the favourite subject of his conversation'; but it had already been grown for some time. Feeding it to cattle made possible improved stock-breeding and consequently better supplies of meat. At the same time the avoidance of the need to slaughter cattle before the winter gave increased supplies of manure, and allowed heavier fertilization and an increased agrarian yield. It is noticeable that English gentlemen travelling in the United Provinces in the eighteenth century paid more attention to farm management, particularly of stock; they began to raise 'Frisian' cattle, and to employ the Dutch plough and the Dutch barn.[17]

The last three chapters have given examples of the Dutch impact upon British economic, intellectual and artistic life. They make no claim to be exhaustive. There are indeed human activities which do not fit easily into any of these categories, for instance the enjoyment of sports and pastimes. In 1662 Pepys 'first in my life, it being a great frost, did see people sliding with their sckeats, which is a very pretty art'. He was a little apprehensive when the Duke of York tried it in St James's Park, 'but he slides very well', perhaps because he had done it when in exile in Holland.[18] The very word 'skates' was Dutch and Hollanders had a reputation for 'sliding'. There is also a rather mysterious connection between the Scots and the Dutch and the game of golf: in 1618 James I put a prohibitive duty on Dutch golf balls imported into Scotland, and there are several Dutch paintings and prints which illustrate the playing of *kolf*, including Cuyp's well-known picture of a boy playing golf; but though the Dutch game was played with a curved club, it seems often to have been played on ice in the Netherlands, and sometimes by children. The links game was in any event developed in Scotland and is much removed from its seventeenth-century predecessor.

CHAPTER ELEVEN

From Utrecht to Belgian Independence (1713–1839)

F rederick the Great's well-known remark that the Dutch Republic was the cockboat to Great Britain's galleon marked the change which had taken place in the respective international positions of the maritime powers by the 1740s. It is true that in 1725 the French government still put the power of the seven provinces as high as that of England, and in mid century the Duke of Newcastle still counted the Republic as one of the four considerable powers. But neither of these assessments was at all realistic in anything other than international finance. In military and naval strength, as in population and natural resources, the Republic fell behind the mighty states of Britain, France, Austria and Prussia, and from 1756 the Seven Years War brought Russia into the centre of European politics too: In a changed world, mainly of powerful absolutist states with large standing armies, the Republic could not compete on equal political terms. Moreover, there was no statesman of the stature of De Witt to make up for the deficiency in strength by intellectual power and a grasp of the diplomatic situation.

It is fair to say that the Republic did not need to compete on equal terms as long as the Utrecht settlement was preserved. Unlike the dynastic rulers, the Dutch had nothing to gain from aggression or from a direct concern in the current succession disputes. Their main interest was, as it had been for several generations, the preservation of the southern Netherlands (which under the terms of the Treaty of

Utrecht had passed from Spain to Austria), and therefore themselves, from French attack. For this purpose they had their line of Barrier fortresses, on which they placed too much weight, and behind this they relied on the well-founded belief that the preservation of Flanders from French attack was still an essential British interest too – as long as the Hanoverians ruled, and not a French-backed Jacobite claimant. As a result, the Dutch made an effort to preserve the Protestant succession in Britain both in 1715 and 1745. They clung to the British alliance which had become traditional, but they had no interest in taking great risks outside their area of immediate concern. The War of the Spanish Succession had imposed a great financial strain and left the Dutch government (from William III's death in 1702 stadholderless except in Friesland and Groningen) with a heavy burden of debt and of taxation to service it.

The British shared the old belief in the importance of Flanders and valued the treaty obligation of the Dutch to send some troops in the event of a Jacobite invasion. However, they thought that this co-operation should extend to other fields, that the Dutch should follow the British lead, and that the Dutch should act with the same energy and strength that they had shown before 1713. They evidently thought that if the Dutch had large sums of money to invest in Britain, they had large resources available to pay for continental armies. They did not appreciate that the Dutch tax-payer was not as comfortably off as the Dutch investor and had little interest in taking a large part in a world-wide Anglo-French conflict. Moreover British statesmen, as they had tended to be since the time of Burghley, were irritated by the complexities of the decision-making process in the Dutch Republic. 'No constitution was ever evolved by the wit of man that contained so many tricks for the delay and for the obstruction of business,' wrote one ambassador, Horace Walpole. British statesmen were inclined to think that Dutch lethargy and degeneracy would be overcome by getting a Prince of Orange into the same position of executive authority as William III had occupied. Heinsius's knowledge of English and his general competence as Pensionary were appreciated by Whig statesmen, but his successors were not equally respected.

In 1715 6000 Dutch troops were despatched to Scotland to cope with the Old Pretender; they were again brought over in 1719, and were ready for embarkation in 1722 at the time of Atterbury's Jacobite plot. In spite of the need for this support against the Jacobite danger, the British minister Stanhope carried on negotiations directly with the French envoy Dubois in 1717. Though the treaty of that year was signed at The Hague and the Dutch were allowed to accede to a Triple Alliance with Britain and France they were not permitted any great part in it. On the other hand the Dutch had no real interest in the crises in the Baltic and the Mediterranean, and Anglo-Dutch relations deteriorated to a point where Stanhope refused the adhesion of the States-General to the 'Quadruple Alliance' which also included Austria. There were Dutch complaints of British haughtiness, and conversely from 1721 there was talk of a British marriage for the young William IV of Orange (the member of the cadet branch of the family in Friesland who had succeeded to the title) to remedy the situation. When William came to England in 1733 to marry Anna, the daughter of George II, he did so in spite of the opposition of the States of Holland and the silence of the States-General. The revival of the marriage connection with the British royal house was obviously unwelcome to many of the regents. However, Horace Walpole was instructed to give the strongest assurances that Britain had no intention of promoting a change in the Dutch constitution, and the bridal pair were reluctantly consigned to the provincial court at Leeuwarden, where William remained stadholder of two remote provinces only. Sir Robert Walpole had no more interest than the Dutch Republic in taking part in the War of the Polish Succession (1733–8). But they had a common concern in putting diplomatic pressure upon the Austrian owner of the southern Netherlands, Charles VI, to withdraw his backing from the new, rival Ostend East India Company.[1]

The resulting obligation to support the claims of Charles's daughter, Maria Theresa, to the Austrian Succession against rival claimants supported by France contributed to the revival of the old anti-French coalition. Once more Britain, the Dutch Republic and Austria stood as allies against France and Spain in the War of the Austrian Succession (1740–8), as in the earlier War of the Spanish Succession. There were, as in the later stages of the previous war, renewed complaints about the inadequate size and quality of the Dutch naval contingent, and to these were now added complaints about the performance of the Dutch forces at the battle of Fontenoy, where 'they ran away and lost us the victory which our own troops had near acquired'. Such recriminations about 'the degeneracy of the Republic's troops' and 'the mutual peevishness arising between the two nations arising from mutual smart' were rapidly allayed when Bonnie Prince Charlie landed in Scotland, and Britain not only needed her own forces from Flanders but was grateful once again for a Dutch contingent. According to Pelham, the Dutch were Britain's only allies, 'for all the rest I look upon as burdens, not as friends engaged in the same interest, and upon equal terms'. But the Dutch troops were again found wanting, not in numbers but in quality, as they had been in surrendering the Barrier fortresses to France and were once again in 1747 when the French went on to invade the Republic. British disillusionment about Dutch military strength might have been qualified by a recognition that the Dutch had no essential interest in the issues now at stake in the war with France – issues concerning Silesia and Italy, and the preservation of the newly-conquered fortress of Louisbourg near the mouth of the St Lawrence for Britain. As it was, the British sought to invigorate the Dutch defence by a revolution similar to that of 1672. The British envoy, the Earl of Sandwich, entered into relations with the Orangist party through the latest member of the Bentinck family, and a British fleet encouraged the revolution which, beginning in Zeeland, made William IV stadholder of all the seven provinces and captain-general. Unfortunately he could not repeat his predecessor's miracle of 1672–4. The British Secretary of State, Newcastle, was told that the commander-in-chief of the key fortress at Bergen-op-Zoom, Cronstrom, was nearly ninety years old – perhaps the oldest commander in history – and that when the French attacked they found both officers and garrison asleep in their beds. The contribution of Dutch credit to the common effort was undervalued by many. In signing the Treaty of Aix-la-Chapelle in 1748 Britain had unwillingly to hand back Louisbourg in order to recover the Austrian Netherlands from French hands.[2]

By the time of the outbreak of the Seven Years War in 1756 the

Diplomatic Revolution had drastically altered the situation. Once more Britain and France were at war, but Louis XV and Maria Theresa were now allies, and for the first time for a century it was irrelevant to think of campaigning to prevent Flanders from being absorbed by France. Twice, in 1756 and 1759, there were rumours of troop transports in French Channel ports threatening an invasion of Britain. Such rumours led British ministers to think of requesting the contingent of soldiers still formally owing by the States-General under the terms of the English alliance. But no request was ever made, though the States-General would probably have provided soldiers had they really been needed. Even Dutch neutrality was fraught with problems, for it revived all the disputes surrounding the claim that 'free ships' meant 'free goods'. It was agreed that trade with a belligerent in contraband was not permissible. However, the question remained whether naval stores, especially timber, amounted to contraband, and there was nearly a clash between British privateers and ships convoying Dutch merchantmen from the Baltic. Nevertheless, these matters were patched up, and Anglo-Dutch friendship was preserved. The most ominous sign for the future arose from the fact that in the minority following the death of William IV in 1751 (the fourth successive minority in the House of Orange), the *gouvernante* or governess for the new infant stadholder, William V, was the English dowager, Anna, who was thought to be an unpatriotic Anglophile ruling with the aid of her favourite Bentinck. In the *De Witten-oorlog*, rival Dutch pamphleteers revived old controversies dating back to the time of De Witt and William III. Once more Orangists sang the praises of the old British alliance, while supporters of republican regents attacked this view of Dutch interests and were thought to be pro-French. The British alliance was becoming the alliance of a party, and not of a nation.[3]

British travellers now thought the Dutch people a shadow of their former selves. Diplomats ceased to find The Hague so agreeable a station. Whereas Prior had spoken of the pleasure of being:

> In a little Dutch chaise, on a Saturday night,
> On my left hand my Horace, a nymph on my right

Chesterfield complained that he was in a land of few temptations, and no opportunities. Fifty years later, Harris on his appointment said: 'I am making up my mind to dullness and gravity; my eyes to black teeth and white lips; my nose to the stench of tobacco and unwashed feet; and my stomach to cheese, butter and herrings.' British diplomats and aristocrats complained disdainfully that Dutchmen were too preoccupied with getting money, forgetting that in Britain covetousness simply took other forms involving landed estates, titles and pensions. According to one traveller, 'money is adored here more than in any other country, where it supplies the place of birth, wit and merit'. Goldsmith and others also criticized alleged Dutch avarice and a decline in Dutch virtues and valour.

> Their much lov'd wealth imparts
> Convenience, plenty, elegance and arts;
> But view them closer, craft and fraud appear.
> Even liberty itself is barter'd here,
> At gold's superior charms all freedom flies,
> The needy sell it, and the rich man buys;
> A land of tyrants, and a den of slaves ...

As this passage indicates, people from the land of the unreformed Parliament were beginning to criticize the land where there were no elections at all as being oligarchical; the Dutch were 'no longer the sons of freedom, but of avarice'. Although according to one observer Amsterdam still had 'a great number of booksellers, who, it is thought, employ twice the presses that work in London' and exported books to London, Goldsmith thought their writers critical rather than creative: 'They wait till something new comes out from others, examine its merits, and reject it or make it reverberate through the rest of Europe. ... All their taste is derived to them from neighbouring nations, and that in a language not their own.' The author of a book on the 'Grand Tour' even criticized their looks: 'Their motion is as disagreeable as their shape, being very heavy and awkward, insomuch that 'tis an easy matter to distinguish a Dutchman from a native of England or France, almost the length of a street by his mien.' Such remarks as these were no longer the war-time abuse of an enemy, as they had been in the previous century, but the patronizing talk of people who thought that the Dutch were a nation with a great past who had fallen from grace.[4]

At the same time some of the old Dutch characteristics were still praised, notably the neatness and cleanliness of their towns, and these were not just the clichés passed on by generations of travellers. Lady Mary Wortley Montagu's impressions of Rotterdam in 1716 were fresh: 'All the streets are paved with broad stones, and before the meanest artificers' doors, seats of various coloured marbles and so neatly kept that I'll assure you I walked almost all over the town yesterday, incognito, in my slippers without receiving one spot of dirt, and you may see the Dutch maids washing the pavement of the street with more application than ours do our chambers.... Here is neither dirt nor beggary to be seen [as in London].... The common servants and little shopwomen here are more nicely clean than most of our ladies, and the great variety of neat dresses ... is additional pleasure in seeing the town.' In another letter she wrote that 'the whole country appears a large garden, the roads all well paved, shaded on each side with rows of trees, bordered with large canals full of boats passing and repassing'. Goldsmith too, in spite of his criticism, praised 'the slow canal, the yellow blossom'd vale, The willow tufted bank, the gliding sail'; the countryside was as neat as the town. The tourist who thought that the Dutch 'suck in with their milk a desire and thirst for gain' thought their neatness a little excessive, 'for they continually wash and rub their goods, even the benches and the least plank, not forgetting the stairs.... Even the very streets are kept wonderfully clean, the servants of each house being obliged every day to wash and rub the pavement before their door.'[5] Boswell struck a discordant note, in an often-quoted letter, in which he said that the principal towns were 'sadly decayed' and full of starving unemployed: at Utrecht 'there are whole lines of wretches who have no other subsistence than potatoes, gin, and stuff which they call tea and coffee; and what is worst of all, I believe they are so habituated to this life that they would not take work if it should be offered to them'. The contrast with the 'golden age' is glaring; but it is not clear how far the inland town of Utrecht was typical, and Rotterdam might have told a quite different story. One hopes that the Dutch opinion of Scots was not founded only on observation of Boswell. A more balanced view is probably that of Joseph Marshall, who visited the Republic in 1768, four years after Boswell and a decade before the disaster of the fourth Anglo-Dutch war. He praised the progressive methods and the prosperity of Dutch agriculture (incidentally finding the cowstalls 'as clean as a parlour', and the cows kept 'as clean as an English gentleman would his racehorse') and made careful distinctions between the different sectors of Dutch trade. On the whole he agreed neither with those who exaggerated Dutch decline, nor with those who thought of commerce as it would have been in the first half of the previous century. 'The truth is that the Dutch yet possess a very considerable commerce ... it is also a fact that for the last twenty years the trade of England has much increased, whereas that of Holland has been on the decline.' High wages, he thought, proved nothing unless it could be shown that wages had not risen elsewhere. A decline in naval power would not matter as long as the Republic was able to remain neutral. 'The happiness and content of the lower classes ... make travelling remarkably agreeable.' Though there was luxury, he found the disparity in wealth between classes less than in other nations, including England. The only danger of sending a young man to Leiden or Utrecht University would be to give him 'a relish for literature' rather than for the ledger, but no taste for extravagance; whereas 'at our universities the man who designs his son for a merchant had better hang him than send him to them'. He thought 'the morals of our youth are incomparably purer at the Dutch universities than the English ones', found the Dutch 'friendly and sincere' and looked forward to a modest prosperity for them.[6]

Unfortunately Dutch neutrality, which since 1713 had been broken only in the War of the Austrian Succession, came to an end in 1780. The War of American Independence at first brought opportunities to Amsterdam merchants who hoped to trade with the rebels through the island of St Eustatius in the West Indies. This became a headquarters of smugglers of arms and gunpowder even though the States-General issued a proclamation against it. According to the British ambassador, even British manufacturers conveyed their goods to America through the United Provinces. Powder, which was said to bring in a profit of 120 per cent, was sent to St Eustatius in tea chests and rice barrels to escape inspection. Seven square miles of barren rocks became one vast storehouse from which American privateers, two of them named after the Dutch governor and his lady, were fitted out. Under insensitive British handling, Dutch resentment against their old commercial and naval rivals grew and feeling for their allies of the past century was transmuted into sympathy for the American rebels against overweening British power. When John Paul Jones anchored at the Texel with English prizes, he was enthusiastically received, and he reported that 'every day those blessed [Dutch] women come to the ships in great numbers – mothers, daughters, even little girls – bringing with them for our wounded all the numberless little comforts of Dutch homes, a tribute that came from the hearts of the people'.[7]

All this was compounded when France entered the war on the side of the rebels. Amsterdam merchants speculated in supplying naval stores to France; Dutch ships were seized as prizes; and once again there were disputes on the question whether naval stores were contraband. After an American emissary had been seized on his way to Holland, and his papers had been found to contain a draft treaty of alliance, Great Britain declared war in December, 1780. As in the former wars the Dutch acquitted themselves creditably in the actual fighting, two small fleets under Parker and Zoutman engaging in the Battle of Dogger Bank which was claimed as a victory by both sides. But the Dutch fleet was too weak to renew the struggle, and Dutch shipping was swept from the seas. This and the capture of St Eustatius by the British fleet under Rodney meant enormous losses to the Amsterdam merchants, and the Republic's trade, which had suffered in previous wars, received a blow from which it did not recover.

The war also brought with it the end of the English and Scots regiments which had served the States-General for the past 200 years. Apart from their services to the Dutch, they had been a training-ground for officers who afterwards gained a reputation in the British army. Of those who remained in the Netherlands, many followed fathers and grandfathers who had grown old in the service, and intermarried with the people among whom they lived, like Hugh Mackay, who married the daughter of the house at Saltbommel

where he was billeted. In the Scots Brigade the marriage and baptismal registers show increasing numbers of Dutch or Flemish wives
(for the soldiers often served in garrisons of the Barrier fortresses)
and children given Dutch names. But officers and children retained
their status as British subjects until in 1782 the States-General
required them to take an oath of allegiance and to renounce their
allegiance to George III. Some returned to Britain to avoid loss of
British nationality, and others followed after the French occupation
in 1795. But others were incorporated into the Dutch forces and a
Mackay was even prime minister in 1888–91.

The moral that the British drew from the war of 1780–4 was that
they must ally with a party in the Dutch Republic to restore the
alliance. Once again, as of old, they looked to the Orangists and the
party of the stadholder William V, rather than the patricians, the
patriot movement and the democrats who sought to reinvigorate
and reform the outworn constitution, and turned to France for
support after the calamities of the war. To help restore the alliance,
the younger Pitt chose as his new ambassador Sir James Harris, who
had been at Leiden University and had learned the Dutch language,
and gave him a generous allowance of secret service funds. William V,
the least forceful of the Princes of Orange, was not loth to be used
in this way. Habit led him to turn to his mother's countrymen.
Though he was scarcely a satisfactory leader and the combination
with Britain served his dynastic interests, it has to be said, if to some
extent with hindsight, that it also served some national interests. The
recent disputes with Britain had been vexatious, and it had become
exasperating, as a former great power, to be subordinated to a
country which had superior resources. But the recent war, in alliance
with France, had only resulted in severe losses. After 1795 the connection with France rather than Britain was to be ruinous to Dutch
prosperity and to lead first to the loss of her colonies and later even
to the loss of her national independence to Napoleon.

Harris was successful in the short term at the expense of alienating
reformist elements in the Republic in the long term. A more dominant personality than the Prince, he acted virtually as a party leader.
He used lavish hospitality to win support, for he professed to believe
that the way to win over a Dutchman was through his stomach. 'I

abhor this dirty work,' he wrote, 'but when one is employed to sweep chimneys one must black one's fingers.' When the Dutch domestic crisis came in 1787 the latest Bentinck ended his letter promising that a port would be ready to receive the British fleet with the words 'Remember 1688.' As it turned out no return expedition was needed, for the allied army of the Princess of Orange's Prussian relative crossed the Dutch border. But Harris got much of the credit from 'the uppermost class of the people' in The Hague, with shouts of *Oranje boven* and *Vivat Wilhelmus und Englandt* (*sic* in his report). He gave supper to the Prince and Princess and three to four hundred guests, and when he became Lord Malmesbury the Prince authorized him to incorporate the Orange device, *Je maintiendrai*, in his arms.[8]

The Triple Alliance of 1788 between Britain, the Dutch Republic and Prussia seemed to guarantee a relationship of mutual support between the British and Dutch in the future. However, relations became soured within seven years. Following the French Revolution the Convention declared war on both British and Dutch, and when the revolutionary armies invaded Holland, the native inhabitants, in contrast to their attitude in 1672 and 1747, were indifferent – or worse. The behaviour of the British troops supposedly 'defending' them, who, for instance, were guilty of pillage, violence and rape at Nijmegen, aroused complaints even from convinced Orangists.[9] The French believed in the slogan *Prenons la Hollande et Carthage est à nous*, meaning that through Holland they would strike at another nation of shopkeepers, Britain. They were spurred on by Dutch radicals like Anacharsis Cloots who had taken refuge in Paris; and in 1795 the Dutch Republic simply collapsed. William V and his family sought refuge in England, where the Prince was accommodated in Kew Palace and, according to contemporary calumny, solaced himself with the servant-girls. Since the Dutch colonies might be a base for a French attack upon India, he was induced by the British to order their governors not to resist the warships and troops sent out to occupy them for George III.

By 1797 Daendels, the commander of the new Batavian Republic, which succeeded the former United Provinces under French protection, was waiting with 30,000 men at the Texel to sail and join a

French invasion of Ireland. With varying degrees of willingness the Republic espoused the French cause, and at one point the troops actually boarded the vessels, only to be driven ashore by bad weather. All possibility of an invasion was eliminated at the Battle of Camperdown, at which the Dutch fought bravely and with 'grim steadfastness' to make 'a dignified exit from the ranks of the great powers'. Only seven of their small remaining fleet escaped, and ten, including seven ships of the line and De Winter's flagship, were captured.[10]

Pitt and his colleague Grenville, however, still believed that the Dutch people were pro-British rather than pro-French and would respond to an invasion mounted in the name of the Prince of Orange. In 1798 there was the first mention of a plan for the union of the southern Netherlands to Holland when France had been defeated and the map of Europe was redrawn. In the meantime France and her satellite republics had to be overthrown, and in 1799 an Anglo-Russian invasion of Holland was planned. It was known that the Batavian government was divided within itself – when the invasion took place a thousand French troops were kept back at The Hague, to watch it. The French were not exactly loved, and knew it. But Britain declined the private overtures of the Batavian president himself, preferring mistakenly to rely on the Orangists. Memories of 1787 and 1794 were not dead, and if 'the alternative to French dominance was British dominance' the Dutch were not enthusiastic. They preferred to wait on events; and an invasion is rarely popular with those who are caught up in it. North Holland, where the British commander Abercromby landed, was reputed to be the least Orangist province in the Republic, and elsewhere Orangists preferred to wait until the British army arrived before they took action. Abercromby's proclamation claimed that they came 'not as enemies, but as deliverers', but it made no reference to the return of the lost colonies, and when he was joined by the stadholder's son, the Hereditary Prince, probably as much support was alienated as was won over.[11]

Abercromby, with 24,000 men, fought his way ashore at Den Helder, at the tip of a peninsula, and was joined by Russian reinforcements, but he soon had to recognize that his task of marching southwards to Amsterdam was impossible. The officers on the few remaining Dutch ships (many of them not Dutch nationals) hoisted Orange flags and became a squadron of the British fleet; but there was no equivalent on land. Daendels's men had resisted the landing with unexpected stubbornness. There were few deserters, and in the words of a British officer, 'the farmers and others within our lines lounged about with their pipes in their mouths, as silent and sullen spectators of an unpleasant disturbance. They were willing enough to sell us their cattle and let us their boats at good prices, but otherwise appeared passive and gloomy.' There was little goodwill to the invaders, and as Abercromby wrote of the better-disposed, 'They will mount an Orange cockade and no more.' With no rising now expected, his forces got no further than Alkmaar, through diffi-cult terrain and bad weather, with battles at Bergen and Egmond. Within a matter of weeks he was thankful to sign a convention allowing him to evacuate Dutch territory without opposition. It should be said that the French commander, Brune, was willing to agree to this; he blamed the failure of his counter-attack at Zijpe upon Dutch cowardice, and conscious of French unpopularity, obviously thought the Dutch forces unreliable. The Hereditary Prince, infuri-ated by the armistice, left for Germany, though his father was given a British pension.[12]

The Treaty of Amiens (1802) brought the return of Dutch colonies except for Ceylon, only for the Batavian Republic to be dragged in again by Napoleon when war was resumed between Britain and France in 1803. This time the colony at the Cape, when seized by the British in 1806, was not returned; Java was left untouched until 1811, when it was attacked with 90 sail and 10,000 men under Minto, and Raffles became Lieutenant-Governor of the occupied territory. Of more immediate interest to Britain, who returned 'Europe's richest colony' after the war, was the probable use of the Netherlands as a base for invasion. This was a danger which British statesmen had always feared and which had dominated British foreign policy since Tudor times. The Batavian Republic was to supply 9000 troops, five ships of the line, five frigates and 250 flat-bottomed boats, or barges, for Napoleon's expedition. Even after the invasion had been called off in 1805, the British government continued to be alarmed by reports of preparations at Antwerp, and it was these that led them to plan an expedition of their own to the Scheldt in 1809.

The Walcheren expedition was even more disastrous than the campaign of 1799; the débâcle led to a duel between two members of the Cabinet, Castlereagh and Canning. With 160 ships, 144 cannon and 38,000 men, it was the largest expedition in British history before the Second World War. It captured the island of Walcheren within a fortnight, culminating in a bombardment of Flushing which lasted two days and two nights. We learn without surprise that, throughout, the Flushing citizens retained a very distant attitude to the British. It was too late; the attack was not pressed home before Napoleon's brother Louis, whom he had made King of Holland in 1806, and Bernadotte collected troops to defend Antwerp. Within 12 days of the capture of Flushing the council of the commander in chief, the Earl of Chatham, declared further operations impossible. 'The old and haughty Chatham, incurably lazy and complacent, was more careful of his turtle, "brought with him on a cart built for the purpose", than of his men'; but it would have taken a genius, or a miracle-worker, to cope with what followed. The troops fell victim to 'Walcheren fever', or malaria with an admixture of dysentery, typhoid and typhus for good measure. Within a month there were 7800 fit soldiers and 8200 sick on the island. In December the expeditionary force was evacuated to England and by February 1810 there were 4000 dead and 11,000 sick.[13]

By this time, however, opinion in Holland was turning decisively against the French. French revolutionary policy, and still more Napoleon's Continental System, entailed a complete prohibition of British imports which meant ruin to the trade which was central to the prosperity of the Dutch. They retaliated by smuggling, particularly in the islands of Zeeland. Over 200 years earlier Cecil had complained that the Low Countries were too easy of access. Every young fellow with a small boat in an obscure creek could have a fling at it, he said; they evaded the customs, they broke the laws.[14] So far as British colonial products, textiles and metallurgical goods were concerned, the Netherlands remained 'the keyhole into Europe' until at least 1805. In this year the French insisted that their coastguards and customsmen should supervise cargos at Dutch ports, with detachments of French troops to aid them if need be. The needs of the Continental System were behind the replacement of the Batavian Republic by the Kingdom of Louis Bonaparte in 1806. But the Kingdom of Holland remained Britain's third best customer after Russia and Denmark, with 4.8 per cent of all British exports and 16 per cent of all colonial re-exports. Louis Bonaparte was sympathetic to the plight of his people, and defended their needs to his brother, saying that trying to put an end to smuggling in the Maas estuary was like 'preventing the skin from sweating', until in 1810 he abdicated under Napoleon's bullying.[15]

Now under unequivocal French occupation the last remnants of Dutch support for the French disappeared. Conscription was the last straw, even leading to riots. The Dutch share in Napoleon's blood-toll in the *Grande Armée* was 15,000, only a few hundred of whom survived the Russian campaign of 1812. The natural alternative was to turn to Napoleon's great rival, Britain, with whose sailors the Dutch smugglers and fishermen fraternized: in 1813 British sloops would hail Dutch fishing boats and throw on board broadsheets with news of Wellington's victories in Spain and accompanying propaganda.[16]

Equally naturally the Prince of Orange was the obvious successor in the Netherlands, and the Hereditary Prince, now William VI, returned to England from Germany in April 1813. It was from England that he landed at Scheveningen at the end of November to become King William I of the Netherlands, with dreams of a kingdom, which not only included Belgium (as agreed with the British Foreign Secretary, Castlereagh), but extended as far as the Moselle. In his proclamation to the Dutch nation he declared that 'independence must be restored with the aid of old allies, under a renewal of the old and new relations of friendship and alliance'. But his son, yet another William, was more popular in England. He had studied the English language and British institutions at Oxford, and had served creditably with Wellington in Spain. He was later to lead a substantial force of Dutch troops at Quatre Bras and at Waterloo, where he was wounded at Mont St Jean. He was sufficiently pre-possessing for real consideration to be given to yet another Anglo-Dutch marriage, between young William and Princess Charlotte, the only daughter of the Prince Regent, who was expected to follow him on the British throne.

Thus for the last time there was a real possibility of union between the two countries, as had been proposed under Elizabeth and Cromwell and had taken place, after a fashion, under William III and Mary II. It would have been purely personal, for there was no intention of assimilating the institutions of the two countries. It would also not have been permanent for, as Castlereagh told the allies against Napoleon, the separation of the succession in the two countries would be ensured by an arrangement that the first son would succeed in Britain and the second, or a collateral branch of the Nassau family, would succeed in the Netherlands. Still, the traditional connection might have been cemented by the personal union, in the way that royal marriages in previous centuries had been used for diplomatic purposes. It was Charlotte herself who broke off the engagement. Not yet 18, she disliked the prospect of staying for even part of the year in Holland, though there were other factors too in her decision. Charlotte was not temperamentally amenable enough to agree to a marriage she did not want, like junior princesses in earlier days, and as heir to the throne could not easily be coerced. Instead she married Leopold of Saxe-Coburg, and never became Queen Charlotte because she died in giving birth to a still-born child in 1817.[17]

The inclusion of Belgium in a Kingdom of the Netherlands was Britain's latest solution to the perennial problem of finding a way to protect the Low Countries from French encroachment. It was intended to set up a solid enough state to put up a resistance there, with Britain going to the rescue if required. But there was no question of compensating William for the loss of some of the Dutch colonies. Under the terms of the Treaty of Amiens Britain was entitled to keep Ceylon, and did so for the sake of the anchorage at Trincomalee which was useful for the defence of the Bay of Bengal and the East India Company's trade with India. Similar reasons led Britain to keep the port of call at the Cape which she had seized; and Liverpool merchants pressed for the retention of the sugar plantations at Demerara on the coast of Guiana. The other colonies were returned, and notably the possessions in the East Indies, to the great disappointment of Raffles, who as Lieutenant Governor had carried out important reforms there in a very short term of office. Considerations of cost may have led the British to forgo the opportunity of acquiring Java when no one could have prevented them from doing so. The fact was that the East India Company had too much on its plate to manage both its possessions on the Indian mainland and those in the archipelago. Raffles was allowed to keep the site of Singapore, which was inhabited only by some fishermen when he seized it in 1819 but was, by virtue of its position, to become a great trading city. Outstanding problems were settled by the Treaty of London in 1824, though there were later to be difficulties with regard to its interpretation over Borneo. To the north of the Straits of Malacca, Malaya was to be in a British sphere of influence, and to the south of the Straits, Sumatra was to be in a Dutch sphere. Merchants of each nationality were to enjoy most favoured nation treatment in the lands of the other.[18]

The Kingdom of the Netherlands, however, lasted only 15 years before the Belgian Revolution of 1830 led to its dissolution. It might be expected that the old friendship, so solemnly reaffirmed at the time of the overthrow of Napoleon, would have led Britain to intervene to reimpose the authority of King William I. Instead of the new quarrel with France which would have resulted, Palmerston and King Louis Philippe co-operated in the setting up of an independent Belgian state. Many thought that this policy, including insistence on freedom of the Scheldt, was carried out in support of British economic aims to set up a small state through which her goods could be poured on to the Continent. But this was scarcely necessary to British economic development in the 1830s, and there is no reason to doubt Palmerston's private statements, when he had no need to conceal the truth, that his guiding motive in wanting an independent Belgium was political. An Anglo-French convention of 1833 imposed an embargo on Dutch commerce and a blockade of the Dutch coast to compel the withdrawal of the Dutch from Belgian territory. When the Dutch refused to yield, a French army laid siege to Antwerp citadel without any British objection.[19]

In 1839 the famous 'scrap of paper' gave the new Belgian kingdom a guaranteed neutrality. It marked a radical change in British policy towards the Netherlands. Since the time of William III and Louis XIV British statesmen had used Dutch help to prevent the French from pushing forward into the key area of Flanders. Now, instead, the same end was to be achieved by a guarantee of Belgian neutrality from the powers, including France. The Low Countries retained their critical importance for British safety; but when they were next threatened, it was by a German and not a French invasion, and Anglo-Dutch relations had to be shaped accordingly.

CHAPTER TWELVE

Modern Times

'Happy is the nation which has no history', and in the century between Belgian independence and the Second World War there were almost no dramatic events in Anglo-Dutch relations. The latest general history of the Low Countries can tell their story with scarcely a reference to Britain in that period.[1] There was no hint of war between the two states; neither had the least thought of intervention in the internal politics of the other. There were no royal marriages, though in 1836 a younger son of the House of Orange, Prince Alexander, was mentioned as one of the possible bridegrooms for Victoria, and he was one of those invited to Kensington Palace. The House of Orange became one of the few royal families not linked in some way by marriage to Queen Victoria with her numerous progeny. Colonial problems were settled without too much difficulty. The remaining Dutch settlements on the Gold Coast, which had long been unprofitable, were handed over to Britain in 1872 in return for a payment of £3790 1s 6½d for stores and fittings. At the same time (though the two transactions were not formally linked) the Dutch were finally given a free hand to deal with the native princes of Acheh in Sumatra, and their East India empire in effect enjoyed British naval protection against possible French or German intervention.[2] Holland was the least of the worries of British statesmen, and at the same time the party political systems, law and administration of the two countries were quite unlike one another.

Yet, though contacts between statesmen and diplomats were less important than in previous ages, contact between the two peoples continued unobtrusively. In economic affairs, British workmen and manufacturers played their part in the slow development of Dutch industry. For example, Ainsworth of Bolton opened his textile school at Goor and introduced the power loom, Wilson set up a bleaching and dyeing works at Haarlem, and Dixon built a cotton-spinning factory at Enschede. From about 1825 the Dutch began to send horticultural products to England. More important, they made an invaluable contribution to the feeding of Britain's growing and indus-trialized population by sending first butter and then, increasingly, margarine. Rotterdam's position near the mouths of the Rhine and Maas became steadily more important as the industries of the Ruhr grew. The port occupied a key position on the commercial routes between Britain and the East, and between Germany and the West. Inevitably the transit trade developed to a degree which encouraged the construction, from 1866 onwards, of the New Waterway making possible improved connections between Rotterdam and the sea.

One consequence was increased passenger traffic between Harwich and the Dutch coast round the mouth of the Rhine. Since 1661 there had been a regular service carrying mail and passengers between Harwich and Hellevoetsluis, but the Dutch-Rhenish Railway Company, which had been chiefly formed of Englishmen, pressed for an improved shipping connection. In 1863 the Great Eastern Company began a weekly service which was so successful that in 1875 it became daily except for Sundays, and in 1893 triumphed over Victorian sabbatarianism. In 1866 9350 passengers were carried between Harwich and Hellevoetsluis; in 1897, when the Hook of Holland was opened, there were 130,000. Obviously some of these were on their way to and from Germany; on the other hand, the Zeeland Steamship Company carried a further 148,000 passengers between Flushing and Queenborough in 1910. There can be no doubt that the scale of personal contacts between British and Dutch vastly increased and peoples who had been only distant neighbours became much closer.[3]

In the last quarter of the nineteenth century, however, these contacts were marred by Dutch indignation at British policy towards their Boer descendants in South Africa who still spoke an Afrikaans form of their language, though there was never any likelihood that this would develop into a crisis between governments. The loss of the small settlement at the Cape in 1806 had not been deeply felt in the Netherlands. In the years that followed young men from South Africa studied theology, medicine and law in the Netherlands, but Britain's annexation of the Boer republics of Transvaal and the Orange Free State in 1877 caused no great excitement amongst the Dutch. The situation changed sharply just three years later. The Dutch counterpart to rising imperialist sentiment in other countries was sympathy for the Boer rebellion which led to the British defeat at Majuba in 1881. It suggested a revival of the old Dutch spirit which, in the eyes of some, might even be a prelude to the reconquest of South Africa for the Dutch race and the redeeming of a missed opportunity in the Dutch past. Funds were gathered for the victims of the war, and thousands signed an appeal to the British nation which was drafted by a central committee for aid to the Boers.

The grant of independence to the Transvaal and the Orange Free State by Gladstone's government solved the immediate problem, but Kruger, who became president in 1883, still looked to the Dutch for support. When he came to London to negotiate a treaty he asked two Dutchmen, one of them the important politician, Dr Abraham Kuyper, to act as his advisers. Later another Dutchman, Dr W. J. Leyds, became his diplomatic representative and afterwards his confidant and highest civil servant. Kruger tried to recruit his civil service from the Netherlands, where a South African society was founded in 1881 to promote relations between the two states. A Netherlands South African Railways Company was formed, though much of the capital seems to have come from Germany. In practice Dutchmen in Kruger's administration and on his railways did not always get on well with the Boers, and the latest Dutch historian of the period concludes that 'by about 1898 Dutch influence in South Africa was already decreasing rapidly'. But the outbreak of the Boer War in 1899 naturally revived and intensified pro-Boer sentiment in the Netherlands.

Many Dutchmen, including Kuyper, had already approved of the German Kaiser's telegram of congratulation to Kruger on the failure of the Jameson Raid in 1896. The outbreak of war was followed by rejoicing at the victory of 'our lingual and racial kinsmen' at Spion Kop, and then, when the course of the war turned against the Boers, by indignation at the hardships suffered in the 'concentration camps'. There were mass meetings at Amsterdam and The Hague, and Dutch public opinion was overwhelmingly hostile to Britain, with an outpouring of pro-Boer literature, which even included children's books. There was talk of a European coalition against the British tyrants in which the Netherlands would take part, as in 1780, but all this was not practical politics. Whatever the feelings of men like Kuyper, official action was limited to sending a warship to Lourenço Marques (Maputo) to bring away Kruger, and to the sympathy shown by Queen Wilhelmina to the exiled president. The fact was that Dutch commerce and the Dutch East Indian possessions still depended on the British navy and its protection against the intrusion of other powers into the Indonesian archipelago, and the mistake of the fourth Anglo-Dutch war was not repeated.[4]

Dutch resentment against Britain did not end with the peace. The South African Society remained active. There was a chair in Afrikaans culture at Amsterdam and a chair in Roman-Dutch law, always to be occupied by an Afrikaner, at Leiden, while Afrikaner theological students also came to Dutch universities. Of future South African Nationalists, Herzog, though his family was of German origin, attended the University of Amsterdam, and Dr Malan obtained his doctorate of theology at Utrecht. The steady, though not large, flow of immigrants included the parents of Verwoerd, who was born at Amsterdam in 1908. In the course of time, however, Dutch opinion turned decisively against apartheid, and even Dutch Calvinist opinion turned against the rigorism of the so-called Dutch Reformed Church in South Africa, especially after the Sharpeville massacre. Nowadays the sense of affinity with the ideals of Afrikanerdom is very slight and it would be a great mistake to think that the Dutch support the present policies of the Republic of South Africa.

The formation of the Union of South Africa in 1909 did something to remove the Dutch sense of grievance at the treatment of the Boers. But it did nothing to encourage a Dutch belief that the Netherlands should join the alliance which included Britain when the First World War broke out in 1914. By that time the economic ties between Holland and Germany were strong. The provision in the original Schlieffen plan for a German advance across southern Dutch territory had been abandoned without becoming publicly known, and the Dutch could see no advantage, and many drawbacks, in going to the aid of Belgium against Germany. As a result, there was no revival of the old Anglo-Dutch partnership to defend Flanders against aggression by the dominant European power. Instead there was to be a repetition of the situation in which a neutral Netherlands, heavily dependent on its trade, suffered from the interpretations of the law of contraband by the belligerents' navies. British orders in council were designed to enforce a blockade of Germany by forbidding the importation into neutral states like Holland of contraband goods which might be transmitted across the German border, and in 1916 any distinction between contraband and non-contraband goods like foodstuffs was dropped. Though the Dutch were supposed to be allowed to import enough for their own needs, and though smuggling into Germany could no more be totally prevented than in the time of Napoleon, Dutch trade inevitably suffered. On the other hand, German adoption of unrestricted submarine warfare in order to enforce a similar blockade upon the British Isles led to the loss of some ships torpedoed by German U-boats. A point was reached in 1917 when Germany threatened to allow the Dutch to freeze by prohibiting the import of British coal unless the Netherlands agreed to their demands, while Britain threatened to let them starve if they did so. In March 1918 the USA and Britain seized the Dutch merchant fleet. However, by the end of the war Dutch sympathies tended to be with the Allies rather than Germany, partly because of their dislike of unrestricted submarine warfare and partly from fear that a victorious Germany might annex Belgium permanently. The fact that the Kaiser was allowed to spend his last years in exile at Doorn was not a reflection of where Dutch sympathies really lay.[5]

During the inter-war period Anglo-Dutch commercial connections were strengthened by the development of Anglo-Dutch companies. The fusion which produced Royal Dutch Shell had already taken place in 1907. The formation of Unilever took place in 1929,[6] and there were other companies which transcended the divide of the North Sea. Whether this would ultimately have been more important than the economic pull to Germany was not clear when Hitler came to power in 1933. There was a minority of Dutchmen, led by Mussert, who supported his National Socialist ideas, but the great majority put their faith in neutrality in the war which was coming. It seemed to have served Dutch interests better than participation in the war of 1914, and might well do so again. Accordingly no steps were taken towards a co-ordinated defence with Britain and France, and the Netherlands did not join in the war in September 1939. In January 1940 the Dutch were disturbed by a radio broadcast in which Churchill attacked the neutrals for 'bowing humbly and in fear to German threats of violence, comforting themselves meanwhile with the thought that the Allies will win', and the foreign minister, van Kleffens, justified the Dutch policy of neutrality.[7]

The weaknesses of this policy were shown in May 1940, when Hitler's attack on his enemies in the west included not only Belgium but the Netherlands, and the latter country was seized in a few days. It led to an occupation lasting five years in which Dutchmen who suffered at the hands of the German invaders and of their collaborators learned to look to London as the centre of resistance to their oppressors. Queen Wilhelmina left in time for England in a British torpedo-boat, followed by her ministers, and thereafter her broadcasts from the BBC had a considerable impact upon the morale of her people at home. The BBC's broadcasts, indeed, had as much influence in the Netherlands as in any other state, as Dutchmen huddled over their sets in secret to listen to words from London, the home of freedom. Equally Dutchmen who had no means of getting away to join the Allied Forces listened gladly to the roar overhead of the Allied bombers which crossed the Dutch coasts on their way to German cities from British bases. The resulting goodwill of Dutchmen towards Britain was considerable. It was not even marred by the incompetence shown in the *Englandspiel*, when a Dutch agent who fell into German hands agreed to continue his radio transmissions to England in accordance with the instructions of his captors. He took care to include in his messages a warning sign (prearranged with the Dutch section of the Special Operations Executive) which should have shown that he was in enemy hands, but the Special Operations Executive paid no attention and sent back details of more agents who were to be flown in. Fifty-seven of these found welcoming German parties in the darkness of the airstrips arranged for rendezvous, and it has been calculated that the deaths of at least 132 victims resulted, with many others imprisoned.[8]

The failure of the Allies at the Battle of Arnhem, fought on Dutch soil in September 1944, led to one more dreadful winter for the Dutch under German occupation. But their very privations, eating bulbs and burning such wood as they could get under the eyes of the German troops, made their rescuers more popular when they finally arrived. At no time in the history of Anglo-Dutch relations were the British more popular in Holland than in the years immediately following the war. This goodwill survived the insistence of Lord Mountbatten and General Christison on behalf of Attlee's government in 1945 that no British soldier be used to bring about the forcible restoration of Dutch authority in Indonesia (though Churchill had told the Dutch ambassador that the Netherlands would get the Indies back).[9] The sense of gratitude has inevitably become muted with time, but the Dutch were anxious that Britain should join the European Economic Community. Many had hopes that British parliamentary experience would have a healthy effect upon the Parliament of Strasbourg – hopes which have, in fact, been disappointed.

In a world now dominated by the superpowers, the two peoples retain largely similar ideals, and it is inconceivable that the Dutch lion and the English dog should ever again be at grips with one another as they were in the seventeenth century. They have many common interests and not only strategic ones. Austen Chamberlain was able to speak of the indispensability of the Low Countries to British defence in 1938, even in the days of air power. If in these days Britain's frontier is on the Rhine or still further east, it remains true that Britain would still have particular qualms about the presence of a hostile power immediately facing her across the North Sea. But the affinities, though unobtrusive, probably go deeper than merely political self-interest: the national of one country may be in the other without feeling a stranger. Their ideals and their problems are not dissimilar: attitudes are liberal (if under strain in the conditions of the 1980s) and at the same time basically undoctrinaire, and (except at election time) relatively free from rhetoric. The Dutch even play cricket, and touring teams have been known to visit The Hague. Facetiousness apart, it is not fanciful to see a community of outlook in open and tolerant societies, formed in contact with one another over a long period of time.

Notes

Introduction

1 J.W. Stoye, *English Travellers Abroad, 1604–1667*, (1952), p. 240.

1 From Boniface to Erasmus

1 Clarendon, *Life* (1827 edn.), II, pp. 334–5.

2 Cit. H. Scherpbier, *Milton in Holland: A Study in the literary relations of England and Holland before 1730* (Amsterdam, 1933), p. 92n.

3 G. C. Homans, 'The Frisians in East Anglia', *Economic History Review* (1957), pp. 189–206; R. H. Hodgkin, *A History of the Anglo-Saxons* (3rd edn., 1952, ch. I); P. Boeles, *Friesland tot de elfde eeuw* (2nd edn. The Hague, 1951).

4 S. Lebecq, *Marchands et Navigateurs Frisons du Haut Moyen Age* (2 vols., Lille, n.d. ?1984), esp I, pp. 23–4, 89–92; H. Loyn, *Anglo-Saxon England and the Norman Conquest* (1962), pp. 23, 26–8, 82.

5 W. Levison, *England and the Continent in the Eighth Century* (1946), ch. III; Govoerdt Schoevaerdt, *Nederlandsche Antiquiteyten*, p. 33, cit. W. J. B. Pienaar, *English Influences in Dutch Literature and Justus van Effen as Intermediary* (1929), pp. 3–4.

6 H. S. Lucas, *The Low Countries and the Hundred Years War* (Ann Arbor, 1929).

7 E. Power, 'The Wool Trade in the Fifteenth Century', in E. Power and M. M. Postan, *Studies in English Trade in the Fifteenth Century* (1933),

pp. 60–2; N. W. Posthumus, *Geschiedenis van de Leidsche Lakenindustrie* (The Hague, 1908), I, p. 422 and ch. IV.

8 T. Fuller, *Church History* (1655), IV, p. 111, cit. A. G. H. Bachrach, *Sir Constantine Huygens and Britain* ... I, 1596–1619 (Leiden, 1962), p. 2; J. Stow, *Annals* (1615), p. 288.

9 H. J. Smit, *Bronnen tot de geschiedenis van de handel met Engeland, Schotland en Ierland* (Rijks Geschiedkundige Publicatien, LXV, LXVI, The Hague 1928), I, pp. VII–VIII and passim; C. te Lintum, *De Merchant Adventurers in de Nederlanden* (The Hague, 1905).

10 J. Davidson and A. Gray, *The Scottish Staple at Veere* (1909).

11 For a recent and well-illustrated description of the Netherlands in the Burgundian period, see W. Prevenier and W. Blockmans, *The Burgundian Netherlands* (Eng. trans., 1986).

12 J. Stow, *Annals* (1615), pp. 246–7.

13 *Cambridge History of English Literature*, III, p. 28.

2 *Allies against Spain*

1 R. B. Wernham, *Before the Armada. The Growth of English Foreign Policy 1485–1588* (1966), p. 290; *Somers Tracts* (1809), I, p. 169, cit. ibid. p. 292.

2 Stow, *Annals*, pp. 570, 575; I. B. Buckwalter Horst, *The Radical Brethren* (Nieuwkoop, 1972), pp. 37, 54–5, 60–2, 136.

3 J. Lindeboom, *Austin Friars: the History of the Dutch Reformed Church in London, 1550–1950* (The Hague, 1950); A Pettegree, *Foreign Protestant Communities in Sixteenth-Century London* (1986).

4 P. Collinson, *Archbishop Grindal* (1979), pp. 134–40.

5 J. S. Burn, *The History of the French, Walloon, Dutch and other Protestant Refugees settled in England, from the reign of Henry VIII to the Revocation of the Edict of Nantes* (1846), pp. 6n.–7n.

6 *Annals*, p. 868.

7 Eng. trans. in W. B. Rye, *England as seen by Foreigners* (1865), pp. 69–73.

8 Wernham, p. 315.

9 P. J. Blok, 'De Watergeuzen in England (1568–1572)', *Bijdragen voor Vaderlandsche Geschiedenis*, 3rd. ser. IX (The Hague, 1896), pp. 226–63.

10 The latest treatment is in N. M. Sutherland, *Princes, Politics and Religion, 1547–1589* (1984), pp. 183–206, who however does not seem to have used Blok's article above. Her general conclusion does not differ from Blok.

11 For these volunteers, see R. Williams, *The Actions of the Low Countries* (1618), in *Somers Tracts* (2nd edn., 1809), I, pp. 329–82, with a modern

reprint, ed. D. W. Davies (Ithaca, N. Y., 1964); D. Caldecott-Baird, *The Expedition in Holland, 1572–1574* (1976); C. H. Wilson, *Queen Elizabeth and the Revolt of the Netherlands* (1970), pp. 27–9.

12 J. Ferguson, *Papers illustrating the history of the Scots Brigade in the Service of the United Netherlands (1572–1782) from the archives at The Hague* (Scottish Historical Society, 3 vols., Edinburgh, 1899–1901).

13 T. Churchyard, *A Lamentable and pitifull Description of the wofull warres in Flaunders* (1578) (dedicated to Walsingham); Williams, pp. 379–80.

14 Cit. J. B. Black, *The Reign of Elizabeth* (1936), p. 289.

15 J. M. Kervyn de Lettenhove, *Relations Politiques des Pays-Bas et de l'Angleterre sous le règne de Philippe II* (Brussels, 1882–1900), VIII, p. 249.

16 Conyers Read, *Mr. Secretary Walsingham and the policy of Queen Elizabeth* (1925), I, pp. 352–62.

17 Cit. J. A. van Dorsten, *Poets, Patrons and Professors: Sir Philip Sidney, Daniel Rogers, and the Leiden humanists* (Leiden, 1962), p. 54.

18 Printed in *Somers Tracts* (1809), I, pp. 410–19.

19 Van Dorsten, as above, p. 106. For Leicester's reception, see R. C. Strong and J. A. van Dorsten, *Leicester's triumph* (1964); for the proclamation appointing him governor-general, *Somers Tracts*, I, pp. 420–1.

20 J. Bruce, *The Correspondence of Leicester during his Government in the Low Countries* (Camden Society, 1844), pp. 338–9.

21 M. W. Wallace, *Life of Sir Philip Sidney* (1915), pp. 344–5, 356; Historical Manuscripts Commission, *Ancaster MSS*, p. 44; *Calender of State Papers Foreign 1586–7*, p. 322; *Cabala*, pt. II (1691), pp. 19, 22, 25.

22 Conyers Read, *Walsingham*, III, p. 159n.

23 J. den Tex, *Oldenbarnevelt* (Eng. trans. 1973), I, p. 183.

24 Conyers Read, *Walsingham* III, p. 358.

25 R. B. Wernham, 'The Mission of Thomas Wilkes to the United Provinces in 1590', in J. Conway Davies, *Studies Presented to Sir Hilary Jenkinson* (1957), pp. 423–55.

26 Historical Manuscripts Commission, *De L'Isle and Dudley MSS*, II, p. 125.

27 Den Tex, I, pp. 159–60.

28 C. Dalton, *Life and Times of General Sir Edward Cecil, Viscount Wimbledon* (1885), I, pp. 80–3.

29 C. R. Markham, *The Fighting Veres* (1888); Vere, *Commentaries*, reprinted in E. Arber, *An English Garner*, VII, p. 133.

30 M. L. van Deventer, *Gedenkstukken van Johan van Oldenbarnevelt* (The Hague, 1860–5), II, pp. 108–19, 161–4, cit. C. H. Wilson, *Queen Elizabeth and the Revolt of the Netherlands*, p. 120.

31 Cf. Anna E. G. Simoni in *Ten Studies in Anglo-Dutch Relations*, ed. J. van Dorsten (Leiden, 1974), pp. 51–71; and cf. H. Hexham, *The Principles of the Art Militarie practised in the Warres of the United Netherlands* (1637).

32 Cit. M. P. Rooseboom, *The Scottish Staple in the Netherlands* (The Hague, 1910), p. 105.

33 C. R. Markham, *The Fighting Veres* (1888), p. 200.

34 C. Dalton, *Life and Times of General Sir Edward Cecil, Viscount Wimbledon* (1885), II, p. 28.

35 F. Dahl, 'Amsterdam – Cradle of English Newspapers', *The Library* (Dec. 1949), pp. 166–178.

3 Mammon and God

1 J. E. Neale, *Elizabeth and her Parliaments, 1584–1601* (1957), pp. 166–83.

2 Symonds D'Ewes, *Compleat Journal of the Votes, Speeches and Debates both of the House of Lords and House of Commons throughout the Whole Reign of Queen Elizabeth* (1682), pp. 489, 505–7, 509–11.

3 *The Letters of John Chamberlain*, ed. N. E. McClure (Philadelphia, 1939), I, p. 38.

4 G. B. Harrison, *An Elizabethan Journal, 1591–1594* (1928), p. 239; I. Scouloudi, *Returns of Strangers in the Metropolis, 1593, 1627, 1635, 1639*, Huguenot Society, LVII, 1985, pp. 57–93; J. Lindeboom, *Austin Friars: the History of the Dutch Reformed Church in London, 1550–1950* (The Hague, 1950), pp. 122–5; Ben Jonson, *The Devil is an Ass*, Act I. sc.i.

5 J. Keymor, *Observations made upon the Dutch Fishing about the Year 1601*, in *The Phoenix* (1707) pp. 222–31; T. Gentleman, *England's Way to Win Wealth* (1614), dedicated to James's Privy Councillor Northampton, in *Harleian Miscellany*, III, pp. 395–409; anon, *The Trade's Increase* (1615), ibid. IV, pp. 212–31.

6 *The British Monarchie: Rare Memorials pertaining to the Perfect Art of Navigation* (1577).

7 T. W. Fulton, *The Sovereignty of the Sea* (1911), pp. 60–144; text of proclamation in Appendix F.

8 V. Barbour, 'Dutch and English Merchant Shipping in the Seventeenth Century', reprinted in *Essays in Economic History*, I (1954), ed. E. M. Carus-Wilson, pp. 227–53.

9 V. Barbour, *Capitalism in Amsterdam in the Seventeenth Century* (Baltimore, 1950).

10 A. Friis, *Alderman Cockayne's Project and the Cloth Trade* (Copenhagen and London, 1927); B. E. Supple, *Commercial Crisis and Change in England, 1603–42* (1959), pp. 33–51.

11 Dryden, *Works*, ed. G. Saintsbury (1883), V, pp. 1–3.

12 J. R. McCulloch, *Select Collections of Early English Tracts on Commerce* (1856, reprinted for Economic History Society, 1952), pp. 115–209.

13 F. Shriver, 'Orthodoxy and Diplomacy. James I and the Vorstius affair', *English Historical Review* (1970), pp. 449–74.

14 G. Edmundson, *Anglo-Dutch Rivalry during the first half of the Seventeenth Century* (1911), pp. 43ff; G. N. Clark and W. J. M. van Eysinga, *The Colonial Conferences between England and the Netherlands in 1613 and 1615* (Leiden, 1951); S. R. Gardiner, *History of England from the Accession of James I to the Outbreak of the Civil War, 1603–1642* (1895), III, pp. 359–61, V, pp. 84–5; Chamberlain, [see n. 31], II, pp. 346, 424, 562–3, 569–70, 602.

15 *Vox Caeli*, pp. 30–1, 43, and *The Belgick Pismire*, p. 49, cit. M. A. Breslow, *A Mirror of England: English Puritan Views of Foreign Nations* (Cambridge, Mass. 1970), pp. 77–8.

16 Barbour, as in n. 9, pp. 29–30.

17 *The Naval Tracts of Sir William Monson*, V (1914), pp. 31–41, 42–6.

18 Gardiner, VII, pp. 176–7, 368–9.

19 Monson, V, p. 234.

20 Fulton, as in n. 7, pp. 209, 266–76, 309–11 and n.

21 A. W. Harrison, *The Beginnings of Arminianism to the Synod of Dort* (1926), esp. pp. 179, 203, 263–4; N. Tyacke, 'Arminianism and English Culture', in *Britain and the Netherlands*, VII: *Church and State since the Reformation*, ed., A. C. Duke and C. A. Tamse (The Hague, 1981), pp. 94–117.

22 J. Dover Wilson, 'Richard Schilders and the English Puritans', *Transactions of the Bibliographical Society*, XI (1910), pp. 65–134.

23 P. Collinson, *The Elizabethan Puritan Movement* (1967), pp. 234, 295–6; B. R. White, *The English Separatist Tradition from the Marian Martyrs to the Pilgrim Fathers* (1971), esp. chs. V–VII.

24 A. C. Carter, *The English Reformed Church in Amsterdam in the Seventeenth Century* (Amsterdam, 1964) passim; K. L. Sprunger, 'English and Dutch Sabbatarianism', *Church History* (1982), pp. 24–36.

25 K. L. Sprunger, *Dutch Puritanism: A History of the English and Scottish Churches of the Netherlands in the Sixteenth and Seventeenth Centuries* (Leiden, 1982). .

26 K. L. Sprunger, *The Learned Doctor William Ames* (Urbana, Illinois, 1954).

27 R. P. Stearns, *The Strenuous Puritan: Hugh Peter* (Urbana, 1954) esp. ch. III.

28 *Calendar of State Papers Foreign, Jan.–Jul. 1589*, p. 344.

29 R. P. Stearns, *Congregationalism in the Dutch Netherlands* (Chicago, 1940), pp. 121–5; cf. Sprunger, *Dutch Puritanism*, pp. 240ff.; H. Trevor Roper, *Archbishop Laud* (1940), pp. 244–57.

30 Sprunger, *Dutch Puritanism*, pp. 70–6, 307–16.

4 The Dutch (or English) Wars

1 Clarendon, *History of the Rebellion*, ed. W. D. Macray (1888), V, pp. 1–2.

2 S. Groenveld, *Verlopend Getij: De Nederlandse Republiek en de Engelse Burgeroorlog, 1640–1646* (Dieren, 1984).

3 Ed. S. R. Gardiner and C. T. Atkinson, *Letters and Papers relating to the first Dutch war* (Navy Record Society, 5 vols. 1899–1912 and 1930), I, pp. 80–2.

4 For the origins of the war, see C. H. Wilson, *Profit and Power* (1957) and J. E. Elias, *Het voorspel van den eersten Engelschen Ooorlog* (The Hague, 1920).

5 S. R. Gardiner, *The Commonwealth and Protectorate* (1894), I, p. 362.

6 Gardiner and Atkinson (as in n. 3), IV, p. 274.

7 Ibid. IV, pp. 351–3.

8 R. Davis, *The Rise of the English Shipping Industry in the Seventeenth and Eighteenth Centuries* (1962), pp. 12–13.

9 Gardiner and Atkinson, V, p. 369.

10 Wilson, *Profit and Power*, p. 75.

11 Gardiner, *Commonwealth and Protectorate*, II, pp. 128, 341–5, 349–53; A. H. Woolrych, *From Commonwealth to Protectorate* (1982), pp. 283–4.

12 C. H. Firth, 'Secretary Thurloe on the Relations of England and Holland', *English Historical Review* (1906), pp. 319–27.

13 D. K. Bassett, 'Early English Trade and Settlement in Asia, 1602–1690', in *Britain and the Netherlands in Europe and Asia*, ed. J. S. Bromley and E. H. Kossman (1968), pp. 83–109.

14 Clarendon, *Life* (1827 edn.), II, p. 333.

15 Ibid. II, p. 310.

16 Ed. J.J. Jusserand, *Recueil des Instructions données aux Ambassadeurs ... Angleterre, 1648–1690* (Paris, 1929), II, p. 205.

17 Ibid. II, p. 399.

18 *The Dutch Storm* (1665); *An Essay upon the late Victory obtained by His Royal Highness the Duke of York against the Dutch upon June 3, 1665* (1665).

19 P. G. Rogers, *The Dutch in the Medway* (1970).

20 J. E. Elias, *De Tweede Engelsche Oorlog als Keerpunt in Onze Betrekkingen met Engeland* (The Hague, 1930).

21 Pepys, 14 June 1667; V. Barbour, 'Dutch and English Merchant Shipping in the Seventeenth Century' in *Essays in Economic History*, I.(1954), ed. E. M. Carus-Wilson, p. 248n.

22 K. H. D. Haley, *An English Diplomat in the Low Countries: Sir William Temple and John de Witt, 1665–72* (1986), ch. 6.

23 Ibid., pp. 32–8, 228–31 and passim.

24 Cit. V. Barbour, *Capitalism in Amsterdam in the Seventeenth Century* (Baltimore, 1950), pp. 101–2.

25 *English Historical Documents, vol. viii, 1660–1714*, ed. A. Browning (1953), p. 854.

26 K. H. D. Haley, *William of Orange and the English Opposition, 1672–4* (1953), passim.

5 Some Seventeenth-Century English Views of the Dutch

1 J. Huizinga, 'Engelschen en Nederlanders in Shakespeares tijd', in *De Gids*, vol. 88, deel 1 (1924), pp. 219–35, 367–83.

2 *The Naval Tracts of Sir William Monson*, ed. M. Oppenheim (Navy Record Society, 5 vols, 1902–14), V, pp. 324–5.

3 O. Felltham, *Lusoria* (1661), pp. 45–6 (written in 1652).

4 *A discourse written by Sir George Downing ... whereunto is added a relation of some former and later proceedings of the Hollanders: by a meaner hand* (1672), p. 55.

5 Pepys, 28 Nov. 1663; *A Discourse ...* , p. 28.

6 Felltham, *Lusoria*, p. 52.

7 Sir W. Petty, *Political Arithmetic* (1691) in *Several Essays in Political Arithmetic* (4th edn. 1755), pp. 91–184.

8 Roger Coke, *Reasons of the Increase of the Dutch Trade* (1641), p. 114; *The Dutch Drawn to the Life* (1664), p. 65. The latter work is mainly a mosaic of quotations.

9 *Diary*, ed. R. Latham and W. Matthews, VI (1972), p. 35 and n. (13 Feb. 1665).

10 L. E. Harris, *The Two Netherlanders: Humphrey Bradley and Cornelis Drebbel* (1961); and his *Vermuyden and the Fens* (1953); H. C. Darby, *The Draining of the Fens* (2 vols., 1940).

11 *John Smeaton's Diary of his Journey to the Low Countries, 1755*, ed. A. Titley (1938).

12 R. Coke, *Reasons of the Increase of the Dutch Trade* (1671), p. 109; J. Child, *Brief Observations concerning Trade and Interest of Money* (1668), pp. 4–5; *The Dutch Drawn to the Life* (1664), p. 8; Fynes Moryson, *An Itinerary ... containing his ten yeeres travell ... 1617* (4 vols., Glasgow, 1907–8), IV, p. 469; *A Late Voyage to Holland* (1691), in *Harleian Miscellany* (1808–13), II, p. 596.

13 Fynes Moryson, IV, p. 213; J. Howell, *Epistolae Howelianae*, ed. J. Jacobs (1890), I, p. 29; Felltham, *Lusoria*, p. 56; *A Late Voyage to Holland, Harleian Miscellany*, II, p. 599; Sir William Temple, *Observations upon the United Provinces of the Netherlands* (ed. G. N. Clark, 1932, revised 1972), pp. 70–1.

14 J. Hall, *Grace Leading unto Glory* (1651), cit. W. I. Hull, *The Rise of Quakerism in Amsterdam* (Swarthmore, 1938), p. 9; *The Naval Tracts of Sir William Monson*, V, p. 314; *The Character of Holland*, ll. 67–74.

15 *The Politia of the United Provinces* in *Somers Tracts* (1809–15), III, p. 634.

16 L. Wolf, *Menasseh ben Israel's mission to Oliver Cromwell* (Jewish Historical Society of England, 1901).

17 Temple, *Observations*, ch. V.

18 W. Carr, *Reflections of the Government ... more particularly of the United Provinces* (Amsterdam, 1688), pp. 28–35 (later editions under different titles); *The Diary of John Evelyn*, ed. E. S. De Beer (6 vols., 1955), II, p. 45; Fynes Moryson, *Itinerary*, I, pp. 93–4; *Life of Marmaduke Rawdon* (Camden Society, 1863) pp. 100–1.

19 Felltham, *Lusoria*, p. 49.

20 Lodewijck Huygens, *The English Journal, 1651–1652*, ed. A. G. H. Bachrach and R. G. Collmer (Leiden, 1982), pp. 41, 64, 54.

21 *The Works of Sir William Temple* (4 vols., 1754 edn.), I, pp. 378–80.

22 Cit. D. Regin, *Traders, Artists, and Burghers: A Cultural History of Amsterdam in the Sixteenth Century* (Assen, 1976), p. 130; H. Peters, *Good Work for a Good Magistrate* (1651), p. 102; Evelyn, *Diary*, II, p. 46.

23 Marmaduke Rawdon, pp. 100–1; W. N. Sainsbury, *Original unpublished papers illustrative of the life of Sir Peter Paul Rubens* (1859), p. 13; *Travels of Peter Mundy*, ed. R. C. Temple (Hakluyt Society, 6 vols., 1907–36), IV, p. 70.

24 Evelyn, *Diary*, I, p. 29, II, p. 39; W. Brereton, *Travels in Holland . . . 1634–35*, ed. E. Hawkins (Chetham Society, 1844), p. 59.

25 *The Dutch Drawn to the Life*, p. 68; *A Late Voyage to Holland, Harleian Miscellany*, II, p. 596.

26 Fynes Moryson, *Itinerary*, IV, pp. 59–60.

27 Peters, pp. 39, 51, 108–9 and passim; Brereton, p. 8; Carr, p. 42.

28 *A Discourse . . .* (as in n. 4), p. 18; *The Dutch Drawn to the Life*, pp. 69–70 (based on *Lusoria*, p. 50); *Somers Tracts*, II, p. 597.

29 *Observations in his Travels upon the state of the XVII Provinces as they stood, 1609*, in *The Miscellaneous Works in Prose and Verse of Sir Thos. Overbury, Kt*, ed. E. F. Rimbault (1890), p. 230; Temple, *Observations*, p. 114.

6 *Orange, Stuart and the Glorious Revolution*

1 Temple, *Observations*, ch. II, and *Works* (1754), III, p. 93.

2 P. Geyl, *Oranje en Stuart, 1641–1672* (Utrecht, 1939), pp. 1–13; S. Groenveld, *Verlopend Getij: De Nederlandse Republiek en de Engelse Burgeroorlog, 1640–46* (Dieren, 1984), pp. 91–100.

3 *The Journal of Thomas Cuningham of Campvere, 1640–1654* (Scottish History Society, 3rd ser. XI, 1928).

4 Groenveld, pp. 100–10, 122–5, 130–3, revising Geyl, pp. 14–31. 40–8.

5 Geyl, pp. 287–312, 329–42 and sources there quoted; Evelyn, *Diary*, ed. E. S. De Beer (1955), III, pp. 471, 476, 555–6.

6 *English Historical Documents 1660–1714*, ed. A. Browning (1953) pp. 866–7.

7 *Correspondentie van Willem III en Hans Willem Bentinck*, ed. N. Japikse, 5 vols. (The Hague, 1927–37), II.i.30.

8 G. Burnet, *History of My Own Time: the Reign of Charles the Second*, ed. O. Airy (1897), I, p. 495.

9 Japikse, *Correspondentie*, II.i.41.

10 K. H. D. Haley, 'The Anglo-Dutch Rapprochement of 1677', *English Historical Review* (1958), pp. 614–48.

11 Temple, *Works* (1754 edn.), I, pp. 254–7.

12 *The Belgic Boar* (1695).

13 E. Campana de Cavelli, *Les derniers Stuarts* (2 vols., Paris, 1871), II, pp. 266, 276; C. Jones, 'The Protestant Wind of 1688: Myth and Reality', *European Studies Review* (1973), pp. 201–21.

14 G. H. Jones, 'The recall of the British from the Dutch Service', *Historical Journal* (1982), pp. 423–35; F. G. Ten Raa and F. De Bas, *Het Staatse*

Leger, 1568–1795 (1911–), VI, pp. 128–131; G. van Alphen, *De stemming van de Engelschen tegen de Hollanders tijdens de Regering van den Koning-Stadhouder Willem III* (Assen, 1938), pp. 8–10.

15 *Journaal van Constantijn Huygens, den zoon* (Werken van het Historisch Genootschap, nieuwe serie, no. 23. Utrecht, 1876), I, pp. 13–50; J. Whittle, *An exact diary of the late expedition of ... the Prince of Orange ... from ... The Hague to ... his arrival at Whitehall* (1689); E. Green, *The March of William of Orange through Somerset* (1892).

16 For biographies of William, see S. B. Baxter, *William III* (1966); Nesca A. Robb, *William of Orange* (2 vols., 1962–6); J. Miller, *The Life and Times of William and Mary* (1974); N. Japikse, *Prins Willem III, de stadhouderkoning* (2 vols., Amsterdam, 1930–3). Among the more recent literature on the Revolution, see J. R. Western, *Monarchy and Revolution* (1972); J. Carswell, *The Descent on England* (1962); J. R. Jones, *The Revolution of 1688 in England* (1972); J. Miller, *James II: a study in kingship* (1978); Lois G. Schwoerer, *The Declaration of Rights* (1981).

7 *Allies against France*

1 R. Coke, cit. G. van Alphen, *De stemming van de Engelschen tegen de Hollanders tijdens de Regering van den Koning-Stadhouder Willem III* (Assen, 1938), p. 1.

2 G. N. Clark, *The Dutch Alliance: the War against Trade, 1688–1697* (1923), pp. 26–7, 37–8, 43, 76; G. N. Clark, 'War Trade and Trade War', *Economic History Review* (1928), p. 269; J. Ehrman, *The Navy in the War of William III, 1689–97* (1953), pp. 353–4; van Alphen, p. 155.

3 Van Alphen, pp. 94–5.

4 H. Horwitz, *Parliament, Policy and Politics in the Reign of William III* (1977), p. 199.

5 G. Burnet, *History of My Own Time: the Reign of Charles the Second*, ed. O. Airy (2 vols., 1897–1900), I, p. 586, and *History of My Own Time* (1724–34), II, pp. 85–6.

6 P. Geyl, *The Netherlands in the Seventeenth Century: Part Two: 1648–1715* (1964), pp. 257–8.

7 *Somers Tracts* (1813), X, pp. 314–18; *The Dear Bargain, or, a true Representation of the State of the English Nation under the Dutch* (n.d. [1690]), ibid. X, pp. 349–77; van Alphen, p. 90.

8 Marion E. Grew, *William Bentinck and William III* (1924), pp. 203, 155.

9 *Speech of Sir John Knight to the Commons, Somers Tracts*, X, pp. 591–6.

10 Van Alphen, pp. 263–5 (printing *The Dutch Guards' Farewell to England* in full); Defoe, *The True-Born Englishman* (1702).

11 *The Correspondence, 1701–1711, of John Churchill, first Duke of Marlborough, and Anthonie Heinsius, Grand Pensionary of Holland*, ed. B. van 't Hoff (Werken ... Historisch Genootschap, 4th ser., I, Utrecht, 1951).

12 *The Dutch Deputies, A Satire* (1705).

13 G. N. Clark, 'War Trade and Trade War', *Economic History Review* (1928), pp. 262–80.

14 D. S. Coombs, *The Conduct of the Dutch. British Opinion and the Dutch Alliance during the War of the Spanish Succession* (The Hague, 1958), p. 131.

15 R. Geikie and Isabel A. Montgomery, *The Dutch Barrier, 1705–1719* (1930), text of the treaties in Appendix E.

16 Coombs, pp. 324, 328.

17 Swift, *Prose Works*, VI, *Political Writings*, ed. Herbert Davis (1951), pp. 1–65.

18 Ibid., pp. 81–117.

19 *Journal to Stella*, ed. H. Williams (1948), pp. 372, 478; Geikie and Montgomery, p. 287; Geyl, p. 322.

20 Geikie and Montgomery, pp. 288, 289–93, 326.

21 Ibid., pp. 335, 356–8.

8 *Economic Exchange: Goods and Investments*

1 1965, 2nd edn. 1984.

2 C. Te Lintum, *De Merchant Adventurers in de Nederlanden* (The Hague, 1905), pp. 213–18.

3 S. G. E. Lythe, *The Economy of Scotland in its European Setting, 1550–1625* (1960), p. 227; T. C. Smout, *Scottish Trade on the Eve of Union, 1660–1707* (1963), pp. 187–8.

4 *Britannia Languens, or a Discourse of Trade* (1680) in J. R. McCulloch, *Select Collections of Early English Tracts on Commerce* (reprinted for Economic History Society, 1952), p. 413; V. Barbour, *Capitalism in Amsterdam in the Seventeenth Century* (Baltimore, 1950), pp. 92–3, 95.

5 Wilson, *England's Apprenticeship* (1965), p. 194.

6 *Britannia Languens*, p. 420; *Dictionary of National Biography*. s.v. J. P. Elers; G. W. Rhead, *Staffordshire Pots and Potters* (1906).

7 C. H. Wilson, *Anglo-Dutch Commerce and Finance in the Eighteenth Century*

(1941), pp. 17–20; R. Davis, *The Rise of the English Shipping Industry in the Seventeenth and Eighteenth Centuries* (1962), pp. 53, 54n, 202–3, 226, 311.

8 C. R. Boxer, *The Dutch Seaborne Empire, 1600–1800* (1965), pp. 272–7.

9 Lythe, pp. 237–45; Smout. pp. 29, 55–6.

10 Wilson, *Anglo-Dutch Commerce and Finance*, esp. pp. 6–7, 24, 28–35, 42.

11 Ibid., pp. 24, 47, 51, 61–2; C. Gill, *The Rise of the Irish Linen Industry* (1925).

12 Barbour, pp. 122–3, 133; Historical Manuscripts Commission, Eighth Report, p. 134.

13 S. Lambe, *Seasonable Observations humbly offered to His Highness the Lord Protector, Somers Tracts*, VI, p. 454.

14 P. G. M. Dickson, *The Financial Revolution in England* (1967).

15 'De joodse entourage van de Koning-Stadhouder', in D. J. Roorda, *Rond Prins en Patriciaat* (Weesp, 1984), pp. 143–55.

16 C. H. Wilson et al., *The Anglo-Dutch Contribution to the Civilization of Early Modern Society* (British Academy, 1976).

17 Wilson, *England's Apprenticeship*, p. 220.

18 Dickson, pp. 309–11, 158; Wilson; *Anglo-Dutch Commerce and Finance*, pp. 90–7.

19 J. Carswell, *The South Sea Bubble* (1960), pp. 165, 199; F. P. Groenveld, *De Economische crisis van het Jaar 1720* (Groningen, 1940), passim; Dickson, pp. 140, 152, 157–8; Wilson, *Anglo-Dutch Commerce and Finance*, pp. 103–8.

20 Dickson, pp. 314–17, 326, 332.

21 Ibid., pp. 321–4.

22 A. C. Carter, 'Britain as a European Power from her Glorious Revolution to the French Revolutionary War', in *Britain and the Netherlands in Europe and Asia*, ed. J. S. Bromley and E. H. Kossmann (1968), p. 118.

23 For the Hopes, see M. G. Buist, *At Spes non Fracta* (The Hague, 1974); for the crises of 1763 and 1772–3, see Wilson, *Anglo-Dutch Commerce and Finance*, pp. 167–88.

24 Dickson, pp. 322–3.

25 J. de Vries, *De Economische Achteruitgang van de Republiek in de Achttiende Eeuw* (Leiden, 2nd edn., 1968), pp. 126–35.

9 *The Exchange of Ideas: Religion, Free Thought and Science*

1 J. A. van Dorsten, *Thomas Basson 1555–1613, English Printer at Leiden* (Leiden, 1961).

2 H. J. McLachlan, *Socinianism in Seventeenth Century England* (1951), citing T. Fuller, *The Church History of Britain* (1845), V, p. 414.

3 C. W. Schoneveld, *Intertraffic of the Mind: Studies in Seventeenth-Century Anglo-Dutch Translation with a Checklist of Books Translated from English into Dutch* (Leiden, 1983); R. L. Colie, 'Spinoza and the Early English Deists', *Journal of the History of Ideas* (1959), pp. 23–46, and 'Spinoza in England, 1665–1730', in *Proceedings of the American Philosophical Society* (1963), pp. 183–219.

4 P. R. Sellin, *Daniel Heinsius and Stuart England* (Leiden, 1968).

5 G. Edmundson, *Milton and Vondel* (1885).

6 J. Howell, *Epistolae Howelianae*, ed. J. Jacobs (1890), I, pp. 31–2.

7 A. L. Drummond, *The Kirk and the Continent* (1956), p. 137.

8 A. R. Hall, 'Huygens and Newton', in C. H. Wilson et al., *The Anglo-Dutch Contribution to the Civilization of Early Modern Society* (1976), pp. 45–59.

9 J. Walker, 'English Exiles in Holland during the Reigns of Charles II and James II', *Transactions of the Royal Historical Society* (1948), pp. 111–25; R. L. Colie, 'John Locke in the Republic of Letters', in *Britain and the Netherlands*, I, ed. J. S. Bromley and E. H. Kossmann (1960), pp. 111–129; R. Ashcraft, *Revolutionary Politics and Locke's 'Two Treatises of Government'* (Princeton, 1986), chs. IX and X.

10 J. A. van Dorsten, *Poets, Patrons and Professors* (Leiden, 1962).

11 R. L. Colie, *Light and Enlightenment: a Study of the Cambridge Platonists and the Dutch Arminians* (1957); P. J. Barnouw, *Philippus van Limborch* (The Hague, 1963).

12 W. I. Hull, *Benjamin Furley and Quakerism in Rotterdam* (Swarthmore, 1941).

13 Drummond, pp. 121, 127.

14 Ibid., pp. 89–108.

15 Ibid., pp. 132, 140ff.

16 G. A. Lindeboom, *Herman Boerhaave: The Man and his Work* (1968); E. A. Underwood, *Boerhaave's Men at Leyden and after* (1977); R. W. Innes Smith, *English Students of Medicine at the University of Leiden* (1932).

17 Drummond, pp. 146–7; N. E. Ossulton, *The Dutch Linguists* (1973), p. 5.

18 W. C. Braithwaite, *The Beginnings of Quakerism* (2nd edn., 1955), pp. 406–13; W. I. Hull, *The Rise of Quakerism in Amsterdam* (Swarthmore, 1938); J. van den Berg, 'Quaker and Chiliast: the "contrary thoughts" of William Ames and Petrus Serrarius', in *Reformation, Continuity and Dissent: Essays in honour of Geoffrey Nuttall*, ed. R. Buick Knox (1977), pp. 180–98; W. Penn, *An Account of W. Penn's Travels in Holland and Germany, Anno*

MDCLXXVII (1694); W. Sewel, *The history of the rise, increase and progress of the Christian people called Quakers* ... (1722; originally in Dutch, Amsterdam, 1717).

19 Schoneveld (as in n.3 above), esp. pp. 121–4; J. van den Berg and G. F. Nuttall, *Philip Doddridge (1702–51) and the Netherlands* (Leiden, 1987).

20 A. G. H. Bachrach, *Sir Constantine Huygens and Britain; 1596–1687: A Pattern of Cultural Exchange* (Leiden, 1962); Ossulton, pp. 19–20.

21 Schoneveld, pp. 122, 120.

22 H. Scherpbier, *Milton in Holland: A Study in the literary relations of England and Holland before 1730* (Amsterdam, 1933), pp. 63, 125, 170–1.

23 Ossulton, pp. 59–62; Schoneveld, passim; W. J. M. Pienaar, *English Influences in Dutch Literature: Justus van Effen as Intermediary* (1929), pp. 43–50.

24 Pienaar, esp. pp. 62, 71, 111, 191, 212–26, 230–6.

25 C. R. Boxer, *The Dutch Seaborne Empire, 1600–1800* (1965), p. 186.

10 The Exchange of Tastes: Houses, Gardens and their Contents

1 N. Lloyd, *History of the English House* (1931), p. 87.

2 C. L. Cudworth, 'Dutch Influence in East Anglian Architecture', *Proceedings of the Cambridge Antiquarian Society* (1937), pp. 24–42; R. Noad, 'The Influence of the Low Countries on the Architecture of Scotland', *Quarterly of the Incorporation of Architects in Scotland* (1928), pp. 101–16.

3 Margaret Whinney and O. Millar, *English Art 1625–1714* (1957), pp. 207–8.

4 For all forms of interior decoration cf. P. Thornton, *Seventeenth Century Interior Decoration in England, France and Holland* (1978).

5 M. D. Ozinga, *Daniel Marot* (Amsterdam, 1938).

6 D. Defoe, *A Tour through England and Wales* (Everyman edn.), I, pp. 166, 175.

7 F. Simpson, 'Dutch Painting in England before 1760', *Burlington Magazine* (1953), pp. 39–42.

8 Whinney and Millar, pp. 60–7; E. K. Waterhouse, *Painting in Britain, 1530–1790* (1953), passim.

9 Pepys, 11 April 1669.

10 Whinney and Millar, pp. 272–5, 282; Waterhouse, pp. 77–8, 111–12.

11 Waterhouse, pp. 117–18, 132.

12 A. G. H. Bachrach, 'J. M. W. Turner's "This made me a Painter"',

in *Light and Sight* (Koninklijke Nederlandse Akademie van Wetenschappen), (Amsterdam, 1974), pp. 41–61.

13 *Dictionary of National Biography* article on Bernard Janssen.

14 Whinney and Millar, p. 106 and n. 4.

15 *John Smeaton's Diary of his Journey to the Low Countries 1755*, ed. A. Titley (1938), p. 29.

16 Defoe, I, pp. 166–7; R. Dutton, *The English Garden* (2nd edn. 1950), pp. 61–2; M. Hadfield, *A History of British Gardening* (1979 edn.), pp. 142, 150n, 151; J.J. Murray, 'The Cultural Impact of the Flemish Low Countries in Sixteenth Century England', *American Historical Review* (1957), p. 852.

17 G. E. Fussell, 'The Low Countries' Influence on English Farming', *English Historical Review* (1959), pp. 611–22.

18 *Diary*, 1 and 15 Dec. 1662.

11 From Utrecht to Belgian Independence (1713–1839)

1 Ragnhild Hatton, *Diplomatic Relations between Great Britain and the Dutch Republic, 1714–1721* (1950); A. C. Carter, *Neutrality or Commitment* (1975); P. Geyl, 'William IV of Orange and his English Marriage', *Transactions of the Royal Historical Society* (1925), pp. 14–37.

2 Historical Manuscripts Commission, *Buckinghamshire MSS*, pp. 114, 122, 133, 139; P. Geyl, *Willem IV en Engeland tot 1748* (The Hague, 1924), esp. pp. 144–5, 213–16; R. Lodge, *Studies in Eighteenth-Century Diplomacy, 1740–1748* (1930), esp. p. 290.

3 A. C. Carter, *The Dutch Republic in Europe in the Seven Years War* (1971), p. 61, and *Neutrality or Commitment*, pp. 41, 83–7; P. Geyl, *De Witten-Oorlog: een Pennestrijd in 1757* (Amsterdam, 1953).

4 These comments have been assembled from C. C. Barfoot, 'A Patriot's Boast: Akenside and Goldsmith in Leiden', in *Ten Studies in Anglo-Dutch Relations*, ed. Jan van Dorsten (Leiden, 1974), pp. 197–230; G. J. Schutte, ' "A Subject of Admiration and Encomium". The History of the Dutch Republic as interpreted by non-Dutch authors in the Second Half of the Eighteenth Century', in *Clio's Mirror*, ed. A. C. Duke and C. A. Tamse (Zutphen, 1985); H. Dunthorne. 'British Travellers in Eighteenth-Century Holland: Tourism and the Appreciation of Dutch Culture', in *British Journal for Eighteenth-Century Studies* (1982), pp. 77–84; J. Nugent, *The Grand Tour* (3rd edn., 1778), I, pp. 40–4; J. Marshall, *Travels through Holland ...* [in 1768], (1772), I.

5 *Letters of Lady Mary Wortley Montague*, ed. R. Halsband (1965–7), I, pp. 249, 250; Goldsmith, *The Traveller*, ll.293–4; Nugent, I, p. 43.

6 F. A. Pottle, *Boswell in Holland, 1763–1764* (1952), p. 281; Marshall, vol. I, esp. pp. 152, 338–48.

7 F. Edler, *The Dutch Republic and the American Revolution* (Baltimore, 1911); and S. Schama, *Patriots and Liberators: Revolution in the Netherlands, 1780–1813* (1977), p. 62.

8 A. Cobban, *Ambassadors and Secret Agents* (1954).

9 Schama, pp. 184, 187–8.

10 Ibid., p. 282.

11 P. Mackesy, *Statesmen at War: the strategy of overthrow, 1798–1799* (1974).

12 Sir Henry Bunbury, *Narratives of some passages in the Great War with France* (1927); E. Walsh, *A Narrative of the Expedition to Holland* (1800).

13 T. H. McGuffie, 'The Walcheren expedition and the Walcheren fever', in *English Historical Review* (1947), pp. 191–202.

14 Conyers Read, *Mr Secretary Cecil and Queen Elizabeth* (1955), p. 298.

15 Schama, pp. 371, 403, 435, 451, 463, 569–76.

16 G. J. Renier, *Great Britain and the Establishment of the Kingdom of the Netherlands, 1813–1815* (1930), p. 104.

17 Ibid., ch.III.

18 N. Tarling, *Anglo-Dutch Rivalry in the Malay World, 1780–1824* (1962).

19 S. T. Bindoff, *The Scheldt Question to 1839* (1945), pp. 201–5.

12 Modern Times

1 E. H. Kossmann, *The Low Countries 1780–1940* (1978).

2 D. Coombs, *The Gold Coast, Britain and the Netherlands, 1850–1874* (London, 1963).

3 J. Peters, 'A Hundred Years of Sea-Communication between England and the Netherlands', *Journal of Transport History* (1963–4), pp. 210–21.

4 Kossmann, pp. 425–7; A. Vandenbosch, *Dutch Foreign Policy since 1815: A Study in small-power Politics* (The Hague, 1959), pp. 72–6, 157–8.

5 Kossmann, pp. 549–50; Vandenbosch, pp. 115–16.

6 C. H. Wilson, *History of Unilever* (1954).

7 Vandenbosch, pp. 281–2.

8 L. De Jonge, *Het Koninkrijk der Nederlanden in de Tweede Wereldoorlog* (The Hague), V (1974), pp. 912–41, and IX (1979), pp. 976–1093.

9 H. Baudet, 'The Dutch Retreat from Empire', *Britain and the Netherlands in Europe and Asia* (1968), pp. 214–21.

Index

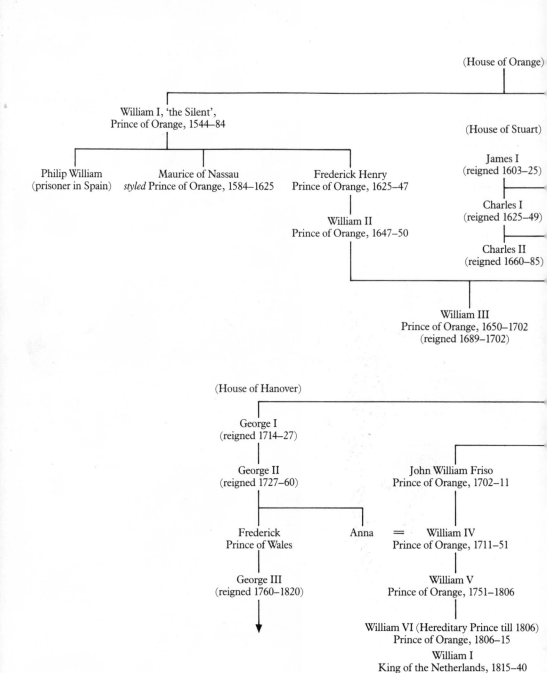

(House of Orange)

William I, 'the Silent',
Prince of Orange, 1544–84

(House of Stuart)

Philip William
(prisoner in Spain)

Maurice of Nassau
styled Prince of Orange, 1584–1625

Frederick Henry
Prince of Orange, 1625–47

James I
(reigned 1603–25)

Charles I
(reigned 1625–49)

William II
Prince of Orange, 1647–50

Charles II
(reigned 1660–85)

William III
Prince of Orange, 1650–1702
(reigned 1689–1702)

(House of Hanover)

George I
(reigned 1714–27)

George II
(reigned 1727–60)

John William Friso
Prince of Orange, 1702–11

Frederick
Prince of Wales

Anna   =   William IV
Prince of Orange, 1711–51

George III
(reigned 1760–1820)

William V
Prince of Orange, 1751–1806

William VI (Hereditary Prince till 1806)
Prince of Orange, 1806–15

William I
King of the Netherlands, 1815–40